Anonymous

AF281711

Proceedings of the Royal Irish Academy

Salzwasser

Anonymous

Proceedings of the Royal Irish Academy

1. Auflage | ISBN: 978-3-84604-848-1

Erscheinungsort: Frankfurt, Deutschland

Erscheinungsjahr: 2020

Salzwasser Verlag GmbH

Reprint of the original, first published in 1870.

PROCEEDINGS

OF THE

ROYAL IRISH ACADEMY.

IRISH MSS. SERIES.

VOLUME I.—PART I.

DUBLIN:

PRINTED BY M. H. GILL,

PRINTER TO THE ACADEMY.

1870.

Price Five Shillings.

LEABHAR NÀ H-UIDHRE.

LEABHAR NA H-UIDHRE, in the library of the Royal
Irish Academy, is the oldest volume now known, entirely in the
Irish language, and is regarded as the chief native literary monu-
ment—not ecclesiastical—of ancient Ireland. The historical and
philological value of the contents of this manuscript is well
known; and to meet the desire for its publication in its integrity,
the Royal Irish Academy has had an exact copy of it executed in
lithograph, elaborately collated with the original. The volume will
be accompanied by PROFESSOR O'CURRY's hitherto unpublished descriptive catalogue of its contents, compiled for the Academy. The
entire edition is limited to two hundred copies, printed on thick,
toned paper, and which can be obtained only by subscribers.

SUBSCRIPTION, £3 3s. PER COPY.

Applications from Subscribers are to be addressed to the TREASURER
OF THE ROYAL IRISH ACADEMY, 19, Dawson-street, Dublin; *or
to the Academy's Publishers,* HODGES, FOSTER, & Co., Dublin;
and WILLIAMS AND NORGATE, Henrietta-street, Covent Garden,
London; 20, South Frederick-street, Edinburgh.

PROCEEDINGS

OF

THE ROYAL IRISH ACADEMY.

IRISH MSS. SERIES.

I.—Descriptive Catalogue of the Contents of the Irish Manuscript, commonly called "The Book of Fermoy." By James Henthorn Todd, D. D., F. S. A. L. & E.

INTRODUCTORY REMARKS.

IN presenting to the Academy a Catalogue of the contents of the ancient Irish MS. commonly called the "Book of Fermoy," it was my wish to have accompanied it by some account of the history of the MS.; but I regret to say that I have found but little to record. I am not sure that the title "Book of Fermoy" is ancient, or that it was the original name of the volume, neither can I ascertain when the MS. was first so called. It is not mentioned under that name by Keating, or, so far as I know, by any ancient authority.* It is not mentioned by Ware, Harris, Archbishop Nicolson, or O'Reilly, in any of their published writings. It has been said that it was once in the possession of the Chevalier O'Gorman; but this has not been established by any satisfactory evidence. There is in the box which now contains the MS. a paper giving a short and very imperfect account of its contents,

---

* A collection of papers relating to the Book of Fermoy was deposited in the Library of Trinity College, Dublin, by the late Dr. John O'Donovan, in 1845. These papers (now preserved in the box H. 5, 7), consist chiefly of extracts from, or references to the Book of Fermoy, made for philological or grammatical purposes.

written about the beginning of the present century, in which it is said to have been then in the possession of William Monck Mason, Esq. This paper is apparently in the handwriting of Edward O'Reilly, author of the Irish Dictionary; but, if written by him, it must have been written at an early period of his life, when his skill in ancient manuscript lore was very inferior to what it afterwards became. Unfortunately the paper is not dated. The Book of Fermoy was sold in London, at the sale by auction of Mr. Mason's books, by the well-known auctioneers, Sotheby and Wilkinson, in 1858. There I purchased it, together with the auto-graph MS. of O'Clery's "Life of Red Hugh O'Donnell," with a view to have both MSS. deposited in the Library of the Academy. For the Book of Fermoy I gave £70, and for the Life of Red Hugh £21, in all £91, which sum was advanced in equal shares by Lord Talbot de Malahide, Gen. Sir Thomas A. Larcom, the late Charles Haliday, and myself; and it may be worth mentioning, to show the rapid increase in the market value of Irish MSS., that the Life of Red Hugh O'Donnell, which in 1858 brought the sum of £21 in a London auction, had been sold in Dublin, in 1830, at Edward O'Reilly's sale, for £3 7s.

The Book of Fermoy might, with equal propriety, be called the Book of Roche. It is a loose collection of miscellaneous documents, written at different times, and in very different hands; a great part of it relates to the family history of the Roche family of Fermoy; but it contains also a number of bardic poems and prose tracts on the general history of Ireland, and a very curious collection of legendary, mythological, and Fenian tales.

It begins with a copy of the *Leabhar Gabhala*, or "Book of Invasions," written in the fourteenth or beginning of the fifteenth century, very much damaged, and imperfect at the end.

Then follows that portion of the book which contains the legendary and mythological tales, written in the fifteenth century. This is in many respects the most interesting and valuable part of the volume; it contains also some historical bardic poems on the O'Connors, or O'Conors of Connaught, the O'Keeffes of

Fermoy, the Mac Carthy, Roche, and other families of the south of Ireland.

The volume concludes with some fragments of medical treatises in the usual exquisitely neat handwriting peculiar to Irish medical MSS. These fragments were certainly no part of the original Book of Fermoy; they probably belonged to the family of O'Hickey, who were hereditary physicians, and whose name occurs more than once inscribed in the margins and blank places of this portion of the MS.

J. H. T.

TRIN. COLL., DUBLIN.

CATALOGUE.

I. A Stave of eight leaves (10½ inches by 8), written in double columns, containing a fragment of the *Leabhar Gabhala*, or "Book of Invasions." The leaves are numbered in the upper margin, 1 to 8, in red pencil, by a modern hand.

Fol. 1. *a.* This page is very much rubbed and defaced, so as to be quite illegible. It begins with the letters Ꞇıo . . . . In the upper margin, in black ink, in a modern hand, is the letter B.

Fol. 1. *b. col.* 1. begins with the words Sem ꝺna ꞃo ᵹab an Aꞅꞅıa, Cam ıꞅ an Aꝺꞅꞃaıc, Iaꝑeꞇ aꞅanꞇoꞃaıꞃ, "Shem settled in Asia; Ham in Africa; Japhet in Europe." This is a short prose account of the establishment of the descendants of Japhet in the principal countries of Europe.

Ibid. col. 2. A short poem, beginning Maᵹoꞇ̇ mac an ıaꝑeꞇ̇ aꞇa cınꞇı a ċlann, "Magoth [read Magog,*] son of Japhet, well known are his descendants."

Ibid. A prose tract, beginning Ƀaaꞇ̇ mac ᵹoımeꞃ m̄c ıaꝑeꞇ ıꞅ uaꝺ ᵹaeꝺıl, "Baath, son of Gomer, son of Japheth, from him are the Gaedil." This short tract contains an account of the building of the Tower of Babel, and the Confusion of tongues, with a tabular list of the

* *Magog.* In the Book of Lecan there is a copy of this poem beginning, fol. 25. b. col. 2. It is there attributed to "Fintan," i.e. Fintan Mac Bochra, the person who is fabled to have survived the Deluge in Ireland.

seventy or seventy-two languages into which the speech of man was divided.

Fol. 2. *a. col.* 2. A short poem beginning berla in bomain bedaib lib, "Regard ye the languages of the world." This is in the Book of Lecan, fol. 26. a. col. 1.

Ibid. Then the history is continued in a prose tract, beginning Sru mac Erru mac gaebil ipe coippad bo gaebilib, "Sru, son of Esru, son of Gaedil, was the leader of the Gadelians." See Book of Lecan, fol. 26. a. col. 2.

Fol. 3. *a. col.* 2. A poem by Gilla Caemhain (ob. 1072), beginning Gaebil glair ocaic gaebil, "Gaedhil Glas, from whom are the Gaedhil." This poem occurs in the Book of Lecan, fol. 26. b. col. 2. & Leabhar Gabhala (O'Clery), p. 60. The poem ends fol. 4. a. col. 2.

Fol. 4. *a. col.* 2. A short prose paragraph, enumerating the several conquests of Ireland, beginning Scuipim bo pcelaib na ngaebil, "I have done with the Stories of the Gaedhil." *Book of Lecan,* fol. 27. a. col. 2.

Ibid. A poem attributed to Fintan (sixth century), beginning Epi ce iappaigcapbim, "Erin, if it be asked of me." See Yellow Book of Lecan, col. 741.

Fol. 4. *b. col.* 1. The narrative is continued in prose to the Deluge. Then follows an anonymous poem,* beginning Capa ip laigni ip luapab gpinb.

Ibid. col. 2. The prose narrative continues to the coming of Ceassair (*pron.* Kassar), grand-daughter of Noah. Then follows a poem (anonymous) beginning Ceappaip canap cdinic pi, "Ceassair, whence came she ?"

Fol. 5. *a. col.* 1. The prose narrative continues to the death of Ceassar at "Carn Cuili Cessrach in Conacht." Then follows an anonymous poem, beginning

    Cecpada cpad bon cup cinb
    po ppic epenn pe nbilinb.

This poem, with a gloss, is preserved in O'Clery's Book of Invasions, p. 3.

Ibid. col. 2. A poem attributed to Fintan, beginning Cain painb bo pinbpamaip. See Leabhar Gabhala (O'Clery, p. 2).

---

* This poem is quoted by Keating.

Fol. 5. b. The history is then continued to the arrival of Partholan, and his death.

Fol. 5. b., lower margin. There is a line of Ogham, in a modern hand, blotted, and with the exception of one or two letters, quite illegible.

Fol. 6. a. col. 1. A poem (anonymous), beginning Ɑ caemaın; ċlaıp cuınɗ caempınɗ, "Ye nobles of the fair-sided plains of Conn." This is attributed to Eochaid Ua Floınn (ob. 984), in the L. Gabhala of the O'Clerys (p. 15), and by O'Reilly (*Writers,* p. lxv).

Fol. 6. b. col. 1. The prose history is continued.

Ibid. col. 2. A poem which O'Reilly, p. lxv. (*loc cit.*), attributes to Eochaidh Ua Floinn, or O'Flynn, beginning Ro bo maıċ ıh muıncıp mop, "Good were the great people." Eochaidh O'Flynn flourished in the second half of the tenth century.

Fol. 7. a. col. 1. A poem headed Ɗo cınpaɗ Papċholan ın poebup, and beginning Papċalan canap caınıc. This poem contains an account of the principal adventures of Partholan, and ends with a notice of the battle of Magh Itha, fought by Partholan against the Fomorians, which is said to have been the first battle fought in Ireland. O'Reilly (*loc. cit.*) attributes this poem to Eochaidh Ua Floınn. It is given in O'Clery's L. Gabhala, p. 9, with a gloss. At the end are the words, ıp ıaɗ pın cpa pcela na .c. ʒabala Ɛpenn ıap nɗılınɗ, "These are the history [or traditions] of the first conquest of Ireland after the Deluge."

Fol. 7. b. The history is then continued in prose to the coming of Nemed, thirty years after the destruction of Partholan's people; with the taking of Conaing's tower in Tor-inis, now Tory island.

Fol. 8. a. col. 2. A poem beginning Ɛpıu oll oıpnıɗ ʒaeɗıl, "Noble Erin, which the Gaedhil adorn." This is preserved in the L. Gabhala of the O'Clerys, with a copious gloss, (p. 25), and is there attributed to Eochaidh Ua Floınn. See also O'Reilly, *Writers,* p. lxvi. The poem ends imperfectly, fol. 8. b. col. 2.

––––––––

II. Next follow sixteen staves, which constitute most probably what remains of the true Book of Fermoy. They are in a very different hand (or rather hands) from the fragment of the Book of Invasions already described, which had probably no connexion with the Fermoy collection of Legendary Tales and Poems.

These sixteen staves are in good hands, probably of the 15th century, and are numbered in the upper margin in Arabic numerals, in a hand of the 17th, and in black ink. The pages are in double columns; size of column, 10.2 inches by 8. A full column contains thirty-six lines.

(1.) The first stave consists of six leaves, and is numbered fol. 23–28, from which it appears that twenty-two leaves have been lost since the folios were numbered, unless the eight leaves of the former part of the volume have been included. The following are the contents of this stave :—

Fol. 23. *a.* The legend of Mór Mumhan (Mór or Moria of Munster), daughter of Aedh Bennain, king of West Luachair (i. e. of West Kerry), and wife of Cathal Mac Finguine,* king of Munster. This tract begins Ɑeḋ ḃennɑın ɲı ıɲloċɲu, ḃɑ meıc ḃec lɑıɲ, ˥ ceoɲɑ ınᵹenɑ ("Aedh Bennain, king of West Luachair, had twelve sons, and three daughters"). A space has been left for an ornamental capital Ɑ, which, however, was never inserted.

Mór was, and is to this day, proverbial for her great beauty. As she approached to womanhood, she was suddenly struck with an irresistible desire to travel, and stole away from her father's house. For some years she continued to wander alone, shunning the haunts of men, and traversing on foot the wilds and forests. At length she arrived at Cashel, in torn and ragged garments, foot-sore, and miserable; but, notwithstanding, her transcendent beauty shone forth, so as to attract the attention of Cathal mac Finguine, king of Munster, who, after some inquiries as to her parentage, finally married her. After this her taste for wandering left her, and she became as celebrated for her wisdom and domestic virtues as for her beauty.

---

* *Cathal Mac Finguine.* Aedh Bennain was the lineal descendant of Cairbre Pict, surnamed Luachra, from Sliabh Luachra, where he was brought up. He died, according to Tighernach, in 619, Ann. Ult. 618, Four Mast., 614. If so, it is difficult to understand how his daughter could have been the wife of Cathal Mac Finguine, who died 787 (Four Mast.). Aedh Bennain is called king of Munster by Tighernach, and king of Iar Mumha, or West Munster, by the Four Masters. But he was really king of Iar Luachair (West Luachair). The district was divided into East and West, and had its name from Cairbre Luachra; it is now Ciarraighe Luachra, or Kerry. See *Wars of the Danes*, p. li, n. ³; lxv. n. ².

Besides the adventures of Queen Mór, this tract contains also the story of the abduction of her sister Ruithchern, the battles fought by their brothers on her account, and the death of Cuana, son of Calchin, King of Fermoy, with whom Ruithchern had eloped. He flourished in the seventh century, and was celebrated for his liberality and hospitality.*

This tale, under the title of Aiċeb Ruiċcearna ṗe Cuana mac Cailcin ["Elopement of Ruithcearna with Cuana mac Cailcin"], is mentioned by Mr. O'Curry in the curious list of ancient tales which he has printed from the "Book of Leinster," *Lectures*, p. 590. A copy of it is preserved in that ancient book (H. 2. 18, Trin. Coll. Dublin); the only other copy (if I mistake not) which is known to exist.

Fol. 24. a. A curious Legend, giving an account of the fifty wonders which occurred in Ireland on the night when Conn of the hundred Battles, King of Ireland in the third century, was born.†

It begins, ḃai ṗinɜen mac lucca aiḃċi ṗamna ın ḃṗuim ṗinɜin, "On Samhain's night (i. e. All Hallow Eve), Fingen Mac Luchta was at Drum-Fingin;" a space being left for an ornamented initial ḃ, which was never inserted. The fifty wonders were related to Fingen Mac Luchta, King of Munster, by a lady named Bacht, who sometimes visited him from the fairy mound called Sith-Cliath, which Mr. O'Curry thought was originally a Tuatha De Danaan mound, now Cnoc Aine in the county of Limerick.

This is a very rare tract, if indeed another copy exists; it contains various topographical, historical, and legendary notices, which throw much light on several superstitious practices not yet entirely forgotten; it records the origin of several roads; explains the ancient names of some rivers, and describes a few of the formerly existing monuments of Tara.

Fol. 25. a. col. 2. A poem of 35 stanzas, beginning, Cıa ṗo aɜ̇aṗ coiṗ um cṗuachaın, "who is it that asserts a right to Cruachan," i. e. a right to the sovereignty of Connaught; Cruachan was the fort or palace of the Kings of Connaught. It is now Rathcroghan,‡ county of Roscommon. The ornamented initial C which ought to have decorated the beginning of this poem was never inserted.

---

* See O'Flaherty, *Ogyg.*, p. 336. ‡ See O'Donovan, (Four Masters, 1223,
† *Ibid.* p. 313. n. ".)

The author of the poem is not mentioned. His object was to arouse Muircheartach, son of John O'Neill, lord of Tir-Eoghain [Tyrone], to assert his claim to the throne of Connaught, in right of his mother Una, daughter of Aedh, King of Connaught, who died in 1274 (Four Masters); which year was therefore the date of this poem, for it must have been written before the successor had been inaugurated; or at least before the confusions consequent on the death of Aedh had come to an end. No less than three Kings of Connaught were set up within that year, 1274, as we learn from the Four Masters, viz.: 1. Aedh (son of Rudraighe, son of Aedh, son of Cathal Croibhdearg), who was murdered in the abbey of Roscommon, after a reign of three months, by his kinsman Rudraighe, son of Toirrdealbach, or Turlogh, son of Aedh, son of Cathal Croibhdearg. 2. Another Aedh, son of Cathal Dall, son of Aedh, son of Cathal Croibhdearg: he was elected by the people of Connaught, but was murdered a fortnight after. 3. Tadg, son of Toirrdealbach, son of Aedh, son of Cathal Croibhdearg, who was permitted to reign for four years, but was slain, in 1278, by the Mac Dermots. It is evident, therefore, that Muircheartach O'Neill (who must have been young at the time), did not yield to the exhortations of the poet to risk his life and fortunes in this troubled sea of factions. The following genealogy, gathered from the present poem, and from the Annals of the Four Masters, will assist the reader in understanding what has been said :—

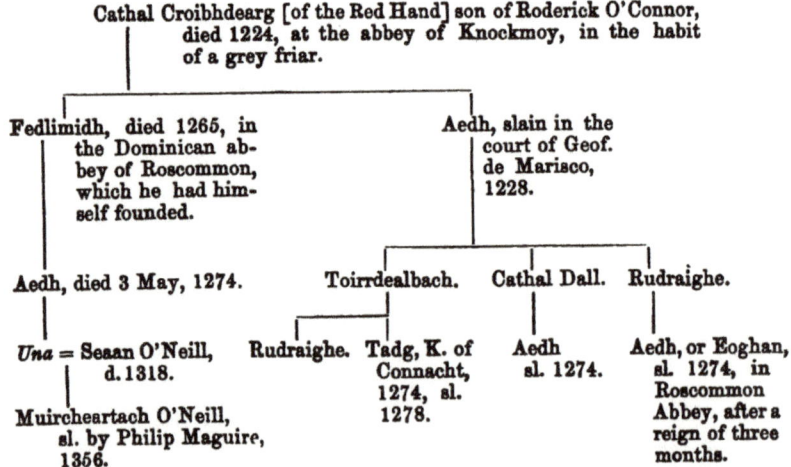

Cathal Croibhdearg [of the Red Hand] son of Roderick O'Connor, died 1224, at the abbey of Knockmoy, in the habit of a grey friar.

Fedlimidh, died 1265, in the Dominican abbey of Roscommon, which he had himself founded.

Aedh, slain in the court of Geof. de Marisco, 1228.

Aedh, died 3 May, 1274.

Toirrdealbach.

Cathal Dall.

Rudraighe.

Una = Seaan O'Neill, d. 1318.

Muircheartach O'Neill, sl. by Philip Maguire, 1356.

Rudraighe. Tadg, K. of Connacht, 1274, sl. 1278.

Aedh sl. 1274.

Aedh, or Eoghan, sl. 1274, in Roscommon Abbey, after a reign of three months.

The present poem is very rare, if not unique; no other copy of it was known to Mr. O'Curry. It belongs to a, class of bardic poems which are extremely valuable for local and family history.

Fol. 26. *a. col.* 1. A poem of fifty-eight stanzas, beginning, Moṇ loıceṛ lucһc an ınɒluıᴣ, "Much do slandering people destroy." The initial M has been written by a modern hand, in the space left vacant for an ornamented letter. The author of the poem, which is addressed to David, son of Thomas O'Keeffe, of Fermoy, was Domhnall Cnuic an Bhile Mac Carthy. It seems that David O'Keeffe had taken offence at some reflections said to have been cast upon him by the poet, who accordingly addressed to him the present poem as a reparation. In it the usual amount of flattery and conciliatory remarks is applied to the wound, the poet denying also the heavy charge brought against him, and putting the blame of it on slandering and backbiting tongues.

This is another of that class of bardic poems throwing light upon local family history. Mr. O'Curry knew of but one other copy of it.

One stanza of the poem (fol. 26. b. col. 1) seems to have been an after insertion, in a space originally left blank for it.

Fol. 27. *a. col.* 1. (six lines from bottom) begins a poem of forty-nine stanzas, the author's name not mentioned. It is in a good hand, by a well practised scholar, but not the same scribe by whom the foregoing poem was written. It begins baıle ṛucһaın ṛıc Єmna, " A mansion of peace is Sith Emna [the fairy hill of Emain.]" The initial letter b is as usual omitted. Five lines at the beginning of col. 2. are obliterated, and nearly illegible, by damp. The poem, which is otherwise quite perfect, is a panegyric on Randal, son of Godfrey, King of the Hebrides, whose royal residence was Emhain Abhla [Emania of the Apples], in the isle of Múilé (*pron.* Moolé), now Mull.

Randal was descended from Godfrey, or Geoffrey, King of Dublin and of the Hebrides, who is surnamed *Mearanach* in the Annals of Ulster, and who died of the plague in Dublin in 1095. Hence, this poem must have been written before that year, for in it the poet exhorts his hero to lay claim to the throne of Ireland, and tells him that the stone which is on the side of Tara would proclaim him as the lawful sovereign. The allusion here is to the celebrated Lia Fail, or stone of destiny, which was said to utter a sound when the true heir of the crown was inaugurated upon it, but to remain silent at the inauguration of an usurper. It is remarkable that the poet speaks of this stone as being

still in his own time at Tara. But notwithstanding his assertion of
Randal's legitimate right to the Irish throne, the prudent poet advises
him to remain in the enjoyment of the ease and happiness which surrounded him in his beautiful island.

The language of the poem is a very ancient and pure style of Irish,
containing, however, a few words peculiar to the Scottish dialect. For
this reason the philological interest of the poem is very great, and that
interest is increased by the historical facts of which it is the only
record. The fairy palace of Eamhain Abhla, or Sith-Eamhna, for
instance, is celebrated in the romantic legends and tales of the Tuatha
De Danaan, but its exact situation was never before known. The present poem identifies it with the residence of the Kings of the Hebrides,
in Mull, in the twelfth century. "This poem alone," wrote Mr.
Curry to me, soon after I had purchased the Book of Fermoy, "is worth
the price you gave for the whole book, and I know of no other copy
of it." Mr. Hennessy has a remarkably fine copy of this poem.

Fol. 28. *a. col.* 1. On the upper margin, in an old hand, is written,
Ⲧⲁⲇⲅ Ⲙᶜ Ⲟⲟⲙⲛⲩⲓⲗⲗ ⲟⲅ. c. c., *i. e.* "Tadg Mac Domhnuill Og cecinit."
In other words, Tadg was the author of the poem, if his name be rightly
decyphered (for the writing is injured and very obscure). The poem
begins, Ⲅⲉⲣⲣ ⲟ ⲃⲁⲃ ⲓⲛⲅⲓⲗⲗ ⲙⲛⲁ ⲙⲩⲙⲁⲛ, "It is a short time since the
women of Munster were pledged," i. e. since they were deemed worth
having pledges given for them. The initial Ⲅ is inserted, with a rude
attempt at ornamentation, by a modern hand.

This poem is a kind of elegy on the death of Siubhan [or Johanna]
daughter of Cormac Mac Carthy; but it gives little information as to
her history, or the time when she lived.

----

(2). The second stave consists of eight leaves, numbered foll.
29–36. Its contents are as follows :—

Fol. 29. *a. col.* 1. In the upper margin is the title of the first tract,
Ⲓⲛⲥⲓⲡⲓⲧ ⲥⲁⲧⲁ Ⲥⲣⲓⲛⲛⲁ, "Here beginneth the battle of Crinna." This
is a remarkably fine copy of this old historical Tale. It is in prose, and
begins ⲃⲁⲓ ⲣⲓ ⲁⲙⲣⲁ ⲣⲟⲣ ⲏⲉⲣⲉⲛⲛ, ⲓ. ⲥⲟⲣⲙⲁⲥ ⲙⲁⲥ ⲁⲓⲣⲧ ⲙⲁⲥ ⲥⲟⲛ ⲥⲉⲃ
ⲥⲁⲧⲁⲓⲅ.* Crinna was a place on the borders of Meath and Louth,

----

* " There was a noble king over Erinn,   the Hundred Combats."
viz., Cormac, son of Art, son of Conn of

in the ancient Bregia, not far from Douth on the Boyne, near Drogheda. There the battle was fought between three Ulster princes, brothers, all named Fergus,* and Cormac mac Art, grandson of Con of the Hundred Fights. Fergus Dubhdedach had usurped the throne, and had, moreover, with his brothers, insulted Cormac at a feast given by him in Bregia. Cormac succeeded in making alliance with Tadg, son of Cian, son of Oilliol Olum, King of Munster, and also with the famous champion Lugaidh Laga. This latter hero had slain Art, Cormac's father, at the battle of Magh Mucruimhe [near Athenry, Co. of Galway], and Cormac demanded of him as an Eric, in reparation, that he should join him on the present occasion, and cut off the heads of the three Ferguses. To this Lugaidh Laga agreed, and in the battle that followed at Crinna, with their united forces, utterly defeated the Ulster princes, and brought their heads to Cormac. By this victory, gained A. D. 254, Cormac became firmly fixed on the throne of Ireland, which he held for twenty-three years.

Another very good copy of this Tale will be found in the Book of Lismore. Keating, in his history of Ireland, has given a summary of it, including most of the legendary and marvellous incidents, which I have not thought it necessary to dwell upon.

Other copies of the Tale are also preserved; but they are very inferior to the copies in the vellum books, the "Book of Fermoy," and the "Book of Lismore." The other copies are on paper, transcribed, no doubt, from ancient copies, but with many mistakes and inaccuracies.

Fol. 32. *a. col.* 1. (line 16). Here begins an ancient prose tale, entitled bruiden mc̄ dareó an̄so sīosana ("The Court of the son of Daire down here") beginning, bui foḋorḋ mor ic aṫeċ-tuaṫaiḃ Erenn an aimsir tri riġ Erenn ["There was a great conspiracy among the Athech-tuatha of Erinn in the time of three kings of Erinn"], the three kings mentioned being "Fiacho Findolaigh (or Fiacha Finnolaidh), King of Ireland; Fiac mac Fidheic-Caich, or Fiac-Caech, King of Munster; and Bres mac Firb, King of Ulster."

This is an account of the insurrection of the people called Athech-tuatha against the Milesian chieftains and nobles in the first century of

* But distinguished by the surnames Fergus Dubhdedach [black toothed], Fergus Foltleabar [of the flowing hair], and Fergus Cas-fiaclach [crooked toothed], who was also called Tene fo Breagha, or "Fire through Breagh," in allusion to his frequent irruptions into Bregia.

the Christian era. It relates to a most difficult and obscure incident
in the history of Ireland—an incident which has been most probably
greatly disfigured by the partizanship of historians, and of which we
have only the account of the ultimately successful party. All revolutions
which have failed in their object are not unnaturally liable to similar mis-
representations. The very name Athech-tuatha is variously interpreted.
Some have sought to identify the people so called with the Attacotti
mentioned by Ammianus Marcellinus, and by St. Jerome, as a tribe of
marauders, who, with the Picts and Scots, caused great disturbance to
the Britons, and are said to have appeared also on the continent of
Europe. But no mention is made of them until the middle of the
fourth century; and in true Celtic pronunciation the name *Athech-
tuatha* bears no similarity to Attacotti. The word *Tuatha* signifies
people, tribes, or the territories they inhabited; but *athech* is the word
whose etymology and meaning make the difficulty. Keating seems to
translate the compound word by ꝺaoꞃ clᴀnnᴀ, the clanns who were not
free, that is to say, the clanns who were under an obligation to contribute
by a rent of cattle and food to their chieftains; in opposition to the Sᴀoꞃ
clᴀnnᴀ, or free clanns who were not under any such rent or tribute. This
is also Mr. O'Curry's interpretation, who tells us that the word *athech*
signifies nothing more than Rent-Payers, Rent-paying Tribes or People.[*]
If this be the true signification, it will follow that in the word Athech-
tuatha we are not to look for an indication of their genealogical descent, but only a description of their civil condition; they were not
free; in other words, they were compelled by an external force or moral
obligation to pay tribute to their chieftains.

This, however, is not the place for a dissertation on this subject,
which very much needs a patient and dispassionate investigation by
competent Irish scholars. It must be enough to say here, that there
seems no reason to suppose these Rent-paying tribes to have been of

---

[*] *People.* O'Curry's Lectures, p. 363.
(O'Donovan's *B. of Rights*, p. 174, n. ▼).
It is to be regretted that Mr. O'Curry
did not give us his opinion on the etymology and origin of the word *Athech* or
Aitheach; his interpretation of it must
therefore rest on his own authority. Lynch
[*Camb. Evers.* p. 65], explains it "ple-
beiorum hominum genus." O'Reilly (Dict.
in voc.) supposes it to be quasi ꝼᴀꞇᴀċ
ꞇuᴀċ, which he interprets "a plebeian."
But ꝼᴀꞇᴀċ or ᴀꞇᴀċ, signifies *a giant*,
and, therefore, Dr. O'Conor explains the
words "gigantea gens." *Rer. Hib. Scriptt.*
vol. i., Proleg. i. p. 74. n. Let it be observed, however, that the word is not
fathach, or *athach*, but *athech*, which is
not necessarily the same thing. See
O'Donovan, *Supplem. to O'Reilly's Irish
Dict. sub vow.*

a different race from the dominant Milesian nobility of the time.
They were dissatisfied with their condition ; they were unable to supply
the extravagant demands of their rulers ; they regarded themselves as
the victims of an intolerable oppression ; they therefore organized a
secret conspiracy to murder the kings, and all the ᴘᴀoᴘ-cᴌᴀɴɴᴀ, "free
clans," or nobles. Their plan was in accordance with the ancient customs of their race. For a year and a half the plot was kept secret,
during which time they laid by cattle and other viands, mead, and
such strong drinks as were then in use, for a great banquet, to which
they invited the kings, above named and their nobles. Fiacha Findolaigh, King of Ireland, was also, it should be mentioned, King of Connaught, so that the three provincial kingdoms, as well as the supreme
power, were represented on the occasion. The unsuspecting guests all
arrived on the appointed day at the Court of Mac Dareo, in a plain
in Breifne, the O'Rourke country, in the present county of Leitrim.
For nine days the guests revelled in all the luxuries of the table; on
the ni nth, especially, the excellence of the viands, the flavour and admirable quality of the drinks, surpassed every thing that had been till
then experienced. All suspicion was lulled; all was joyousness and
noise, and goblets circulated, until at midnight, the royal party—kings,
chieftains, nobles and their followers—all lay senseless in the utter
helplessness of intoxication. This was the moment so long looked for
by their treacherous entertainers. The Athech-tuatha arose, and basely
murdered their unconscious guests. Not a man was suffered to escape,
and the plain in which the *Bruidhen mac Dareó* (or Court of Mac Dareo)
stood, was thenceforth justly named *Magh Cro*, or the Plain of Blood.

The insurgents were completely successful; but their notions were
not republican, and they at once placed upon the vacant throne one
Cairpre-cind-chait, or Cairpre of the Cat's head, who had been their
principal leader in the massacre.

All the "free tribes," it is said, had been entirely extirpated, with
the exception of the queens of the three murdered kings, who by some
means escaped. They were each pregnant, and having found refuge in
Alba, or Scotland, soon after gave birth to three princes, by whom was
afterwards restored the ancient race of the murdered sovereigns.

It is not possible of course to receive all this as authentic history;
but that some such event did take place cannot be doubted. The bards,
who were always in the interest of the chieftains and royal races, can-

not be supposed to have gratuitously invented a tale so dishonourable to their race and sovereigns; and the very inconsistencies of the history, the different order in which the succession of kings, during and after the revolution, is given by different bardic historians and annalists, clearly show that attempts were made to tamper with the truth. Keating gives the succession of supreme kings of Ireland thus:—[the dates are the supposed years of the accession of these sovereigns to the throne]:—

B. C. 12. Crimthann Nia Nair, killed by a fall from his horse.

A. D. 4. Feradach Finn-Fectnach, son of Crimthann Nia Nair.[*]

A. D. 24. Fiacha Finn, slain by his successor.

A. D. 28. Fiacha Finnolaidh (son of Feradach Finn-Fechtnach), slain by the Athech-Tuatha.

A. D. 54. Cairbre Cinn Chait, the usurper, king of the Athech-Tuatha.

A. D. 59. Elim, son of Connra.

A. D. 79. Tuathal Techtmar, son of Fiaca Finnolaidh; escaped in his mother's womb from the slaughter of the nobles.

The "Four Masters" give the order of events and dates as follows:—

B. C. 8. [74]. Crimthann Nia Nair.

A. D. 10 [90]. Cairpre Cinn-Chait.

A. D. 15 [95]. Feradach Finn-fechtnach, son of Crimthann Nia Nair; died A. D. 36.

A. D. 37 [116]. Fiatach or Fiacha Finn, slain by his successor.

A. D. 40 [119]. Fiacha Finnfolaidh, slain by the Athech-Tuatha.

A. D. 57 [126]. Elim Mac Connra, slain by his successor.

A. D. 106 [130]. Tuathal Teachtmar.

O'Flaherty retains the same order of the events, but alters the dates to the years which I have put in brackets.

The account given by Tighernach is as follows:—

A. D. 79. Crimthann Nia Nair: died A. D. 35.

A. D. 85. Feradach Finn-Fechtnach.

A. D. 110. Fiacha Findolaidh, or Findfolaidh.

[A. D. 128. Elim Mac Conrach, or Mac Connra, is mentioned as king of Emania only.]

A. D. 130. Tuathal Teachtmar.

It is curious that Tighernach makes no mention whatsoever of the rebellion of the Athech-Tuatha, and their Cat-headed king. Fiacha Finn-

---

[*] *Nia-Nair*, or Niadh-Nair, "hero of Nar," his wife's name.

olaidh is said to have been slain in his palace of Tara, or as others say, in Magh Bolg, by Elim Mac Conrach, king of Ulster, who was himself killed in the battle that followed, by Tuathal Techtmar, in vengeance for the death of his father.*

It will be seen that these accounts, each given by high authorities, are not only widely discrepant, but also utterly inconsistent.

This tale of the slaughter of the nobles is enumerated among the curious list† of ancient tales published by Mr. O'Curry from the "Book of Leinster," under the title of Aṅgaɩn Caɩppe Cɩnn Caɩc pop paep clannaɩb hEpenn, "Slaughter of the free clans of Erinn by Cairpre Cinn-chait." There is a copy of it in the Trin. Coll. MS. H. 3. 17, and another which Mr. O'Curry calls "a detailed, but not very copious account," in the MS. H. 3. 18. (*Lectures*, p. 264.)

Fol. 33. *a. col.* 1. (Five lines from bottom) is a tale with this title—Aɩn bɩapoɩbe ɩn cep pop ulcaɩb pó pɩp, "This was how the debility came on the Ultonians," beginning Cɩb bɩapaɩbe an cep pop ulcaɩb? .nɩn., "Whence [proceeded] the debility that was on the Ultonians? not difficult *to tell.*"

The story is this: Crunnchu, son of Agnoman, was a rich farmer‡ of Ulster, whose wife had died. Not long afterwards, as he was sitting in his house alone, a strange woman, well clad, and of good appearance, entered, and seated herself in a chair by the fire. She remained so until the evening without uttering a word, when she arose, took down a kneading trough, went to a chest, as if she was thoroughly at home, took out some meal, kneaded it, baked an excellent cake, and laid it on the table for the family. At night Crunnchu, perceiving her excellent qualities, proposed to her to become his wife; to this she consented,

---

* *Father.* See Tighernach, *Rer. Hibern. Scriptt.* tom. ii. p. 29. An instance of the confusion which exists in the history of these events is furnished by Mr. O'Curry. In one place (*Lectures*, p. 263) he tells us that Fiacha Finnolaidh was slain by the insurgents at Magh Cro; in the very next page (p. 264) he says, that Fiacha succeeded to the throne after the death of Cairpre Cinn Chait, but was afterwards slain by a second body of rebels at Magh Bolg. For both statements he could have cited high authority; but it is curious that he does not seem to have perceived their discrepancy.

† *List.* Another list of these tales is given in the MS. H. 3. 17. in Trin. Coll. Dublin. See O'Donovan's Catalogue.

‡ *Farmer.* The word so translated is aɩceach in the original; the very same word which occurs in the disputed compound Aɩceach cuaca, "the farmer or tribute-paying tribes," of which we have already spoken.

and they lived together in great happiness and prosperity, until she became pregnant.

At this time the great annual fair of the Ultonians was proclaimed, and Crunnchu pressed his wife to accompany him thither. This, however, she refused on the ground of her approaching accouchement; so Crunnchu went alone. The sports consisted of sham fights, wrestling, spear-throwing, horse or chariot racing, and other athletic games. In the race, the horses or chariots of the King of Ulster (the celebrated Conchobhair Mac Nessa*), carried off the palm from all competitors. The bards and flatterers of the Court extolled the royal horses to the skies; they were the swiftest in the world—nothing could compete with them. In the excitement of the moment, Crunnchu publicly denied this statement, and declared that his own wife could excel in fleetness the royal steeds. He was immediately seized, and detained in custody until his words could be put to the proof. Messengers were sent for his wife; she urged her condition and the near approach of the pains of childbirth; but no excuse, no entreaty, was suffered to prevail; she was carried by the messengers to the race course, and forced to run against the king's fleet horses. To the surprise of all, she outran the horses, and reached the goal before them; but in the very moment of her triumph she fell in the pains of labour. Her agonies were increased by the cruel circumstances which had prematurely caused them; but she brought forth twins—a son and a daughter. In the irritation of the moment she cursed the Ultonians, and prayed that they might be periodically seized with pains and debility equal to that which they had compelled her to undergo. And this was the *Ces* [debility or suffering], or as it was also called, *Ces naoidhean* [infant or childbirth suffering†], of the Ultonians.

A tale called Cochmaꝛc mná Cꝛuinn, "Courtship of the wife of Crunn," or Crunnchu, is mentioned in the ancient list‡ of Tales, published by Mr. O'Curry, from the Book of Leinster (*Lectures*, p. 586). The

---

* *Conchobhair Mac Nessa.* O'Flaherty dates the beginning of his reign B. C. 13, and his death, A. D. 47.

† *Childbirth suffering.* It is added that this plague continued to afflict the Ultonians for nine generations. The Book of Lecan says during the reign of nine kings, to the reign of Mal Mac Rocraidhe, A. D.

180. But there were but seven reigns from Conchobhar Mac Nessa to Mal, inclusive. See the list given O'Conor, *Stowe Catalogue*, pp. 101, 102.

‡ *List.* It is also in the corresponding list in Trin. Coll. MS. H. 3. 17, under the title of *Tochmarc mna Cruinn mc Agnomain.* O'Donovan's Catalogue, p. 819.

story is also given in the *Dinnseanchus*, where Crunnchu's wife is named *Macha*, and she is mentioned as one of three ladies so called, from whom Ard-Macha, or Armagh, may have had its name.*

Mr. O'Curry states (*ibid.* note), that the whole of this tale is preserved in the Harleian MS. 5280, in the British Museum.

Fol. 33. b. col. 2. On the upper margin we have Cιnαeτ .h. αpτα-ӡαιn .cc. "Cinaeth O'Hartigan cecinit." This poet, called by Tighernach the chief poet of Leth Chuinn (the northern half of Ireland), died A. D. 975. The poem here attributed to him begins Ɖoɫuιɔ αιllιll ιp ιn cαιllιɔ ι cuɫɓpeαɔ, "Ailill went into the wood in Cul-breadh." The object of the poem is to describe the manner of death, and places of interment of the seven sons of Aedh Slaine, King of Ireland, A. D. 595 to 600.

Several good copies of this poem exist in the Academy's collection, and in that of Trinity College. The present copy is one of the best of them.

Fol. 33. b. col. 2. (eight lines from bottom). A poem headed Ϝoτh-αɔ nα cαnoιne .cc., "Fothadh na Canoine [of the Canon] cecinit," beginning Cepτ cech pίӡ co péιll, ɔo clαnnαιɔ neιll nαιp, "The right of every king clearly, of the children of noble Niall;" the next lines add, "except three, who owe no submission so long as they are in power, the Abbat of great Armagh, the King of Caisil of the clerics, and the King of Tara."

This poem was addressed to Aedh Oirnighe, when he became king of Ireland in 793, by Fothad of the Canon, so called because he gave a decision, which was regarded as a law or Canon, exempting the clergy from military service. (See O'Curry, *Lect.*, pp. 363, 364; Four M. 799, and O'Donovan's note *, p. 408). Fothad was tutor, as well as poet, to King Aedh Oirnighe, and in the present poem gives that sovereign advice as to his conduct in the management of his kingdom.

There is a damaged copy of this poem in the Book of Leinster; and other copies, more or less perfect, in the Academy, and in Trinity College. The present is a very good copy, and quite perfect.

---

* *Name.* Book of Lecan, fol. 266. b. b. [pagination of lower margin]. The original, with a translation, and a curious poetical version of the story, are published by Dr. Reeves in his "Ancient Churches of Armagh," p. 41, sq. See also Dr. S. Ferguson's agreeable volume, "Lays of the Western Gael," pp. 23 and 233.

On the upper margin of fol. 34. b. col. 1. a modern reader of the volume has written his name thus:—" Uıℓℓ. ua heaʒɲa," "William O'hEagra, 1805." The O'hEagra are called by O'Dugan* "kings" of Luighne, the present barony of Leyny, in the county of Sligo. The name is now O'Hara.

Fol. 34. b. col. 2. A tract headed ınƀaɲƀa Mochuƀa aɲ Raıċın, "Banishment of Mochuda out of Raithin." It begins Mochuͬͬa mac ꝑınaıℓℓ ƀo cıaɲaıʒı Luacɲa a ceneℓ, "Mochuda, son of Finall, of Ciariaghe Luachra [now Kerry] was his family."

This is a curious and valuable account of the banishment of St. Mochuda† from Raithin, now Rahan, near Tullamore, King's County, and his settlement at Lismore, where he founded a celebrated school and episcopal see in the seventh century. The banishment of this holy man from his original seat at Raithin seems to have been due to the jealousy of the neighbouring clergy, and is said to have been owing partly to his being a native of Munster. The names of all the clergy who took part in this proceeding are given (a singularly curious list),—and the conduct of the joint kings of Ireland, Diarmait and Blathmac, is severely censured.

This tract ends fol. 36. b. col. 2. imperfectly, the next leaf (fol. 37) of the MS. being lost.

---

(3). The third stave consists of six leaves; the first leaf is numbered 38, showing that the loss of fol. 37 has taken place since the numbering of the leaves in black ink, which has been already spoken of.

Fol. 38. *a.* begins imperfectly. This leaf has been greatly damaged and stained. It contains the life of St. George, of which the Academy possesses a very fine copy in the Leabhar breac.

The present copy ends fol. 42. b. col. 2.

Fol. 42 *b. col.* 2 (eight lines from bottom), is a short legend, entitled,

---

* *O'Dugan.* See Topogr. poems transl. by O'Donovan, p. 59.

† *St. Mochuda.* He is also called St. Carthach. A beautiful woodcut of the round window of the Church of Raithin (still nearly perfect) may be seen in Dr. Petrie's Essay on the Round Towers.

Dr. Reeves is of opinion that the expulsion from Raithin had some connexion with the Paschal controversy. Tighernach records it at 636 in these words: "Effugatio Cairthaigh a Raithin *in diebus Paschæ;*" and it is remarkable that St. Cummian's paschal letter was written in 634.

Scel ꞃaicꞃach na muice annꞃo ꞃioꞃ, "The story of the pigs' Psalter down here;" it begins Eꞃpuc ampai bo hi cluain mc noiꞃ," "There was a noble bishop at Cluain-mic-nois." The name of this bishop was Coenchomrach; see Mart. of Donegal, July 21 (p. 199). He died 898 (Four M.) which was really 901. The present copy of the legend is damaged, but other copies exist in the Academy's collection. The original scribe seems to have written as far as line 9, col. 2. fol. 43. a., and to have left the tract unfinished, but it was afterwards taken up where he had left off, and completed by another hand, on the next page. This continuation begins line 10, fol. 43. a. col. 2., under which a line is drawn in modern ink. The portion of the column thus for a time left blank is now occupied by the following curious note by the Scribe of the life of St. George, already noticed :—

Cꞃaiꞃ laiꞃꞃ in mbꞃcuiꞃ ꞃo ꞃain ꞃeoiꞃꞃi o uilliam offceaꞃa, bo baibic mac muiꞃiꞃ mhic ꞃꞃain bo ꞃoicꞃi, ⁊ bo biaꞃ bliaꞃna in ciꞃeꞃna an can bo ꞃoꞃibaꞃ anꞃo hi .i. mile bliaꞃan ⁊ ceicꞃi .c. bliaꞃan ⁊ ꞃechc mbliaꞃna beꞃ ⁊ ba ꞃioic; ⁊ in baꞃa la ꞃioic bo mi nouemꞃ. bo cꞃiꞃnuiꞃeꞃ anꞃo hi, ⁊ a ꞃaiꞃicaꞃiuꞃ bo bi ꞃꞃian incan ꞃin ⁊ a caincꞃen bo bi inc eꞃꞃai; .a. bo biꞃ leiciꞃ bomnach in bliaꞃan ꞃin, ⁊ a 15 bo biꞃ nuaꞃmiꞃ oiꞃ, ⁊ iꞃe ainꞃ ꞃennaꞃ bociꞃeꞃnaꞃ ꞃanuaiꞃ ꞃin bo lo .i. miꞃcuꞃ, ⁊ 6 laeca aꞃ ꞃon in concuꞃ.

A prayer along with this life of St. George, from William O'Hiceadha [O'Hickey], for David, son of Muiris, son of John Roitai [Roche], and the year of the Lord when this was written here was a thousand years and four hundred years, and seventeen years, and two score [1457]; and it was finished here the twenty-second day of the month of November; and the Sun was in Sagittarius at that time, and the Moon was in Cancer; A was the Dominical Letter, and 15 was the Golden Number, and the planet that dominated at that hour of the day was Mercury, and 6 days on account of the concurrent.

The year here designated, whose Sunday letter was A, and golden number 15, was 1457-8; that is, from 1 January to 24 March, was called 1457, according to the old style reckoning; and from 25 March to the end of the year was 1458. It is not worth stopping to explain the astrological characteristics.

This note is followed by four lines of consonant and *Coll* Ogham, in which the two modes of writing are mixed up together in a way which renders it very difficult to read them; and the difficulty is greatly increased by the injury sustained by the lower corner of the MS., which renders one-third of each line illegible.

(IV.) The fourth stave contains but five leaves, numbered in the same hand as before, 44–48. It is greatly damaged by damp and dirt.

Fol. 44. *a.* Here commences a Tract on the Destruction of Jerusalem under Vespasian and Titus, taken apparently from the account given by Josephus; it is of considerable length, and ends fol. 48. a. col. 2. It begins ᴅa bliaᴅan ceachpachaᴅ baᴅap na huiᴅaiᴅi, &c., "The Jews were 42 years, &c."

Fol. 48. *b.* is occupied by a poem, but so obliterated by dirt and damp that it cannot be easily decyphered, at least without giving more time to the task than I have now at my disposal.

———

(V.) The fifth stave contains eight leaves, numbered as before, from 49 to 56. The leaves are all injured in the outer margin.

Fol. 49. *a. col.* 1. On the upper margin, in the handwriting of the original scribe, now nearly obliterated, are the words in nomine pacpip ⁊ pilii ⁊ rpipicup pancci. amen; under which is written, in a later hand, the title of the following tract: Coᴄmapc Cpeblainne, "The Courtship of Treblainn." It begins Ppoech mᴄ piᴅaiᵹ polc puaiᵹ o piᴅ piᴅaiᵹ ⁊ o loᴅ piᴅaiᵹ, &c., "Froech, son of Fidach of the Red Hair, of Sidh Fidaigh, and of Loch Fidaigh," &c.

The tale belongs to the time of Cairbre Niafar, called in many of these tales erroneously King of Ireland; he was in fact only King of Leinster; but because he dwelt at Tara, he is sometimes called King of Tara, which led to the mistake. He was contemporary with Concho-bhar Mac Nessa, and therefore flourished about the end of the first century.[*] Treblainn was his foster daughter, although daughter of a Tuatha De Danann chieftain. The story is as follows:—

At this time there dwelt in the west of Connaught a young chieftain, named Froech, son of Fidach, of the race of the Firbolgs. He was as distinguished for his remarkable beauty as for his valour. His

---

[*] *Century.* See O'Flaherty, *Ogyg.* p.   Rer. Hib. Scriptt. vol. ii. p. 14). 273; and *Tighernach,* B. C. 2. (O'Conor,

fame having reached the ears of the lady Treblainn, she contrived to convey to him a hint, that it would not be displeasing to her, if he would ask her in marriage from her foster-father. In this there was nothing, perhaps, absolutely improper—at least for a young lady brought up at an Irish Court in the first century. But whether she exceeded the rules of decorum or not I do not pretend to say, when she went a step further, and gave her lover to understand that, if her foster-father refused his consent, she was quite prepared to take the law into her own hands, and elope with him. Froech, at least, saw no impropriety in this declaration of her independence. His vanity was flattered, and he at once communicated with King Cairbre on the subject. As the lady had foreseen, however, his suit was refused, and in accordance with her promise, she managed to elude the vigilance of her guardians, and eloped with her beloved, who soon after joyfully made her his wife.

Like all tales relating to the Tuatha De Danaann, this story is full of curious necromantic and magical narratives, some of which are perhaps worthy of preservation.

In the list of ancient tales published by Mr. O'Curry from the Book of Leinster is a legend, called *Tain bo Fraech*, "the Cowspoil of Fraech," which, notwithstanding the difference of title, Mr. O'Curry thought was the same as that now before us. *Lectures*, p. 585, n. (115). Mr. Hennessy thinks it a different tale, although the hero was the same.

Fol. 51. a. col. 1. A tale beginning buí coipppe cpom mac ꝼepabaiᵹ mic luᵹach mic balldin mic bpepail mic maine moip, a quo .l. maine Connachc. "Coirpre Crom* was the son of Feradach, son of Lugaidh, son of Dallan, son of Bresal, son of Maine mór, a quo Hy Maine in Connacht, &c."

This is a short legend giving an account of how the iniquitous Cairbre Crom, King of Hy Maine, in Connaught, was murdered and his head cut off; and how he was afterwards restored to life by the miracles of St. Ciaran of Clonmacnois, who replaced his head, but in such a manner that it remained from that time forward somewhat stooped, a circumstance from which Cairbre received the name of *Crom*, or *the Stooped*.

---

* *Cairpre Crom.* See the genealogical table in Dr. O'Donovan's "Tribes and Customs of Hy Maine."

This story is interesting in consequence of the topographical information it contains. Seventeen townlands are enumerated which the grateful king, on the restoration of his head, conferred upon St. Ciaran and his church for ever.* See Proceedings of the Kilkenny Archæological Society, New Ser. vol. i. p. 453.

The present is a very excellent copy of this legend.

Fol. 51. *b. col.* 1. (line 14), a tract beginning Ríʒ uaρal oiρmíóneaó oiρeóóa óo ʒaó ρlaiceṁnuρ ρóóla ρecc naill .i. conó .c. cachaó mac ρeíólimíʒ ρeócmaíρ, "Once upon a time a noble, venerable, famous king assumed the sovereignty of Fodla [i. e. Ireland], viz., Conn of the Hundred Fights, son of Fedhlimigh Rechtmar." This is a full account of the exploits, reign, and manner of death, of the celebrated Conn of the Hundred Battles, called by O'Flaherty,† Quintus Centimachus. He was treacherously slain by his kinsmen near Tara, on Tuesday, 20 October, A. D. 212, according to O'Flaherty's computation. The history is continued after the death of Conn, until the accession of his son Art-aonfir, or the solitary (so called because he had murdered all his brothers), who was slain at the battle of Magh-Mucruimhe, near Athenry,‡ in the county of Galway, A. D. 250, by his successor and nephew, Lugaidh. The revolutionary times§ that followed are passed over briefly until Cormac, son of Art, the commencement of whose reign is dated by O'Flaherty from the battle of Crinna, A. D. 254; his glories‖ and

---

* *For Ever.* O'Donovan, *ubi supra*, p. 15. 81.

† *O'Flaherty*, *Ogyg.* p. 144, 313.

‡ *Athenry.* O'Flaherty, *Ogyg.* p. 327.

§ *Times.* The chronology, as well as the succession of so called kings, is very confused in this part of Irish history. The following is O'Flaherty's arrangement of the events :—

Art Aonfir, King of Ireland, slain at the battle of Magh Mucruimhe by his successor, A. D. 220.

Lugaidh Laga or Mac Con. In 237, his followers appear to have given him the title of king, which he disputed with Art. After the battle of Cenn-febrath (dated by O'Flaherty, 237), he fled beyond sea. In 250 he became undisputed king, having slain his rival and uncle, Art; but in 253 he was expelled by Cormac, son of Art, and took refuge in Munster. Cormac, however, was himself also driven into Connaught, by Fergus Dubhdedach [of the Black Tooth], who seized the kingdom, but was soon after slain by Cormac at the battle of Crinna, A. D. 254. From this event O'Flaherty dates the beginning of Cormac's reign, although Lugaidh Laga was allowed to retain the name and pomp of king to 267 or 268, when he was murdered at the instigation of Cormac, by the Druid, Ferchis mac Comain, *Ogygia*, p. 151.

‖ *Glories.* See O'Flaherty's panegyric, *Ogyg.* p. 336.

successful government are then described, until the story comes to the following romantic event which lost him the crown :—At the south side of Tara dwelt the family of Fiacha Suighdhe, brother of Conn of the Hundred Battles, and consequently Cormac's grand-uncle. These people were called Deisi, i. e. Right-hand, or Southern people, from their position in reference to Tara ; and subsequently Deisi Temrach, or Deisi of Tara, to distinguish them from the Deisi of the county of Waterford. The barony of Deece, in the county of Meath, still preserves their name. Some time before, Cormac had sent out his son Cellach in command of a party of warriors to assert his right to the Boromean tribute, or annual tax of cows, which had been imposed upon the men of Leinster about 150 years before by the King Tuathal Teachtmar. Cellach returned with the cows; but, as an insult to the Leinster men, he had brutally carried off 150 maidens. Amongst these was one named *Forrach,* who did not belong to the Leinster families liable to the cow tribute, but was of the neighbouring race of the Deisi, the allied tribe descended from Fiacha Suighde. In fact, Cellach had carried off, and reduced to slavery, his own cousin.* When this became known to her uncle, or grand-uncle, Aengus Gaei-buaibhtech, he undertook to avenge her. He had announced himself as the general avenger of all insults offered to his tribe, and for the better discharge of this duty carried with him a cele-

* *Cousin.*—The following Table will help the reader to understand this relationship :—

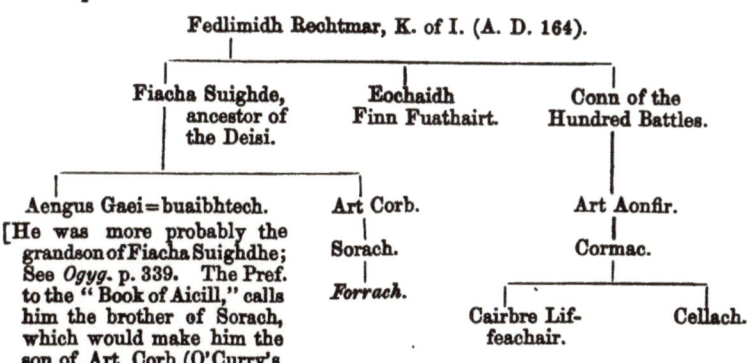

Fedlimidh Rechtmar, K. of I. (A. D. 164).

Fiacha Suighde, ancestor of the Deisi.   Eochaidh Finn Fuathairt.   Conn of the Hundred Battles.

Aengus Gaei=buaibhtech.   Art Corb.   Art Aonfir.
[He was more probably the grandson of Fiacha Suighdhe; See *Ogyg.* p. 339. The Pref. to the " Book of Aicill," calls him the brother of Sorach, which would make him the son of Art Corb (O'Curry's   Sorach.   Cormac.

Forrach.   Cairbre Liffeachair.   Cellach.

Lect. p. 48), and this seems to have been O'Flaherty's judgment. *Ogyg.* p. 340. The *Seanchas na relec,* first published by Dr. Petrie (*Round Towers,* p. 98), makes him the son of Eochaidh Finn Fuathairt. This must be wrong, for the whole story hangs on his being of the Deisi; but it shows how old the confusion about his genealogy was.]

brated javelin, called *Gaei-buaibhtech*, or poisonous dart. He immediately went to Tara, and found his kinswoman at a well called Nemnach, near Tara, engaged with the other captives in carrying water to the royal residence. Without delay he led her to his own house, and having put her in safety, returned to Tara; there he sought the presence of the king, behind whose chair stood the young prince Cellach. Aengus, after some words of angry altercation, struck Cellach with his formidable spear, and slew him in his father's presence. On withdrawing the spear, the blade touched King Cormac's eye, and blinded him for ever; the other end of the spear-handle at the same time struck Setna, the king's house steward, in the heart, and killed him on the spot. In the confusion Aengus escaped, and safely reached his home.

It was then the law that personal blemishes, such as the loss of a limb or an eye, incapacitated the sovereign from the active government of the kingdom; Cormac therefore left Tara, and retired to Aicill, or Acaill, now the hill of Skreen, where he had a residence. He resigned his crown to his son Cairbre Liffeacair, although for nearly a year Eochaidh Gonnat, grandson of Fergus Black Tooth, took advantage of the confusion, and usurped the throne; two years afterwards Cormac was accidentally choked by the bone of a salmon which stuck in his throat.

At Acaill, Cormac is said to have compiled the curious book of Brehon Laws, called the "Book of Acaill," of which two copies now exist in the Library of Trinity College, Dublin, and one,[*] a much more valuable and perfect MS., in the Stowe collection, now in the possession of the Earl of Ashburnham. In the Preface to this work is an account of the loss of Cormac's eye, and the deaths of his son and steward, essentially the same as that given in the tract before us, although differing in many of the details. Mr. O'Curry has published an extract from this Preface, from the Trinity College MS., E. 3. 5 (*Lectures*, p. 43; and Append. xxvii. p. 511).

The "Action" taken by King Cormac, to recover damages from the Deisi for the loss of his eye, and for the double murder of his son and steward, is extremely interesting, as illustrating ancient criminal proceedings under the Brehon Law; and these proceedings are much more clearly described in the tract before us than in the Preface to the Book of Aicill. Cormac first sent his Brehon, Fithal, to demand reparation from

---

[*] *One.* See Dr. O'Conor's Stowe Catalogue, vol. i. p. 282 (No. **xxxvii.**)

Aengus and his tribe, and to dictate the terms that would be accepted. These were referred to an assembly which, in due time, met on the hill of Uisnech ; the terms of reparation were insisted upon by Daire, Cormac's youngest son, who represented his father on the occasion, and were the following :—1. That the Deisi should no longer hold their territory in the neighbourhood of Tara of free patrimony, but by service. 2. That they should own themselves the vassals* and tributaries of Cormac and his descendants for ever.

These terms were indignantly rejected by the Deisi, whose an- cestor, Fiacha Suighde, was the elder brother of Cormac's grandfather Conn of the Hundred Battles : the result was a series of wars, and a lasting feud, which ended in the expulsion of the Deisi from Meath, and their wandering in different parts of Leinster and Munster for many years, until they settled at length, in the fifth century, in the present county of Waterford, in a territory where the two baronies of Decies without Drum, and Decies within Drum, still bear testimony to their emigration.

But these subsequent adventures of the Deisi† are not included in the present tract, which ends abruptly, and perhaps imperfectly, on fol. 55. b. col. 2.

There is no other copy known of this important historical tale, which is well worthy of publication.

This tract, although written in prose, contains, like all such bardic tales, some poems inserted into the narrative. The following are the initial lines of these poems :—

bronan pola peir crogaṁ (5 stanzas). Fol. 51. b. col. 2.

Puil cuinb bo cuaig potalmain (11 stanzas). Fol. 52. b. col. 2.

Cri pludiöig gaċ en bliaban (9 stanzas). Fol. 53. a. col. 1.

Cigiö aṁna imcolaiñ cuinb (9 stanzas). *Ibid.* col. 2.

---

* *Vassals.* The legal steps by which the free tribes were to be reduced to the state of tributaries and vassals are minutely described, and are extremely important as illustrating the Brehon Laws, and the con- dition of civilization at the time when the Book of Aicill was compiled.

† *Deisi.* In the Trinity College MS. H. 2. 15. p. 67. a. col. 1. (ten lines from bottom), is a tract " On the blinding of Cormac mac Airt, and the expulsion of the Deisi from Meath." In H. 3. 17. col. 720. is also an account of the blinding of Cormac ; and col. 723, line 27 of the same MS., is an account of the Gaibuaibhtech, or poisonous dart with which Aengus in- flicted the wound.

Rı mac ꝓeıổlımıᵹ ampa conn (2 stanzas). Fol. 53. b. col. 1.
Ꞇꞃı mıc a cunn poᴄualа (7 stanzas). *Ibid.* col. 2.

Fol. 56. a. This leaf contains a long poem of fifty-eight stanzas, written across the full page, and not in columns; it occupies the whole of this, and nearly the next page. The poem is anonymous, composed in praise of David Mac Muiris Roche, and begins, Ꝺleaᵹaꞃ cunổꞃaổ ổo ᴄoṁall, "A covenant must be fulfilled." It gives a curious account of various border battles, forays, and plunderings by the Lord of Fermoy, whose hospitality and other virtues the poet celebrates. Mr. O'Curry told me that he had never seen another copy of this poem.

(VI.) The sixth stave contains six leaves numbered in continuation, and in the same hand as the foregoing, from fol. 57-62. The double columns are here continued.

Fol. 57. a. col. 1. A short legend, beginning, Ꝺpoıle ổuıne ꞇꞃuaᵹh boᴄꞇ, "A certain miserable poor man." This is a story of a miserably poor man who came one day to beg for alms from King David. David had nothing to give, and the poor man asked him to give him at least a blessing in his bosom; David did so, and the beggar wrapping his cloak closely round the place where David had pronounced the words of blessing, hastened home; there he cast his cloak into a well, which immediately became full of great fish. The poor man sold the fish, and soon became immensely rich, &c., &c.

Ibid. (line 19). A legend beginning, Ceıꞇꞃe haıꞃổı an ổomaın .ı. ꞇoıꞃ, ⁊ ꞇıaꞃ, ꞇeꞃ, ⁊ ꞇuaıᵹh, "The four cardinal points of the world, viz., East and West, North and South." This is an account of the persons (*four*, in accordance with the points of the compass), whom God willed to live through and survive the Deluge, in order that the history of the world after that great destruction of all monuments might be preserved. The margin is injured by damp; but enough remains legible to see that one of these was Fintan, son of Lamech, to whom it was committed to preserve the history of the Western world, viz., Spain, Ireland, and the countries of the Gaedhil. He is fabled to have lived in the South West of Kerry, to the middle of the sixth century. Another was Firen, son of Sisten, son of Japhet, son of Noah, who was appointed to preserve the history of the North, from Mount Rifia to the

Mur Torrian, or Tyrrhene Sea. Fors, son of Electra, son of Seth, son of Adam, was to preserve the history of the East; and Annoid, son of Cato,* . . . . son of Noah, was responsible for the history of the South.

Fol. 57. a. col. 2. A tract beginning Oa mac ampa la .ōō., " Two celebrated sons had David." The margin is greatly injured, and not easily read. This seems to be some worthless legend of David and his son Solomon.

Ibid. (line 18). The Life and Martyrdom of St. Juliana, beginning Oo bi apoile uppaiɟi. Her martyrdom is commemorated in the Irish Calendars of Aengus and Maelmuire O'Gormain, as well as in the Roman Martyrology, at Feb. 16.

The Life of St. Juliana ends fol. 58. a. col. 1. line 33.

Fol. 58. a. col. 1. (line 34). Begins a tract with the following title : Cuapurcbail luōáip rcaipiot, " The account of Judas Iscariot." This is one of the innumerable legends connected with the voyages of St. Brendan. The beginning of the tract is injured.

Fol. 58. b. col. 1. The beginning of this tract is injured. It is a legend of the wanderings of two of St. Columcille's priests or monks, who, on their return to Hy from Ireland, were driven by adverse winds into the northern seas, where they saw strange men, and great wonders. The details may not be altogether worthless, as it is possible that there may be a substratum of truth.† On the upper margin, a modern and bad hand has written, meapuɟaō clepeach coluimcille, " Wanderings of Columcille's clerks." This tract begins O caimic ōepeaɟ piɟe ⁊ plaiteṁnup ōomnaill mc aeōa, mc ainmipech. Ends fol. 59. b. col. 1.

Fol. 59. b. col. 1. This tract is headed beacha baippe Copcaiōe aṅpo pip, " The Life of Barre of Cork, down here." It begins Mobaippe ōá. ōo chonnaccaiō ōo iapcineol, &c., " Mobairre was of the Connachtmen by family." Ends fol. 60. col. 1. There appears now a considerable defect between fol. 59 and 60, which had taken place before the folios were numbered, and is not noticed in the count ; four pages at least must be missing. Some paper copies of this life are extant.

---

* Some words in the MS. are here illegible.

† *Truth.* In the Trinity College MS. H. 2. 16 [col. 707 al. 711, line 29] is a tract entitled Eaōcpa Clepech Coluimcille, " The Adventures of Columcille's clerks."

Fol. 60. *a. col.* 1. The title is written in a bad modern hand, beaca molaʒa, "Life of St. Molaga." The tract begins Molaʒa ⱃ. ꝺⱃepaⰉꝺ muⰉʒⰉ ꝼene a cenel, .Ⰹ. ꝺe uⰉꝺ cuⱃcpaⰉꝺ, &c., "Now Molaga, his race was of the men of Magh Fene, i. e. of the Hy Cusgraighe." St. Molaga was the founder of the Church and Monastery of Tech Molaga, now Timoleague,* county of Cork, and of many other churches in Ireland. The present tract is extremely valuable for its topography and local allusions. The tract ends abruptly, as if the scribe had never quite finished it; but there is nothing lost. Ends fol. 61. b. col. 1.

Fol. 61. *b. col.* 1. This tract is headed Ɇaccpa CopmaⰉc m̄c ⱭⰉpc, "Adventures of Cormac Mac Airt." It is one of the many fairy tales and romantic stories of which that celebrated hero has been made the subject. It begins Ꝼeccuⱃ ꝺo ⰦⰉ Copmac huⰉ CuⰉnn a LⰉacⱃuⰉm, &c, "Once upon a time Cormac, grandson of Conn, was at Liatruim, i. e. Tara." This story has been published, with a translation, by the Ossianic Society,† along with the tract called "Pursuit after Diarmuid ODuibhne and Graine, daughter of Cormac Mac Airt;" edited by Mr. Standish H. O'Grady. It is to be regretted, however, that the Society should have selected so bad a copy of this tale for their text; they had not of course, at that time, access to the excellent and ancient copy now before us; but in the "Book of Ballymote," in the Library of this Academy, there is a copy much fuller and better than that which they have published.

Fol. 62. *b. col.* 1. A legend entitled Ɑcⱃo anc aꝺꝺaⱃ ꝼanaⰦaⱃ Ⱖomnach cⱃom ⰦuⰦh, "This is the reason why Crom Dubh Sunday was so called," beginning Laꞇ . . . . ꞃoⰦe caⰉnⰦeach naeⰮ anoⰉⱡen ꝉoⱃa [cⱃe] . . . . "One day that Saint Cainnech was in the island of Roscrea," he saw a great legion of demons flying over him in the air. One of them came down to the island, and Cainnech asked him where the devils were going. He replied that a good friend of theirs, named Crom-dubh, had died that day, and they were going to take possession of his soul. 'Go,' said the saint, 'but I charge you to return to me here on your way back, and tell me how you have fared.' The demon after some time returned, but limping on one leg

---

* He is better known as the founder of Ath-cross-Molaga (now Aghacross, n. of Fermoy), and Temple-Molaga.

† *Society.* Transact. vol. iii. (1855), p. 212.

‡ The MS. is here illegible.

and groaning with pain. 'Speak,' said the saint; 'what has happened to you?' 'My Lord,' said the demon, 'we seized upon Crom-dubh, certain that our claim to him was good, but suddenly St. Patrick, with a host of saints and angels, appeared, who assailed us with fiery darts, one of which struck me in the leg, and has left me lame for ever. It seems that Crom-dubh's charities and good works were more than a balance for his sins; so the saints took possession of his soul, and put us to flight.'"

(VII.) The seventh stave contains now ten leaves, foll. 63-72; numbered as before; written in double columns.

Fol. 63. *a. col.* 1. A tract beginning Ochτεριη uзuρτ ba hαιρῦηι αη bοmαιη αηb ρο зειηιρ Cριρτ, &c., "Octavianus Augustus was emperor of the world when Christ was born, &c." This is a history of the birth, life, and death of our Lord, with the succession and acts of the Roman emperors, to the destruction of Jerusalem under Titus. The lower margins are much injured; on the upper margin of fol. 63. a. col. 2. is some writing in a hand of the sixteenth century, now nearly illegible. On the left-hand margin of fol. 64. a. is scribbled the name "uιll ηα heaзρα, 1805," i. e. William O'Hara, and on the lower margins of fol. 70. a. and b. is the same name without the date. On the upper margin of fol. 72. a. is written "Εmαηuεl," but not in the hand of the original scribe.

This tract ends fol. 72. a col. 1. line 10.

Fol. 72, *a. col.* 1. (line 11). A tract beginning Ɑροιle oзlach bo bí ιη abbαιηe bρumαηαιз, "A certain youth was in the abbey of Drumanach," now Drimnagh, county of Dublin. This is a foolish story. The youth, at Easter time, with a sword in his hand, lay down on the side of the hill upon which the abbey was built, and there fell asleep; when he awoke he found himself transformed into a comely maiden.

Fol. 72. *b. col.* 1. A tract beginning Ɖα bροη ρlαchα ηιme, "The two sorrowful ones of the kingdom of heaven," viz., Enoch and Elias. This is a tale of which we have other copies. There is one, slightly defective at the beginning, in the "Leabhar na hUidhri."

(VIII.) The eighth stave contains four leaves only. It is evidently very defective. The first page is marked 73, in a modern hand; the remaining leaves are numbered in red pencil, in Mr. O'Curry's hand, 74, 75, 76; but there are traces of the older pagination which seems to have been 79, 80, 81, and 82. This Mr. O'Curry found to be wrong, and altered it accordingly.

Fol. 73. *a. col.* 1, to *col.* 2. line 10, seems to be the conclusion of the tract on Enoch and Elias. See fol. 72. *b.*

Fol. 73. *a. col.* 2. from line 11 to the end is in a different hand. It is a collection of extracts translated into Irish from St. Ambrose. It begins, ḃpiaċpa annpo o Ambpopiup, "These are the words of Ambrose."

Fol. 73. *b.* is blank.

Fol. 74. *a.* The remainder of this stave is written across the pages at full length, and not in double columns.

On this page begins a poem of which the Academy possesses a complete copy in the O'Gara MS. From this it appears that the author was Donnchadh Mór O'Daly,* abbat of Boyle, in the first half of the thirteenth century. The subject of the poem is religious; it consisted originally of seventy-one stanzas (284 lines), as appears from the O'Gara MS., but there now remain in the present copy only thirty-one stanzas, owing to a loss of several leaves between fol. 74 and 75. The poem begins—

Ᵹabum ḃechmaḋ ap nḃana
Ɗo Ɗia map ap ḃiñᵹmala.

"Let us give tithe of our poems
To God, as it is meet."

Ends imperfect; fol. 74. b.

Fol. 75. *a.* A poem on the Signs of the Day of Judgment, by the same author.† It wants nine stanzas at the beginning, as appears

---

* *O'Daly.* See O'Reilly, "Transact. Iberno-Celtic Soc.," p. lxxxviii.   † *Author.* See O'Reilly, *ibid.* p. xc. no. 17.

from the O'Gara MS.; but twenty-six stanzas remain, ending on the present page, ninth line from bottom. This poem began

Ᵹaɼb eıɼᵹe ıᵭna an bɼaċa

"Fierce the uprising of the Signs of the Judgment."

Ibid. Line 8 from bottom. A poem in praise of the B. V. Mary, beginning,

Ɑ ṁuıɼe, a macaıɼ aɼ naċaɼ
ɼo ċaċaıᵹ ᵹaᵭ boᵭuɼ,

"O Mary, O Mother of our Father,
Who hast appeased all grief."

This poem is anonymous; no other copy of it is known. It is of considerable length, and ends fol. 76. b. line 10. Several words in the last few lines are rubbed and illegible.

Fol. 76. *b.* line 11. A poem headed Mıanna Coɼmaıc mıc Ɑıɼc, "The Desires of Cormac Mac Airt." It begins—

Mıan Coɼmaıc cıᵹı cempa, oᵹlaᵭ claıċ ɼe cıᵹeɼna,

"The desire of Cormac of the house of Tara, a soldier mild towards his Lord."

The poem consists of twelve stanzas, and is here anonymous; but O'Reilly[*] attributes it to Flaithri, son of Cormac's brehon Fithil, which is ridiculous. Copies of it are common, but this is an old and valuable one.

Ibid. line 12 from bottom. A poem of eleven stanzas, headed, Ᵹeɼoıb ıaɼla boċum na ɼuaċa beᵹa ɼoɼıɼ, "Earl Gerald that composed the little hateful things down here." This was Gerald, fourth Earl of Desmond, who succeeded his half-brother in 1349. He died, or was murdered, 1397.[†]

The poem, which is anonymous, begins—

Ƥuaċ lem ɼuaċha mıc mıc Cuınn,

"Hateful to me what was hated by the son of Conn's son."

It is very much rubbed, and difficult to read.

---

* O'Reilly. *Ibid.* p. xxiv.
† He was celebrated for his learning, and was surnamed the Poet. Lodge,

Peerage, vol. i., p. 65. The Four Masters call him *Geroid un dana*, "Gerald of the poems." (A. D. 1588, p. 1796.)

(IX.) The ninth stave contains four leaves. The pagination has been altered as before, by Mr. O'Curry, who has marked the leaves in black pencil in the upper margin, changing to 77, 78, 79, 80, what were before 74 [an attempt seems to have been made to erase this number, and it is evidently not in the same hand as the other old pagination] 74, [repeated in the old hand], 75, 76. We shall here follow Mr. O'Curry's pagination. This stave is written in double columns, as before.

Fol. 77. *a. col.* 1. A poem beginning O mnaıb aınmnıᵹcep epı, "From women Eri is named," alluding to Fodla, Banba, and Eri, the wives of the Tuatha De Danann Kings, whose names are frequently given by the bards to Ireland. The poem ends on the following page, col. 1, line 14. It is in many places illegible; but it seems to be a panegyric on the daughter of O'Brien, who was married to David,* son of Morris Roche.

Fol. 77. *b. col.* 1. line 15. A poem headed Eoᵹan mac conchobaıp hı balaıᵹe. cc., "Eogan, son of Conchobhair O'Dalaighe, cecinit." This poet, Eoghan, or Owen, son of Connor O'Daly, is not mentioned by O'Reilly, or elsewhere, as far as I can find. The present poem is a panegyric on the same wife of David, son of Muiris Roche, to whom the preceding relates; but it gives us the additional information that her name was *Mór*, and that she was the daughter of Mathgamhain (or Mahon) O'Brien, of the county of Clare. The poem begins—

Nı pd hınbṁe ıp meapca móp,

"Not for her wealth [only] is Mór to be estimated;"

so that she was probably a great heiress in her day. The poem ends fol. 78. a. col. 1.

Fol. 78. *a. col.* 1. line 7 from bottom, a poem with the heading Cepball mac conchobaıp ı balaıᵹe .cc., "Cearbhall, son of Conchobhair O'Dalaighe, cecinit." This poet must have been the brother of the preceding; but I can find no account of him. The poem is an

---

* *David.* See above, fol. 56. a.

elegy on the death of the above-mentioned Mór, daughter of Mahon
O'Brien. It begins—

Olc an cumċaċ an cuṁa,

" An ill covering is sorrow."

This poem ends fol. 78. b. col 2.

Fol. 79. *a. col* 1. An anonymous poem of sixty stanzas (240 lines),
beginning—

Ⱥ ceġ beġ ciaġaır a ceġ mór.

" From a small house people go to a big house."

This is a panegyrical poem on Diarmait O'Brien, son of the celebrated Torrdealbhach, or Torlogh, the hero of the well-known historical
romance called the "Wars of Torlogh," or "Wars of Thomond."*

The margins are greatly injured, and in many places illegible; but
there is an excellent copy of it in the O'Conor Don's MS. where the
authorship is ascribed to Godfrey Fionn O'Daly,† a poet who died in
1386, or 1387.

Fol. 79. *b. col.* 2. A prose tract entitled Caċ alṁaıne ro, " The
battle of Almhain here." It begins boı cocaḃ mor ecır caċal mc
pınġuıne rı leċe moḃa ⁊ ⱸerġal mac maeıleḃuın rı leċe cuınḃ
rı ré cıan, " There was a great war between Cathal mac Finguine,
King of Leth Mogha [Munster], and Ferghal, son of Maelduin, King of
Leth Cuinn [K. of Ireland]; during a long time." This famous battle
was fought A. D. 722 (see Tighernach in anno), at the Hill of Almhain, now the hill of Allen, in the county of Kildare. See " Four Masters," and "Chron. Scotor." ad ann. 718.

There is another copy of this tract in the Library of Trin. Coll., H.
2. 16.

Fol. 80. *b. col.* 2. A legend of Longarad of Disert-Longarad, in
Ossory, beginning, Lonġaraḃ coırⱸınḃ amuıġ cuaċac : the story is,
that Longarad refused to allow St. Columbcille to see his books, whereupon the saint of Hy prayed that the books might become useless to
every one after the death of their owner; accordingly, on the night of
Longarad's death the satchels fell from their racks, and the books be-

---

* *Thomond.* See O'Curry's Lectures,
p. 233, *sq.*

† *O'Daly.* O'Reilly mentions this au-

thor, and notices several of his productions,
but not the present poem, *ubi supra,* p.
ciii.

came illegible for ever. See Mart. Donegal, 3 Sept. p. 234. Reeves, Adamnan, p. 359, *n.* Book of Obits of Christ Church, Introd., p. lxxi.

(X.) There is a loss of some leaves between this and the forego-ing stave. The tenth stave contains eight leaves, numbered in the old hand from fol. 85 to 92, written in double columns.

Fol. 85. a. col. 1. A prose tract beginning Ⱂeaⱅⱅ naen ⰱan-ⰱeaċaⰱ ⱂiaċna ⱂinⰰ mac ⰱaeⰰain meic muⱂceⱂⱅaiⰷ m̄c muⱂe-ⰱaiⰷ m̄c eoⰷain ṁeic neill aⱀeiⱂinⰰ amaċ co ⱂainic a loċlanⰰaiⰱ. "Once upon a time Fiacna Finn, son of Baedan, son of Muirchertach, son of Muredach, son of Eoghan, son of Niall, went forth from Ire-land until he came to the Lochlanns." This is a copy—the only known copy—of the life of Mongan, son of Fiachna, King of Ulidia in the sixth century. It is mentioned in the list of ancient tales published by Mr. O'Curry,[*] from the "Book of Leinster," under the title of Єⱅⱂa Monⰷain mic Ⱂiaċna, "Adventures of Mongan, son of Fiachna." The first part of the tract is occupied by the adventures of Fiachna, Mongan's father, who in his youth had visited the country of the Loch-lanns, or Scandinavia, where Eolgharg Mor, son of Maghar, was then king, and lying ill of a fatal disease. The physicians declared that no-thing could cure him but the flesh of a perfectly white cow, with red ears; after searching the whole country, only one such cow was found, the property of an old woman,[†] whose sole possession it was. She agreed to accept four of the best cows in exchange for her own, provided the Irish prince Fiachna became security for the performance of the promise. To this the king's steward induced Fiachna to agree; but soon after, the death of his father compelled him to return with haste to Ireland, to take possession of his inheritance as King of Ulidia. He had been scarcely settled on his throne when the old woman appeared before him,

---

[*] *O'Curry.* Lect. p. 589. Mr. O'Curry adds in a note, "This tale is not known to me." But there is an abridged copy of it in Trin. Coll. Library.

[†] *Woman.* The original word caillⰵaċ (cucullata) may signify either *a nun,* or an old woman wearing a hood, or cowl. White cows with red ears are mentioned more than once in Irish History. Cathair Mór, in his will, bequeathed 100 such cows to Nia Corb (*Mart. Donegal, Introd.* p. xxxvi.); and Matilda, wife of William de Braosa, is said to have offered 400 cows, all milk white, but with red ears, to Isabelle, the queen of King John of England, in order to purchase her intercession with John. *Leland, Hist. of Ireland,* i., p. 191, quoting Speed (8vo. Dublin, 1814). For these references I am indebted to Mr. Hennessy.

to complain that the king's word had been broken, and that she had never received the promised cows. Fiachna offered her eighty cows to make good her loss, but she refused to receive any such compensation, and demanded that he should invade Scandinavia with an army, and take signal vengeance on the king for his breach of faith. This Fiachna, in consequence of his promise, considered himself bound to do, and landed with an army in the kingdom of the Lochlanns, challenging the false king to battle. In a series of battles the Irish were defeated, owing to Druidical influences which were brought to bear against them; for we are told that flocks of poisonous sheep, who were really demons, issued every day from the Lochlann King's pavillion and destroyed the Irish soldiers. Fiachna, therefore, resolved to take the field against these strange enemies, and did so notwithstanding all his people could say to dissuade him. When he appeared at the head of his troops he beheld a knight approaching him in rich and gorgeous apparel. The knight promised him victory over his Druidical enemies, provided Fiachna would give him a gold ring which he wore on his finger. Fiachna gave him the ring, and the knight produced from under his cloak a small hound with a chain, which he gave to the Irish king, saying, that the hound if let loose upon the magical sheep would soon destroy them all. The stranger knight then said that he was Manannan Mac Lir, the celebrated Tuatha de Danann Navigator and Necromancer, and instantly vanished; immediately after, however, he appeared in Fiachna's Court in Ireland, and presented himself to the queen in the exact likeness of her husband, wearing also his signet ring. The queen never doubted his identity, and admitted him without scruple to her bed. Fiachna, having vanquished his enemies, returned home, and found his wife pregnant from the stranger, but he had no difficulty in conjecturing from her story who the stranger was. In due time a son was born, and named Mongan, but three nights after his birth he was carried off by Manannan, who kept him, and educated him until he was sixteen years of age. At that time Fiachna was deposed and slain by a pretender to the throne, and Manannan brought back Mongan to receive his reputed father's crown. What follows is the most curious part of this tale, containing the history of Mongan's dealings with Brandubh, King of Leinster, and recording several curious and seemingly authentic historical facts, with the origin of many legends and superstitions, frequently alluded to elsewhere, but of which this valuable tale contains the only ancient explanation.

This tract is well worthy of publication. It occupies eight pages of the MS., and ends fol. 88. b. col. 2.

Fol. 89. *a. col.* 1. A tract begining Ⱃeachⱃ naen ba ⱃoiбe conn .c. caⱅhað mac Ⱇeiðlimiᵹ ⱃecⱅmaiⱃ mic Ⱅuaⱅhail ⱅechⱅmaiⱃ mic Ⱇeⱃaɒaiᵹ ⱇinð ⱃechⱅnaiᵹ, &c.

Conn of the Hundred Battles, when in the midst of his glory as King of Ireland (at the close of the second century), lost by death his wife Eithne Taebhfada [of the long side, i. e., the tall], daughter of Bris-lind Bind [the melodious], King of Lochlann, or Scandinavia. To dispel his grief, he repaired to the hill of Howth, and derived some consolation from watching the sea. One day he beheld a boat approaching with rapidity without the agency of any rowers. It soon arrived, when a beautiful woman, in splendid garments, who seemed to have been its only occupant, stepped ashore, advanced to Conn, and sat fami-liarly beside him. She proved to be Becuma Cneisgel [of the fair skin], daughter of Eoghan, of Inbher [now Arklow], a famous Tuatha de Danann chieftain, and wife of Labhraidhe Luaith-clamh-ar-cloidem [of the swift hand at the sword], another chieftain of the same race who dwelt at Inis Labhrada, in Ulster. Her history was this: she was found guilty by her tribe of a too great intimacy with the son of Manannan Mac Lir, whereupon, on the very day when she ap-peared before Conn, she had been expelled from her people by the great assembly of the Tuatha de Danann, who sentenced her to be sent adrift upon the sea in a self-moving boat; and she was carried, as we have seen, to the place where Conn was sitting. After some con-versation, Conn proposed to make her his queen, but she declared that she preferred to marry his son Art, of whose fame she had heard, and whom she loved, although she had never seen him. Conn pressed his own suit, and the lady at length consented, on the condition that Art was to be banished from Ireland for a year. This was done, but on his return at the end of the year, Art was challenged by Becuma to play with her a game of chess. Art won, and imposed upon his stepmother the task of procuring for him the magical wand which the great Irish legendary hero Curoi Mac Daire used to carry in his conquests. Then are described the travels of Becuma through all the fairy mounds and mansions of Ireland in search of the wand, which at last she discovered, and brought to Art. This is a very curious portion of the tale, as illus-trating the fairy mythology of the Irish. Art, on receiving the wand, challenged her to another game, but this time he lost, and his stepmother imposed upon him the task to seek for, and bring home with him, Delbh-chaemh [beautiful form], a lady of transcendent beauty, daughter of Mongan. Art inquired where Delbh-chaemh was to be found, but the only information he could get was, that she resided in an island of the sea. With this clue he set out in search of her, and his adventures are described. He brings her home with him at length; and the tale concludes with the repudiation and banishment of Becuma.

This tract is valuable, and ought to be carefully studied, if ever the history of the legendary lore and fairy mythology of Ireland should be written.

Fol. 92. b. A poem headed Maelmuᵽe maᵹᵽaιᴄ .ᴄᴄ., "Mael-muire Magrath cecinit." This poet flourished about 1390, according to O'Reilly, who does not, however, mention the present poem, which begins, Mιᵽι a aιmι aᵽ hιnᴄaιb ᵽ́eιn, "I put myself, O Emma, upon thine own protection."

This is a panegyric upon Emma, daughter of the Earl of Desmond, and was evidently written during her lifetime. This was Maurice, the first Earl, who was married in 1312 to Margaret, fifth daughter of Richard de Burgo, the red Earl of Ulster. At the end of the poem the scribe has signed his name Mιᵽι bomnall oleιᵹ . . . . . . "I am Domhnall O'Leig . . . . . " the rest of the name is illegible.*

(XI.) The eleventh stave contains four leaves only, written across the page, and not in double columns. They are numbered in the old hand, fol. 93–96. This stave is very much injured, and in many places utterly illegible; the application of tinc-ture of galls by some former possessor has blackened alto-gether several passages.

Fol. 93. a. This is a poem of thirty-eight stanzas, written in a most beautifully regular hand. It is anonymous, and seems to be a pane-gyric on David Roche of Fermoy. The first line is illegible.

Ibid. (fifth line from bottom). A poem in the same hand, with the following heading, which gives the author's name: Comaᵽ, mac ᵽuaιᴆᵽι mᴄ bιaᵽmaᴆa mecᵽaιᴄ .ᴄᴄ., "Thomas, son of Ruaidhri (or Rory), son of Diarmaid Magrath, cecinit." The poem begins,

---

* *Illegible.* The name was probably of a scribe Domhnall hua Leighin in ano-
O'Leighin, now Lyons. We find the name ther place. See fol. 96. a.

Ceic oιρbeρc an ιɱheριɜ,
Um oιρbeρc ρe hιnɒιne aɜ ɒιall.

" The wealth of royal nobility,
With the nobility of wealth contends."

This poem seems to be a panegyric, probably on the same David Roche, who is the subject of the preceding. It is greatly injured at the margins.

Fol. 83. *b.* (14th line from bottom). A poem (anonymous) of thirty-three stanzas, in praise of the same David Roche, of Fermoy. The first line is illegible; it is in the same beautiful hand as the foregoing.

Fol. 84. *a.* (line 20). A poem in praise of David, son of Muiris Roche. It is anonymous, and in the same hand as the preceding, consisting of thirty-one stanzas, beginning,

Ɜeρρ ɜo laιbeoρaιɒ an lιa ρáιl,

" It is short until the Lia Fail speaks."

This means that the claims of David Roche to be King of Ireland will soon be acknowledged by the voice of the Lia Fail, or Druidical Stone of Destiny, at Tara, which was fabled to utter a peculiar sound whenever the true heir to the crown of Ireland was placed upon it.

Fol. 94. *b.* (line 8). An anonymous poem of twenty-eight stanzas, in the same hand, in praise of the same David, son of Muiris Roche. The first line is illegible.

Fol. 94. *b.* (line 9 from bottom). A poem whose author is recorded in the heading, which is now nearly illegible, Ɒonchaɒ mac Eoɜaιn O Ɒalaιɒe .c̄c̄., " Donogh, son of Owen O'Daly, cecinit." It is in praise of the same David Roche, but the first line is illegible. The first half of the next page is blackened and rendered utterly illegible by tincture of galls. I cannot say whether it contains a continuation of O'Daly's poem, or a different article.

Fol. 95. *a.* (half down the page). An anonymous poem of thirty-four stanzas in praise of the same David Roche, of Fermoy, beginning ɒa ριɒι ƒeolca aρ ƒen nɜall, " In two ways is woven the property of the foreigners." This poem ends on the next page, the second part of which is blank.

Fol. 96. *a.* Here is a very curious and valuable list of lands which

once formed part of the vast estates of the Roches of Fermoy. It is in
many places now totally illegible, but enough might still be recovered
to be of considerable interest; especially if it were decyphered with
the aid of a local knowledge of the names of the places mentioned.
The first line is illegible, with the exception of the words IS ᵹᴙᴀ . . . . .
The last nine lines of this page are less obliterated than the rest, and
were thus translated for me by Mr. O'Curry, soon after I obtained possession of the MS.; they are curious, as fixing the date of this inventory of the lands of the Roche family.*

"[It was in the time of] Daibith mor mac Muiris do Roidsigh [David
the great, son of Morris Roche], that Domhnall h. Leighin† wrote this
first; and I, Torna, son of Torna h. Maoilconaire‡ wrote this present
chart for David, son of Muiris, son of David, son of Muiris, son of
Daibith mor; and for Oilen, daughter of Semus, son of Semus, son of
Eman, son of Piarois [Pierce], at Baile Caislean an Roitsigh,§ the
fortress of the authors and ollavs, and exiles, and companies of scholars
of Ireland; and from which none ever departed without being grateful,

---

* From this curious document it appears
that an inventory of the lands belonging to
the Roche family was made in the time of
David Mór, or the Great, son of Morris
Roche, by Donnell O'Leighin, or Lyons.
Of this older document the present page
is a copy made by Torna, son of Torna
O'Mulconry, for another David, whose descent from David Mór mac Muiris is thus
given:—

David Mór mac Muiris.
|
Muiris.
|
David.
|
Muiris.
|
David, who was, therefore, the great-
great grandson of David Mór; he was
married to Oilen, or Ellen, daughter of
James, son of James, son of Edmund, son
of Pierce Butler; and it would seem that
this branch of the Butler family bore the
name of Mac Pierce, to distinguish them

from other branches. The chart, or charter, as it is called, was transcribed in
the year 1561, at Castletown Roche, then
the seat of the Roche family, where scholars, poets, ollaves, exiles, &c., were received with hospitality, and invited to
consider it as "their fortress." The names
of the witnesses who were present at the
transcription of the document are then appended to it. These are, William, son of
James, who is called Sionanach, or of the
Shannon; Edmund Bán (or the white), son
of John Ruaidh (or the red), son of . . . .
Garoid (or Gerald), son of Edmund, who
is called the Ceithernach, or Kerne [i. e.
soldier or champion] of the House of Roche;
Godfrey O'Daly, son of Cerbhaill (or Carroll) Beg (the little), "with many others;"
whose names are not given.

† Domhnall O'Leighin, now Lyons.

‡ Mulconry.

§ Now Castletown-Roche, barony of
Fermoy, county of Cork.

according to the laws* of *Laoich-liathmuine,* to this couple, i. e., to the Roche and to the daughter of Mac Piarois; and may God give them counsels for prosperity and for light a long time in this world, and the Kingdom of God in the next, without termination, without end. And these are the witnesses that were present at the writing of this out of the old charter, namely, the Sionanach,† i. e. William Mac Semuis, and Emann Ban, mac Seain Ruaidh, mac [a name erased here], Garoid mac Emaind, i. e. Ceithernach of the House of Roitsech; and Diarmaid h. Leighin, i. e. the Ollav of the Roitsech; and Gotfraid h. Dalaighe, mac Cerbhaill beg, and many others along with them. Anno Domini 1561 is the age of the Lord at this time."

On the next page is a similar document in the same handwriting, considerably damaged at the margins; it appears to be a schedule of the rents in cash payable to the Roche, for certain denominations of lands enumerated.

A careful search ought to be made amongst our MSS., both in the Academy and in Trinity College, for another copy of these curious documents. A second copy would materially assist in decyphering them, and they are of great interest and curiosity, not only to the family history of the Roche, but to the local topography of the country.

Fol. 97 is wanting.

(XII.) The twelfth stave contains five leaves (including one leaf loose), numbered 98–102. This stave is in double columns.

Fol. 98. *a. col.* 1. The first five or six lines are injured by the application of galls. In the first line the following words are legible:—
. . . . . bc. ap mile iappin popgab papcalan. . . . . .

The tract begins imperfectly; it gives an account of the early colonists of Ireland, and of Tuan mac Cairrill, who survived the deluge, and remained in Ireland to the coming of St. Patrick. The tract ends fol. 98. b. col. 1.

----

* The laws of Laoch Liathmuine, i. e., the laws of the most unbounded hospitality. Cuana, son of Ailcen or Cailchine, lord of Fermoy, was called *Laoch Liathmuine,* or Hero of Cloch Liathmuine, in the parish of Kilgullane, barony of Fermoy. See *Four Masters,* A. D. 640, and O'Donovan's notes.

† This seems a kind of nickname, signifying " of the Shannon."

Fol. 98. *b. col.* 1. A poem of ten stanzas (anonymous), on the relative length of life of man and other animals, as well as the time allowed for the duration of fences and tillage in fields. It begins:—

> bliaban bon cuaille co cepc
> A cpi bon gupc na glaṗbepc
> Na ċuṗ ⁊ na aċ cuṗ
> An cṗeṗ na cṗepcuṗ.

> "A year for the stake by right,
> Three for the field in its green bearing,
> In fallow and in second fallow,
> And the third in its third fallow."

Fol. 99. *a. col.* 1. There is here a loss of one or more leaves, not noticed in the pagination. On the corner of the upper margin is the number 208, which would seem to show that more than 100 pages of the volume are lost. Fol. 99. a. contains the last page of the tale of the Lady Eithne, daughter of Dichu, of whose history we shall speak at fol. 111. a. *infra.*

Fol. 99. *b. col.* 1. An anonymous poem, of which the first thirty-four stanzas now remain, a leaf or more having been lost between what are now fol. 99 and 100, although not noticed in the pagination. It is a dialogue between the aged Eagle of Ecaill (Achill island) and Fintan, who had preserved the history of Ireland since before the Deluge,* in which Fintan gives an account of the primitive history of Ireland and its early colonists. The poem begins:—

> Appaib pin a eóin eacla!
> inbiṗ buin abbuṗ heaċcpa
> aca agam gan cṗéna
> ċagulluim a hein beṗla,

> "It is old thou art, O Bird of Eacaill,
> Tell me the cause of thy adventures;
> I possess, without denial,
> The gift of speaking in the bird language."

Fol. 100. *a. col.* 1. The last seven stanzas of a poem, imperfect, owing to the loss of the leaves already noticed. The names of "Cormac," and also that of "Diarmaid mag Carthaigh," occur in it.

---

* *Deluge.* See above, fol. 57, a. col. 1.

Ibid. Then follows a collection of eighteen short poems, ending on fol. 103. b., intended, apparently, for the instruction of Cormac, son of Diarmaid Mac Carthy. These poems are driftless and unintelligible; Mr. O'Curry thought that they may have been school lessons, or exercises for the young Mac Carthy, for the author seems to have been his tutor. They are not worth the time it would take to catalogue them more minutely. In some of these poems the O'Briens of Cluain-Ramh-fhada, now Clonrood, near Ennis, are mentioned. On the corner of the margin of fol. 100. a. is the number 2012, probably intended for 212. On the corresponding margin of fol. 101. b. is what seems the number 204; and there is a similar pagination which seems to be 209 on fol. 102. a.; but the last figure in all these paginations is very uncertain.

(XIII.) The thirteenth stave contains eight leaves, numbered foll. 103 to 110; the folios 105 to 110 have a second pagination in the upper margin, 154 to 159. The first two leaves of this stave are written across the pages, and not in double columns.

Fol. 103. *a.* A poem whose author is announced in the following heading:—Muıpcheaptach O Ꝃloınn .cc., "Muircheartach (or Mur-toch) O'Flynn, cecinit." This poem is in praise of two ladies, Mór and Johanna, who appear to have been the daughters of Owen Mac Carthy, and to have been in some way connected with the family of Roche, of Fermoy. It begins, Ceac ba banᵹan paic Caıpıl. "The Rath (or fort) of Cashel is a house of two fortresses." Ends next page.

Fol. 103. *b.* A poem of fifteen stanzas, headed, Eoᵹan mc aenᵹup ıbalaıᵹ .cc., "Eoghan, son of Aongus O'Daly, cecinit." This poem is in praise of Johanna, wife of David Roche, of Fermoy. It begins, Nel pıᵹna óp paic luᵹaıne, "There is a queenly cloud over Rath Ugaine."

Fol. 104. *a.* & *b.* Here are six more of the short, meaningless poems which were already noticed, fol. 100. a., and which Mr. O'Curry thought were written for Cormac son of Diarmaid Mac Carthy. These are in the same handwriting, and relate to Diarmait's son as well as to some female of the family who is not named. Except for the language, they are quite worthless.

Fol. 105. *a. col.* 1. Here begins an ancient religious tale, or legend,

known under the name of Impuim ċuραιᵹ ua coρρα, "Navigation*
of the curach [canoe or boat] of O'Corra." It begins Ϝlαċḃρuᵹαιḃ
ceḃach compαmaċ ρóċineaρaρ ḃo cuiᵹeaḃ conaċc.

As Mr. O'Curry has given a full and minute account of the contents
of this tale (Lect. xiii. p. 289. sq.), it will be unnecessary to say anything on the subject here. The O'Corra, and the company of nine
who formed the crew and passengers in their boat, are invoked in the
Litany of Aongus the Culdee. If that work be genuine, and written,
as Mr. O'Curry supposed, about 780 (a date scarcely credible), this
would give a very high antiquity to the legend; not that the tale or
legend, as here given, can pretend to such antiquity, for it is manifestly
of a much later date, but Mr. O'Curry's argument is, that the O'Corra,
if they have been invoked as saints in a litany of the end of the eighth
century, must have lived long before that time; this, however, assumes
the litany to have been written at the date he assigns to it, and that we
have it now uninterpolated, and in its original state; both these as-
sumptions, I need hardly say, are extremely improbable.

109. *col.* 1: A short tract entitled, Rıᵹaḃ nell noiᵹiallaiᵹ oρ
clann Ɇchaċ, aṅρo, "Inauguration of Niall of the Nine Hostages over
the clann Eochaidh here." It begins, ḃoi Ɇochaḃ muiᵹmeḃin ρι
Ɇρenn maḃun i cρich conaċc i coṁṗoccuρ ḃo lochuiḃ Ɇρne. The
object of this tract is to show how it came to pass that Niall succeeded
his father as King of Ireland, although he was the youngest of his
father's sons.

The original ink having become faint, has been gone over in some
places with black ink.

Fol. 110. *a. col.* 2. A tract headed Ceρca ᵹρeᵹa anḃρo, "Greek
questions here." This seems a silly and worthless production.

(XIV.) The fourteenth stave contains six leaves, numbered from
111 to 116, written in double columns.

Fol. 111. *col.* 1. A tract without title, beginning Aρḃρiᵹ cρoḃa
coρᵹρach clann. It contains the legend of Eithne, daughter of Dichu,
a very curious addition to the Tuath De Danaan mythology of Ireland;

----

* *Navigation.* Lit. rowing. In the list   entitled Impam hua Coρρα. "Row-
of ancient tales published by Mr. O'Curry,   ing [or Navigation] of O'Corra." Lect.
from the Book of Leinster, this tale is   p. 587.

for this tract has hitherto been unknown to us, and no other copy of it is known to exist.

The tale opens by an account of the Milesian invasion of Ireland, and their overthrow of the Tuatha De Danaan, the joint reign of the brothers Heber and Heremon, and the battle of Geisill, in which Heber fell, and Heremon became sole monarch of Ireland. After this the chiefs of the Tuath De Danaan appointed over themselves two supreme chiefs, viz., Bodhbh Dearg and Manannan Mac Lir. The latter being the great astrologer and magician of the tribe, was entrusted with the duty of selecting for them habitations where they might lie concealed from their enemies. Accordingly he settled them in the most beautiful hills and valleys, drawing round them an invisible wall impenetrable to the eyes of other men, and impassable, but through which they themselves could see and pass without difficulty. Manannan also supplied them with the ale of Goibhnenn, the Smith, which preserved them from old age, disease, and death; and gave them for food his own swine, which, although killed and eaten one day, were alive again, and fit for being eaten again, the next, and so would continue for ever.

The story then goes on to tell how the great Tuatha De Danaan mansion of Brugh na Boinne, near Slane, on the banks of the Boyne, had passed from the possession of Elcmar, its true owner, into that of Aengus, youngest son of the Daghda Mór, or great king of the Tuatha De Danaan. Elcmar was the foster-father of Aengus, and Manannan Mac Lir suggested to him to ask his foster-father for the palace. Meanwhile Manannan, by his art, deprived Elcmar of the power of refusing, and drove him forth, with all his family, to seek other habitations. Thus Aengus took undisputed possession of the palace, and there he dwells to this day, surrounded by an impenetrable and invisible wall, drinking Goibhnenn Smith's ale of immortality, and eating the never-failing pigs.

But it so happened that when the spell was put upon Elcmar and his family, which compelled them to abandon their home, part of the household was absent. This was Dichu, Elcmar's chief steward, with his wife and son. They had gone to seek some additional dainties for the distinguished company that Elcmar was then entertaining, one of whom was Manannan himself. The steward finding his old master gone, entered into the service of Aengus, and things went on as before.

Soon after this a daughter was born to Manannan, to whom he gave the name of "Curcog," from a tuft of golden hair which appeared on the crown of her head when she was born. On the same night a daughter was also born to the steward, Dichu, and she was named Eithne.* Aengus, according to the old fosterage customs, received both daughters to be brought up at his court.

When the girls grew up, Eithne was appointed one of the maids of honour to wait upon Curcog; but she refused to eat; and nevertheless continued in good health and plumpness. This was a great mystery, and gave much uneasiness to her friends; but Manannan discovered the cause. It appeared that on a former occasion she had received an insult from Finnbar, a Tuatha De Danaan chieftain of the hill Cnoc Meadha, who had been on a visit at her foster-father's. Her pure soul so resented this insult that her guardian demon fled from her, and was replaced by a guardian angel sent by the true God. From that time she was unable to eat any pagan food, and was miraculously sustained by the power of God.

Aengus and Manannan had at this time two lovely milch cows, giving an inexhaustible supply of milk. These cows they had brought home from India, whither they had gone on some necromantic voyage; and as India was then a land of righteousness, it was proposed that Eithne should live on the milk of these cows, which she consented to do, milking them herself.† Things went on so, and Eithne continued to live with, and wait upon the lady Curcog, at Brugh na Boinne, from the days of Heremon to the reign of King Laeghaire, son of Niall, and the coming of St. Patrick,‡ a period of about 1450 years.

At this time, St. Patrick still living, Curcog and her ladies, finding the weather sultry, went to bathe in the Boyne, after which they returned home, all except Eithne, whose absence they did not at first perceive, as neither did Eithne perceive that she had wandered from them. Her astonishment was great, when she returned to the shore, to find her companions gone. The fact was, that the influence of the true faith

---

* *Eithne.* "Sweet kernel of a nut."

† *Herself.* It seems that she was wont to milk her two cows in two golden *medars,* or methers; and that this tale was, therefore, called Alꞇꞃom ꞇiᵹe ꝺa ṁeꝺaꞃ, i. e. "The fosterage of the house of the two medars." But the medars do not seem to occupy a very prominent place in the story, as it is told in the Book of Fermoy.

‡ *St. Patrick.* In the text he is called mꞇailᵹin, "the shaven head," fol. 115. a. col. 2. line 8 and 17; in another place (ibid. line 5 from bottom), he is called Patrick Mac Alpuirn." St. Patrick, *Apost. of Ireland,* p. 411.

was now in the land, and had destroyed the power of her *feth-fiadha*, or veil of invisibility, when she threw it off with her other garments on going into the river. She therefore became an ordinary woman, unable to see through, or penetrate the invisible wall which protected her former associates from mortal gaze. She wandered on the north side of the Boyne, in great perplexity, ignorant of the cause of her dilemma; every thing to her eye was changed, and she could no longer find those paths and places which had been for so many centuries familiar to her. At length she came to a walled garden, in which stood what seemed to her a dwelling-house. A man, in a garb which was new to her, sat at the door and was reading in a book. He proved to be a recluse, and was sitting at the door of his church. She spoke to him, and told him her history. He received her kindly, and brought her to St. Patrick, by whom she was instructed and baptized.

One day she was sitting at the church of the recluse on the Boyne, when a great noise and clamour, as of a great multitude surrounding them, was heard, but it was not seen from whence the voices proceeded. Eithne, however, at once recognized her former friends, and discovered that Aengus and his household had gone forth in search of her, and when they could not discover her (for she was now invisible to them) they set up a loud wail and lamentation. At this she was so deeply affected that she swooned away, and was at the point of death. This shock she never recovered. She died, her head leaning on St. Patrick's breast, and was buried with due honour in the little church of the recluse, which from that time received the name of Cill-Eithne, or Eithne's Church.

The hermit's name was Ceasar; he was son of the King of Scotland, and one of St. Patrick's priests. He abandoned his little church on the death of Eithne, and retired to the wood of Fidh-Gaibhle, in Leinster, where he cleared for himself a field, in which he built another hermitage, called, from his name, Cluain-Ceasair.

The story of Eithne is continued on fol. 115. a. col. 1, in a quite different hand, and ends fol. 116. b. col. 1, line 12 from bottom.

Several poems are inserted into the latter part of the tale, viz.:—

Oena bam a cana pen. Fol. 115. a. col. 1. line 7 (a poem of three stanzas).

Oenum impob inirnimuch. Fol. 116. a. col. 1, line 28 (seven stanzas).

ɢoɩρɩɓ ṁe a muɩnꞇɩρ nɩṁe. "Call me, ye people of Heaven."
Fol. 116. a. col. 2, line 14 (six stanzas).

Cluɩꞇꞇɩρ lɩɓ ꝑeꝑꞇ ꝑɩaɩl eꞇne. "Let the generous Ethne's grave
be dug by you." Fol. 116. b. col. 1. line 30 (thirteen stanzas).

Fol. 116. *b. col.* 1. (line 10 from bottom). A poem with the title
Eoᵹan moρ u ɓalaɩᵹ .cc̄., "Eoghan mor O'Daly cecinit." It begins
Ceaᵹaρc mɩρɩ a Muɩρe, "Teach me, O Mary." The first four or
five stanzas are greatly rubbed, and in part illegible; the entire poem
seems to have consisted of nineteen stanzas.

* * *

(XV.) The fifteenth stave contains seven leaves, numbered from
fol. 117 to fol. 123. On the upper margin of fol. 117, *a.* col.
1, are the words ɩhꞃ maρɩa, "Jesus Maria."

Fol. 117. *a. col.* 1. A poem of thirty-seven stanzas (anonymous),
on the Crucifixion of our Lord, His descent into Hell, His Resurrection, and His Ascension into Heaven, accompanied by the souls whom
He had delivered from the Limbus patrum. The poem begins,

Eɩρeɩρᵹɩ ɓo eɩρɩᵹ Dɩa,

"A resurrection in which God arose."

It is written in a very beautiful and remarkable hand.

Fol. 117. *b. col.* 2. A poem with the heading ɓꞃɩan o huɩᵹɩnn .cc̄.,
"Brian O'Higgin, cecinit." This is a panegyric on David, son of
Muiris, or Maurice Roche, of Fermoy, enumerating all the places in
Munster from whence he had carried off plunder and spoil. The poem
contains sixty-two stanzas; it begins, Cɩnɓuρ ɩcꞇaρ ρeɓ ρuɩρᵹɩ,
"How is a gift of courtship paid." Brian O'Higgin is not mentioned
by O'Reilly. But the Four Masters record the death of Brian, son of
Fergal Ruaidh Ui Uiccinn, or O'Higgin, "head of his own tribe,
oɩɓe, or Superintendent of the Schools of Ireland, and preceptor in
poetry,"—on Maundy Thursday, 1477. He seems to have been a Connaught poet. The poem ends fol. 119. a col. 1.

Fol. 119. *a. col.* 1. A poem (of thirty-six stanzas), whose author is
given in the following title: Seaan oᵹ mac ρaɩꞇ .cc., "Shane (or

* *Magrath.* Not mentioned by O'Reilly.

IR. MSS. SER.—VOL. I. H

John) Óg [i. e. Junior] Mac Raith, or Magrath,* cecinit." It begins,

Ʒach ꝼonn ʒuꝼeꞃuıḃ muıġe,

"All lands *are good until* [compared with] Fermoy."

This is a poem in praise of the territory of Fermoy and its lord, David, son of Morris Roche, and his wife Joan. It ends fol. 120. a col. 1.

Fol. 120. *a. col.* 1. A poem headed, OMaocħaʒan .c̄c̄., "O'Maothogan, cecinit." This poet is not mentioned by O'Reilly, but he was certainly of Munster. His poem begins, Ꝼaḋa ıꞅ mná maıṫı mná Muṁan, "Long have the women of Munster been noble women." It is a panegyric on Cathilin, who seems to have been the mother of David, son of Morris Roche, of Fermoy. The poem consists of thirteen stanzas of an unequal number of lines. It ends fol. 120. b. col. 2.

Fol. 121. *a. col.* 1. A poem headed Coꞃmac mac Eoġaın u Ḋalaıʒ, .cc., "Cormac, son of Eoghan O'Daly, cecinit." A panegyric on Cathilin, daughter of Tadhg Mac Carthy, and on David, son of Morris Roche, who seems to have been her son. The poem begins,

Ḋlıġım ıc aꞃ mꝼeaꞃaċt ʒꞃáıḋ,

"I am entitled to payment in right of my office."

This poem consists of thirty-nine stanzas of the usual number of four lines each.

Fol. 121. *b. col.* 1. (eight lines from bottom). A poem headed, Ua maeṫaʒan, .c̄c̄., ı ꞅeaan "OMaethagan, ceciṁit, i. e. John." This is a panegyric on Morris, son of Morris Roche, of Fermoy, and his son David. It begins, Ꝼoꞃmaḋ aʒ caċ le clu Muıꞃıꞅ, "All men envy the fame of Muiris." It consists of twenty stanzas of an unequal number of lines, and is written in a good hand, but in faint ink. The poem ends fol. 122. a. col. 2. After which, in a space that was originally blank, is written, apparently by the same hand that wrote the pagination, these words in English: "The former pages of this Book, from the beginning to this page, was 288."

Fol. 122. *b*. This page was originally blank, but is now covered with idle scribbling. Amongst these are the following: ḋo ḃı an leabaꞃ ꞅo aꞃ na aꞃꞅcꞃıbaḋ le uıllıam ua heaʒꞃa anno ḋn̄ı 1805, ambaıle aṫa clıaṫ, "This book was re-written by William O'Hara,

A. D. 1805, in Baile-atha-cliath, i. e. Dublin." Again, ' uıll. ua heaʒna Ꝺ.Ꞇ. 1806, Jan. 29, 1806."

I am sorry to be obliged to add that Mr. O'Curry condescended to write his respectable and honored name amongst such wretched scribbling, thus:

Ꞓóʒan ó Comṗaıꝺe,
Ꞇbcccꞇuın.

Another note is this: Ꞇeaꝺaıꝛ beannaċꞇ aꝛ anmaın ṗꝛoınꝛıaꝛ uı locıꝺe aꝛ ꝛon ꝺe ꝛna cceaꝛꝛaꝺ, "Give a blessing on the soul of Francis O'Hickey, for the sake of God, and his friends (?)."

Fol. 123. *a.* (written across the page, without columns). An anonymous poem of fifty-two stanzas, in praise of Cathilin, daughter of Tadhg Mac Carthy, who has been already mentioned. It begins,

Ꝺıleꝛ ʒac en ꝺuıne a eıꝺꝛeċꞇ, "Every one has a right to his inheritance."

Fol. 123. *b.* (13 lines from bottom, very much rubbed, and in many parts illegible), is a poem of which the author is named in the title, Ꞹaıꞇhıaꝛ móꝛ o cıllın .c̅c̅., after which we have the words in a later, but contemporary hand, uıle cꝛıoꝺ oꝛ ṗaꝛ.

The writing is so effaced that neither the number of stanzas nor the first line can be ascertained.

(XVI.) The sixteenth stave consists of five leaves, numbered by Mr. O'Curry (in entire disregard of the old pagination), fol. 124, 125, 126 [127 omitted], 128, 129. On fol. 125 the old pagination seems to have been 77; on fol. 126 it is clearly 94, and on 128, 78. On the other leaves it is obscure. This stave is written in double columns.

Fol. 124, 125, 126, contain fragments of the ancient tale Ꞇoċmaꝛc Ꞓımıꝛe, "Courtship of Eimire," or Eimer, by the celebrated Ulster champion Cuchullainn (ob. AD. 2). Mr. O'Curry gives a full abstract of this tale (Lectures, p. 278, *sq.*) A perfect copy of this curious legend is in the British Museum, from which Mr. O'Curry tells us he made a careful transcript for his own use (ibid. p. 282). Two other copies belong to the Royal Irish Academy, one in the Leabhar na h-Uidhré, and the other partly on paper and partly on parchment. Both are imperfect, as is also the copy now before us. There is also in the Royal Irish Academy an indifferent modern copy made from the British Museum text.

Fol. 127. Mr. O'Curry appears to have omitted to number this page by mistake. It is not likely that a leaf could have been lost since his pagination was written, as the book has never since been out of my possession.

Fol. 128, 129. These leaves contain a fragment of the old historical tale of ḃꞃuiᵹeaɴ ḃa ḃeaꞃᵹa ("Palace of Da-Dearga"), or the death of Conaire Mór, King of Ireland, at the house of Da-Dearga, a farmer of Leinster of noble birth, who kept a mansion celebrated for hospitality, at a place in the upper valley of the Dodder, the name of which is yet partly preserved in that of Bothar na Bruighne, "Road of the Bruighean, or Palace," on the River Dodder, near Tallaght, in the county of Dublin. At this place Conaire Mór was slain, and the palace burned by a party of pirates, in the 60th year of his reign (A.D. 60, according to O'Flaherty's date, *Ogyg.* p. 138, 273).*

––––––––

The remainder of the volume consists of some fragments of medical MSS. in a very much injured condition. These fragments do not appear to have formed any part of the collection now called the Book of Fermoy.

––––––––

(XVII.) This stave consists of four leaves marked on the lower margins Ꞓ 1, Ꞓ 2, Ꞓ 3, Ꞓ 4. The upper margins are greatly injured throughout, and no traces remain of any older pagination.

This is a fragment of a medical MS. imperfect at beginning and end. It never formed a part of the Book of Fermoy. We have found the

––––––––

* O'Curry, (*Lect.* xii. p. 258, *sq.*). O'Donovan's note, p. 90. *Conf.* Four Masters, A.M. 5160, and

name of O'Hickey scribbled more than once on the margins and elsewhere in the Book of Fermoy, and, as the O'Hickeys were hereditary
physicians, we may fairly conjecture that this is a fragment of one of
their professional MSS. which has got mixed up with the Book of
Fermoy.

(XVIII.) A fragment in a small and beautiful medical hand,
consisting of two leaves, marked both on the upper and
lower margins, ℮ 5, and ℮ 6.

This fragment seems to contain part of a treatise on the liver and
organs of generation. On page 2 of ℮ 5, begins a tract, the first
sentence of which (as is commonly the case in medical MS.) begins
with some words in Latin: ꝺe epace [hepate] ec ꝺe eius
uaretace [sic] complexiones [sic] loquamur ; the tract
then translates this into Irish, and proceeds in the same language.
Perhaps these Latin sentences may indicate that the work was translated from some Latin original. It would be of great importance to
philology, and enable us, no doubt, to fix the true meaning of many
old Irish names for plants and medicines, if the original Latin could
be discovered.

On page 2 of ℮ 6 is a tract beginning, ꝺe membRORum
ꝫeneraciuorum [opera]cionibus e[c eorum] qua-
licacibus, which then proceeds in Irish, as before.

(XIX.) A fragment imperfect at beginning and end, consisting
of two leaves, in a good medical hand. Mr. O'Curry did
not put any paging on these leaves, nor are the remains of
any former pagination now visible.

On the first page of the second leaf begins a tract on the liver, with
these words: uiRcus nacuralis esc in epace que cum
peR uenar ab membra in cper biuibicur uircucer ꝛc.

(XX.) A fragment, five inches by four, containing the conclusion of what seems to have been a religious tract. It was evidently cut from the upper part of the leaf of some book for the sake of the blank parchment that surrounded it.

It contains twenty lines, ending with the word ꝼiniꞇ, and is written in a very good and scholarlike hand.

The back of this fragment was originally blank, and now contains some scribbling, of which I can read only the following words :—

> Qn ainm Dia [sic] ꝺon. . . . .
> cen Coꞃꝺelbach ui Domnaill maille . . . . .
> le ꝼeil ṁaicheꞇae ꝼoꞃꞇ . . . .

INDEX TO THE BOOK OF FERMOY.

II.—SOME ACCOUNT OF THE IRISH MS. DEPOSITED BY THE PRESIDENT DE ROBIEN IN THE PUBLIC LIBRARY OF RENNES. By the Rev. JAMES H. TODD, D. D., F. S. A., Senior Fellow of Trinity College, Dublin.

IT is now upwards of one-and-twenty years since I laid before the Academy a detailed account of an Irish MS. in the Bibliothéque Impériale of Paris*, which had been described, and a very beautiful *fac-simile* of a page of it engraved, by M. Silvester, accompanied by letter-press from the pen of M. Champolion Figeac, in the fourth volume of the "Palæographie Universelle." In the description accompanying this engraving M. Champolion maintains the opinion that the Paris MS. is the same which was sent from Britanny, upwards of a century ago, by the President de Robien, to the Benedictines of the Congregation of St. Maur, compilers of the "Nouveau Traité de Diplomatique," of which they have given a full account in that learned work†.

On comparing this description, however, with the MS. in Paris, I saw reason to doubt the opinion of M. Champolion, and in my former paper I endeavoured to show that the Paris MS. must have been a different book from that which the learned authors of the "Traité de Diplomatique" have described as the MS. of the President de Robien‡. My arguments were drawn from the fact that the description of this latter MS. given by the Benedictines, and the *fac-similes* of portions of it engraved in their plates, did not at all agree with the Paris MS. I concluded, therefore, that there were two Irish books, distinct from each other, although containing some of the same matter—the one, that described by Champolion, and now in the Library at Paris, of which the Benedictines make no mention ; the other, the MS. which had been sent to them from Britanny by M. de Robien, of which they have given a minute description.

---

* See "Proceedings of the Royal Irish Academy," vol. iii., p. 223.

† Tom. iii., p. 200.

‡ Christophe Paul Gantron de Robien, President a mortier au Parlement de Bretagne. Mort de 1751 a 1756. (Querard, "La France Litteraire," tom. viii., p. 82, where see an account of his writings). He was the founder of the public Library of Rennes, to which he left all his books.

When I read to the Academy, one-and-twenty years ago, my former paper on this subject, I was ignorant of the existence of this latter MS.*; but afterwards I found reason to believe that it was preserved in the town Library of Rennes, in Britanny; and during my very agreeable visit to that country, in August last, I went to the Library in search of it. I remained at Rennes for three or four days, for the express purpose of examining this MS.

I found that my former conclusion was fully borne out; the Rennes MS. agreed exactly in every particular with the description given of it by the Benedictines. It had been given to the Library by the President de Robien, about the middle of the eighteenth century; and in its contents it coincided partially with the MS. at Paris. Clearly, then, there were in France two distinct Irish MSS., as I had formerly concluded, and M. Champolion was wrong in his conjecture that the MS. now in the Bibliothéque Impériale was the same as the De Robien MS. which had been sent from Britanny to the Benedictines.

But before I proceed to speak of the contents of this latter MS., I must return my grateful thanks to M. de la Bigne Villeneuve, Librarian of Rennes, for his courtesy in affording me every possible facility for examining it; although I had called upon him without any introduction, he received me with the greatest kindness, assisted me to the utmost of his power, and permitted me to transcribe from the MS. whatever was necessary for my purpose.

The volume in size is what would probably be called a small folio, and is thus described by the authors of the "Nouveau Traité de Diplomatique" (Dom Tassin, and Dom Toustain):—

"La notice† de ce MS., tres difficile à lire, porte, qu'il contient des fragmens de piété

---

* I ought to have known that this MS. is mentioned by M. de Vaines in his "Dictionaire raisonnée de Diplomatique," vol. i., p. 456. He follows the errors of his predecessors in regarding the MS. as of the 11th or 12th century. It has been more recently noticed by Mr. C. P. Cooper, in the Appendix A. to his (not yet published) "Report on the Records" (Supplement to App. A., p. 44), where he has printed a very inaccurate and imperfect account of the MS. by one of his foreign correspondents. See also another very useless notice of this MS., "The Literary Remains of the Rev. Thomas Price:" *Llandovery*, 1854, vol. i., p. 20.

† The "Notice" here alluded to is a MS. paper inserted at the beginning of

et de morale, plusieurs traductions soit en vers, soit en prose, des sermons de S. Ambrose, et de son Traite de la Confession, la Généalogie des ancièns Rois et des prémières familles d'Irlande. Cette partie du MS. est uné des plus considérables. Sa largeur est de sept pouces et demi, sa hauteur de neuf et plus. Il est a deux colones et l'on y rencontre de tems en tems quelque lignes de latin avant les genéalogies. L'écriture en est toute semblable a l'anglo-saxone. Beaucoup de lettres initiales des ouvrages et des chapitres sont dans le meme goût que celles du MS. de S. Ouen de Rouen, d'on nous avons tîré l'alphabet saxon de lettres initiales serpentines. On trouve dans le commencement du MS. irlandois beaucoup d'articles, qui commencent par *labrum* en plus grosse écriture saxone*."

The Benedictines speak of this MS. (that is to say, of the first portion of it) as written "vers la fin du xii⁰ ou commencement du xiii⁰ siècle," and notice certain contractions (such as ⊤c for "et cætera;" .ı. for *id est* ; 2 for *est*), which the antiquaries of the period regarded as characteristic of that date. Their words are these :—

"S. Bernard y est cité de cette sorte : *Ut dixit Bernardus in sermone de beata Maria Virgine, &c.* Cette abbreviation, ⊤c., qu'on trouve plusièurs fois dans ce mſ. est remarkable, ainsi que les autres abbreviations de cette écriture saxone de la fin du xii⁰ siècle, ou du commencement du suivant. Les antiquaires qui donnent† au moins neuf cent ans a des mſſ. en lettres saxones, nous sauront gré d'en avoir produit un plus recent d'environ trois siécles et demi‡."

To this it may be added that S. Thomas Aquinas and S. Bonaventure are quoted, who flourished in the middle and latter half of the thirteenth century, and that the character of the writing, to every one acquainted with Irish palæography, indicates unmistakeably the end of the fifteenth century as the period at which the MS. was written.

With respect to the contractions alluded to as indications of the date

---

the Rennes volume, giving a description of its contents in English, written about the middle of the seventeenth century, by a person who was very imperfectly acquainted with the Irish language, and wholly ignorant of its palæography. He attributes to the MS. a much higher antiquity than it really possesses, and his opinion has evidently been the cause of the

mistakes made by later writers on the subject.

* "Nouv. Traité de Diplom.," tom. iii. p. 200.

† "Journal Historique," Avril, 1755, p. 289.

‡ "Nouv. Traité de Diplom.," tom. iii., p. 228.

of the MS., the Benedictines further say (they are speaking of what they call the "demi-uncial" Saxon square character, followed by the "minuscule :")—

"Le MS. de M. le président de Robien nous a donné le modèle suivant* : *Zelus dommus tue cometit me, id est.* Le *z* a eté laissé en blanc comme lettrine dans le MS. L'*m* est redoublée en *domus,* l'*e* simple est mis pour *œ* dans *tue,* et le *t* prend la place du *d* dans le mot suivant; en sorte qu'on lit *cometit* an lieu de *comedit*—mais rien n'est plus singulier que l'abreviation des mots *id est,* signifiés par un *i* ayant deux points à ses cotèst†."

But the contractions which these learned writers deemed so peculiar are to be found in all the later, as well as in the earlier Irish MSS., and indeed are in use with the Irish scribes to the present day, so that they are no criterion of age whatsoever. With respect to the use of *e* for *œ*, the double *m* in *dommus* for *domus,* and the *t* for *d* in *cometit*, it will be enough to refer to the valuable remarks of Dr. Reeves, on the orthography of Latin in Irish MSS., in the preface to his edition of Adamnan's "Life of St. Columba‡."

I believe the foregoing extracts from the "Nouveau Traité de Diplomatique" contain all that the learned compilers of that work have said as descriptive of the MS. of the President de Robien. A comparison of these extracts, and of the *fac-similes* in the plates, renders it quite certain that their MS. was the book now at Rennes, and not the volume preserved in the Paris Library.

I proceed now to give some account of the contents of the de Robien MS.; but in quoting from it I shall not attempt to preserve the contractions. To represent them accurately would require an especial fount of types.

The book is not all written in the same hand. It consists of fifteen portions—or, as printers would now call them, *signatures* or *staves*—containing an unequal number of leaves. This inequality may arise from the loss of some leaves of the original MS.; but this is not always the case. The following is a Table of these "signatures:"— .

---

* Alluding to a *fac-simile* of this passage given in one of their plates, *Planche* 47.

† Ib., p. 229.

‡ Reeves, *Adamnan,* p. xvi., xvii.

No. 1 contains		10 leaves.
„ 2	„	8 „
„ 3	„	8 „
„ 4	„	10 „
„ 5	„	10 „
„ 6	„	10 „
„ 7	„	10 „
„ 8	„	8 „
„ 9	„	10 „
„ 10	„	5 „
„ 11 [not numbered]		5 „

Then begins another hand, and the remaining signatures of the volume are numbered thus—

No. 10 [bis] containing		8 leaves.
„ 11 [bis]	„	8 „
„ 12	„	8 „
„ 13	„	6 „
„ 14	„	8 „

So that the total number of leaves now in the volume is 132; unless I have made a mistake in the number of leaves I have assigned to the signature No. 11 (not numbered), which in my notes is, I am sorry to say, somewhat obscure.

Fol. 1. 22 b. col. 1.—This portion of the MS. is all in the same handwriting, and contains a series of short religious tracts or sermons on the Christian virtues or duties. To these is prefixed a preface, which begins :—

Ðeo paꞇꞃı caꞃıꞃꞃımo Peꞇꞃo beı ᵹꞃacıa Poꞃꞇuꞃenꞃı .ı. an onoıꞃ bıa aꞇhaꞃ ꞇ peabaꞃ baꞃ cınbꞃɔnab an Leabaꞃ ꞃo.

Deo Patri carissimo Petro Dei gratia Portusensi, i.e. in honour of God the Father and of Peter, for whom this book was begun.

I know not who the Peter here spoken of was. We should probably read *Portuensi* instead of *Portusensi;* and, if so, he was probably a bishop of Porto, or Portus Augusti, at the mouth of the Tiber, near Rome; but the transcriber, in the Irish translation which follows the Latin words, seems to have imagined that S. Peter the Apostle was intended. There was a Peter bishop of Porto at the beginning of the twelfth century, to whom S. Bruno, bishop of Segni and abbat of Monte Casino, addressed one of his epistles*, on the forced investiture of the Emperor Henri by Pope Paschal, A. D. 1111.

Then follow the short religious tracts or sermons, each beginning with the words Labꞃum anoıꞃ, " Let us now speak . . . ." The

---

* Ceillier, " Hist. des Auteurs Eccles.," .   trum," (Lugdun.), tom. xx., p. 788. tom. xxi., p. 102, 107; " Biblioth. Pa-

Benedictines, in a passage already quoted, have mentioned these words, which they did not understand, but which attracted their attention, because of their frequent occurrence, and because they are written in a larger and peculiar character. They serve to identify the Rennes MS. with that which had been sent to the Benedictines by the President de Robien, inasmuch as they do not occur at all in the Paris MS.

Fol. 23. a. col. 1.—A tract beginning

Ɍouec ın pꞃıncıpıo uıꞃꞃo maꞃıa meo .ı. coꞃ[u]ꞃcaòcaıꞃı muıꞃe ban- cıꞃeꞃꞃa bam a coꞃach mobeıꞃcı. oıꞃ aòeıꞃ auꞃ. naem . . . .

Fovet in principio virgo maria meo, i. e. May the Lady Mary comfort me in the beginning of my work, for Saint Augustine says . . . .

This tract occurs also in the Paris MS., and it was one of the evidences on which M. Champolion relied in support of his opinion of the identity of that MS. with the volume described by the Benedictines. He has given a very correct *fac-simile* of it*, in which it will be observed that the words "virgo maria meo" are so much contracted as to be decyphered with difficulty—in fact, I myself, in my former paper, failed to decypher them†. Twenty years ago I was not so well skilled in reading the contractions of such a MS., as I am now; and I am glad to have this opportunity of acknowledging my error. But in the Rennes MS. the words are written without contractions, and are quite easily read. I neglected to transcribe the passage quoted from St. Augustine; for my notes were necessarily made in great haste. The Tract was probably translated from the Latin, and the passage from St. Augustine would possibly have helped us to identify or discover the original work.

The Tract ends fol. 24. l.

Fol. 25. a. col. 1.—A Tract beginning "Ut dixit Bernardus in sermone de beata Maria Virgine ꞉c̄." The rest is in Irish; but I unfortunately omitted, as before, to transcribe the quotation. Ends fol. 27. a. col. 2.

Similar religious tracts follow to fol. 35. a. col. 2., where we have a

---

* See the "Palæographie Universelle;" tom. iv., Planche, 130 (Sir Fred. Madden's Translation, vol. ii., p. 641).

† "Proceedings of Royal Irish Academy," vol. iii., p. 227.

Treatise on Confession, which begins thus [a space is left in the margin for an initial ornamented ı or ɑ]:—

[1] Sıaᴅ ṗo na ṗe cumȝıll ᴅeȝe ᴅlıȝıṗ an ṗaeıṗıᴅın ᴅo beıt́ ınċı amaıl aᴅeıṗ ṗanccuṗ comaṗ, ṗa .u. ᴅeıṗᴅınȝ ᴅon lebaṗ ṗen abaṗaṗ ṗuṗṗa quaṗcum ṗummaṗum ᴅeoıma quınca ᴅe ıncencıone.

"These are the sixteen conditions that confession requires to have in it, as Saint Thomas says in the 5th Distinction of the book which is called Supra quartum, the fifteenth of the Sums, De intentione."

The reference here is to the great works of St. Thomas Aquinas on the Sentences (in Librum Quartum Sententiarum Distinct. xvii. 39. 4. 4. 1., according to the present mode of citing; and 3 Summ. q. 9. 4. 4. 1.)* where the sixteen conditions of confession are given in these verses :—

" Sit simplex, humilis, cónfessio ; pura, fidelis,
Atque frequens, nuda, discreta, libens, verecunda,
Integra, secreta, lacrymabilis, accelerata,
Fortis, et accusans, et sit parere parata."

Fol. 37. b., in the margin, in the handwriting (as I believe) of old Charles O'Conor, of Belanagare, is the following note :—

Iṗ cenc ᴅuıne an Eṗınn ᴅo nıṗ [for ȝnıṗ] a ṗaeıṗınᴅ maṗ aᴅeıṗ an leabaṗ ṗo.

"Scarcely a man in Erinn makes his confession as this book directs."

Fol. 44. b. col. 2.—There is here a note, in a very bad hand, difficult to read, and in very ignorant spelling, to the effect that the writer had here inscribed his name (which is now illegible) in the year 1755. He adds "Nannetiis," which, I presume, signifies that his name was written here at Nantes.

Fol. 45. a. col. 1.—A collection of sayings gathered from the works of St. Augustine, beginning

Aᴅeıṗ Au. cıᴅbe bȝ. . . .

"Augustine says that whoever is . . ."

Fol. 47. a. col. 2.—Here are continued the short tracts or sermons noticed by the Benedictines, beginning

Labṗum anoṗ ᴅon cṗocaıṗe. . . .

"Let us now speak of mercy."

---

* These references do not agree with the number of the distinctions and questions as given in the text. But it is not worth while to attempt to reconcile such discrepancies, which are probably only evidence of the ignorance or carelessness of transcribers.

In this Tract are quoted SS. Augustine, Gregory, Isidore, Ambrose, Bonaventure.

Fol. 52. a. col. 2.—We have here the following very curious note :—

Loċc ḋon leḃaṗṗa Roṗṗ ḃṗoin a cṗıċ .h. nEċaċ Muman, ⁊ peaṗṗa ḋo Seon Manḃauıl, ṗıḃeṗı ḋo muımḃ- ċıṗ ṗíẓ Saẋan ḋo ṗaccaıḃ Saẋa la ṗeıle Mıċıl, ⁊ ḋo ṗıḃlaıẓ moṗan ḋo cıṗcaıḃ ın ḃomuım, maṗ aca an Ḟṗaınẓc ⁊ an almaın, ⁊ anċṗlıẓeḋ aṗṗın co hlaṗuṗalem : ⁊ cıḃ bé lé ḃuḋ aıl ḋol ḋṗeċaın an cíṗe ṗın aṗ ṗon cuṗ coẓ Cṗıṗc ḃa popul ṗeın hı maṗ ċıṗ caıṗṅẓeṗı, ⁊ ḃo cṗıḃlaıẓ ḃa ċoṗaıḃ naemca ṗeın hı, ⁊ con- ḃeṗṗa moṗan ṗenmoṗa ⁊ cecaıṗcc ḃa popul ınncı, ⁊ coṗ coẓ a maċaıṗ ⁊ hé ṗeın ḃo ḃṗeċ ⁊ ḃo aḃlacaḋ ınncı ; ⁊ maṗ a ḃuḃaıṗc ṗe cuṗ bé ṗeın ṗı na ıuḃaıẓe ; aṗ ṗon ṗeḃuṗ an coṗaẓ ṗın cuc an cíṗ, ⁊ aṗ ṗon naeṁcaċc an cı ḃo cṗıḃlaıẓ hí, ⁊ ḃo coẓ a páıṗ ḃo ṗaẓḃaıl a ponẓc ceṗc meḃóın an ḃoṁaın ın nlaṗuṗalem, ınnuṗ comaḋ ẓaṗ ḃá ṗẓelaıḃ ⁊ ḃa cṗeıḃım ṗoċcaın aṗ an ınaḃ ṗın ṗaıṗ ⁊ ṗıaṗ, ḃuḋḃeaṗ ⁊ ḃuḋ cuaıḋ ; ⁊ ıṗ ann ḃo ċuıṗ ṗé an ṗṗıṗacc naem ḃocum a aṗṗcal ḃomnaċ Cınẓcıḃıṗı, ⁊ ḃo ċuıṗ ṗo cecṗıḃ haıṗḃıḃ an ḃomaın ıac ḃo cṗılaḋ cṗeıḃım ⁊ cṗaḃaḋ ḃo ċıneḃaıḃ an ḃomaın ; ⁊ cıḃ bé le ḃuḋ aıl a ṗíṗ ḃo beıċ aıẓcı ınc ṗlıẓeḋ ḃuḋ ṗeṗṗ ḃo ḃul aṗ caċ ċıṗ co hlaṗuṗalem ⁊ na Loċc naemca acaıḃ na cımcıll, ınḃeo- ṗaıḃ Ḟınẓın mac Ḋıaṗmaca mıc Ḋomnaıll mıc Ḟınẓın mıc Ḋıaṗmaca moṗn hí Maċẓaṁna hí, óıṗ ıṗṗe ḃo ċuıṗ an leḃuṗṗa a beṗlaı ⁊ a laıḃın,

"The place of this book is Ross-Broin in the territory of Ui-Echach-Mumhan and the person [i. e. author] of it, John Mandavil, a knight of the people of the king of the Saxons, who left Saxon- land on Michaelmas day, and traversed many of the lands of the world, as France and Germany, and the way from thence to Jerusalem. And, whoever has a desire to go to see that land*, because Christ had selected it for His own people as a Land of Promise, and traversed it with His own holy feet, and uttered many sermons and instructions to His people in it, and chose that His Mother and Him- self should be born and interred in it, and as He said that He Himself was King of the Jews—or because of the excellence of the produce the land furnished, and the ho- liness of Him who traversed it, and who chose to receive His passion in the very central point of the world—in Jerusalem— so that it might be convenient for His fame and His faith† to reach from that place eastwards, and westwards, southwards and northwards. And it was in it that He sent the Holy Spirit to His Apostles on Pentecost-sunday, and sent them to the four quarters of the world, to sow the seed of faith and devotion in the tribes of the world ;—and whosoever would wish to know the best way to go from every country to Jerusalem, and to the Holy places that are around it, Finghin son of Diarmait, son of Domhnall, son of Finghin, son of Diarmait Mor O'Math

---

* The Holy Land.

† That is Faith in Him, or His Religion.

L

a ʒneıʒo ⁊ a habna a nʒaeıbılʒe, bo
cɲeolab na ɲlıʒeba aɲ muıɲ ⁊ aɲ cíɲ
co hIeɲuɾalem, ba ʒaċ aen le buṫ
mıan bol ba oılıcɲı ann, ⁊ co ɾɾuċ
Oɲɲċannaın, ⁊ co ɾIꝛab ɾıoın, ⁊ caċ
ɾlıʒeb no ʒabaıɾ ɾeon oɲın amaċ,
⁊ bo ınbıɾın caċ ınʒnab bo con-
naıɾcc ɾeon aɲ baeınıb ⁊ aɲ ċıɲ-
ċaıb an bomaın a coıcċınne; ⁊ bob
ı aoıɾ an Cıʒeɲna an can bo ɲınbı
ɾeon a eaċcɲa .ı. mılı blıaban ⁊
cɲı ceb, xxxıı blıabna. Ɑ aoıɾ ın
cɲaċ bo cuıɲ Ƒınʒın a nʒaoıbılʒo
ꝛo beıɲeb hé .ı. mılı cccc. lxx. ıı.
blıabna; ⁊ bo bı ɾeon ceıcɲı blıabna
.x. aɲ .xx. ıc cuaɲcuʒab an bomaın;
⁊ aɲ nımꝛob bo bo ɾoım bo baınʒ-
nıb ın papa a leaban.

Iɾ ıacc ɾo na cıʒeɲnaba bo bı
oꞃ cınn Ʒaoıbel ın uaıɲ bo cuıɲ
Ƒınʒın ɾo a nʒaoıbılʒc. ı. Caḃʒ
mac Oomnaıll oıcc mıc Caıbʒc na
maınıɾcɲeċ mıc Oomnaıll oıcc ınna
Mac Caɲċaıʒ móɲ, ⁊ Oıaɲmaıc
macCaıbʒc mıc Aṁlaıḃ ına .h. cSu-
labaın beɲɲe,⁊ Oonnċab mac Oıaɲ-
maca mıc Oomnaıll mıc Ƒınʒın, ⁊
Oomnall cona mḃɲaıċnıb, oꞃ cınb
.h. nEċaċ; ⁊ Coɲmac mac Oonn-
ċaba mıc Oomnaıll ɲıabaıʒ oꞃ cınn
.h. Caıɲꝛɲe; ⁊ Oıaɲmaıc mac Oomnaıll ɲıabaıʒ ana mac Caɲċaıʒ
Caıɲꝛneċ; ⁊ Oomnaıll mac Oomh-
naıll mıc Oomnaıll cluaꝛaıʒh oꞃ oınn
cꝛleċca Oıaɲmaba ɲeṁuın ; ⁊ Ƒınʒın mac Meıc Con meıc Mıc Con
ṁıc Ƒınʒeın ına O Eıbeɲꝛceoıl móɲ ;
⁊ Coɲmac mac Caıbʒ mıc Coɲmaıc
oꞃ cınn Muɲʒɲaıbı; ⁊ Oonnċab

gamhna (O'Mahony) will tell it; for it was
he that put this book from English, and
from Latin, from Greek, and from He-
brew, into Irish, to show the ways on
sea and on land to Jerusalem, to every
one who may wish to go in pilgrimage thither, and to the river Orrthan-
nan [i.e. the Jordan], and Mount Sion; and
[to describe] every way that John[*]
proceeded from that out; and to relate
every prodigy that John saw amongst
the peoples and countries of the world
in general. And the age of the Lord
when John made his journey was one
thousand years, and three hundred and
thirty-two years. His age[†], when Finghin put it ultimately into Irish was
one thousand, four hundred and seventy-
two years. And John was thirty-four
years visiting the world, and on his return
to Rome the Pope confirmed his book.

"These are the Lords who were over
the Gaeidhel when Finghin put this into
Irish, viz :—Tadhg[‡], son of Domhnall óg,
son of Tadhg of the monastery, son of
Domhnall óg, as Mac Carthaigh Mór; and
Diarmait, son of Tadhg, son of Amhlabh,
was the O'Sullivan Berre; and Donnchadh,
son of Diarmait, son of Domhnall, son of
Finghin, and Domhnall, with their brothers,
over Ui-Echach; and Cormac[§], son of
Donnchadh, son of Domhnall Riabhach,
over Ui-Cairpre; and Diarmait, son of
Domhnall Riabhach, as the Mac Carthaigh
Cairbrech; and Domhnall, son of Domh-
nall, son of Domhnall Cluasach over
Slicht-Diarmada-Remhair[‖]; and Finghin,
son of Mac Con, son of Mac Con, son

---

* i. e. Sir John Mandeville.

† i. e. Our Lord's age, or the era of A. D.

‡ This was Tadhg, called Liath, or the
grey. See " Life and Letters of Florence
MacCarthy," by Daniel MacCarthy, p.452.

§ See 4. M. 1477, and " Life of Florence
MacCarthy," p. 453.

‖ " The descendants of Diarmait Remhair," or the Fat.

og mac Coinnbealbaig mic bniain
mic Machgamna inna .h. bniain;
⁊ Enni mac Eogain mic Neill oig
ina .h. Neill, ⁊ cnen cneana Congail
ag Conn mac Aeda buidi mic bniain
ballaig, ⁊ benbnachain a achain ina
.h. Neill buidi; ⁊ Aed Ruad mac Neill
gainb mic Coinnbelbaig an Fina
ma .h. Domnaill; ⁊ cnen ichcain
Connachc aigci; ⁊ Feidlim mac
Coinnbelbaig mic Aeda mic Coinnbelbaig ina .h. Concubain; ⁊ cadge
caoch ma c Uilliam iCellaig ma .h.
Cellaig; ⁊ Uilliam mac Aeda mic
bniain ina agaid bon caob cain bo
fucca; ⁊ Eogan mac Munchada hi
Madugain an cnil nAnmchada; ⁊
Munchad mac Muincencaig mic
Donnchada Caemanaid na nig an
laignib; ⁊ Cachain mac Cuinn mic
an Calbaig an ibh Concubain; ⁊
cadc mac laigen mic nuaidni ina .h.
Duinn; ⁊ Sean mac Maolnuanaigh
mic Caidge mic Caidge na nig an
'Eilib; ⁊ Gilla na naomh mac Caidg
mic Gilla na naomh an ib Meachan;
ec alii mulci an Eininn o nunn amach
nach nimcan an baig chuimne.

of Finghin, as O'Edirsceoil [O'Driscoll]
Mór; and Cormac, son of Tadhg[*],
son of Cormac, over Musgraidhe; and
Donnchadh óg, son of Torrdealbach, son of
Brian, son of Mathgamhain, as the O'Brien;
and Henry, son of Eoghan, son of Niall
og, as the O'Neill; and the power of Trian-
Conghail[†] was with Conn, son of Aedh
Buidhe, son of Brian Ballagh; and the
brother of his father was the O'Neill
Buidhe; and Aedh Ruadh, son of Niall
Garbh, son of Torrdelbach-an-fhina, was the
O'Donnell, (and he had the power of lower
Connacht); and Feidhlim, son of Torrdelbach, son of Aedh, son of Torrdelbach, was
the O'Concobhair; and Tadhg Caoch, son
of William O'Cellaigh, was the O'Cellaigh; and William[‡], son of Aedh, son
of Brian, was opposed to him on the
eastern side of the Succ; and Eoghan[§] son
of Murchadh O'Madughain [O'Madden]
was over Sil-Anmchada; and Murchadh,
son of Muirchertach, son of Donnchadh
Caemhanach, was king over Leinster; and
Cathair, son of Conn, son of the Calbach
[the Bald] over the Ui Conchobhair[‖]; and
Tadhg, son of Laighen, son of Ruaidhri,
was the O'Duinn; and John, son of Maol-
ruanaigh, son of Tadhg, son of Tadhg, was
king over the Eile[¶]; and Gilla-na-naemh,
son of Tadhg, son of Gilla-na-naemh, over
the Ui Meachair[**]; et alii multi in Erinn
from that time forth, who are not reckoned
for commemoration.

Then follows the Irish translation of Sir John Mandeville's travels
to fol. 68. b. col. 2.

---

[*] Slain, 1495, 4. M.

[†] A name for the district of Clanaboy, or
inheritance of Clann-Aedha-buidhe.

[‡] See Geneal. Table, No. 32, in O'Donovan's "Hy Many," p. 96.

[§] Ibid., No. 31.

[‖] That is, the O'Connor Failghe.

[¶] That is, the Eile-O'Carroll.

[**] The Cineal Mechair, whose tribe name
was Ui-Cairin, whence the barony of Iker-
rin, Co. of Tipperary. The name is now
Meagher.

I have decyphered and translated from my rough notes the foregoing very curious document, by the able assistance of my friend Mr.
W. M. Hennessy. We learn from it that this book was transcribed at
Rossbroin, "in the country of Hy nEchach Mumhan," now Ivaugh*,
the territory of O'Mahony, in the county of Cork. Rossbroin, now Ross-
brin, was a castle of the O'Mahonys, in the parish of Skull, barony of
West Carbery.

"The person," that is to say, the author of the original work of
which this MS. contains an Irish translation, was Sir John Mandeville, "a Knight of the people of the King of the Saxons," whose well
known travels in the Holy Land were so popular in England, and indeed in Europe, in the 14th and following centuries. It has not, I believe been hitherto known that there was an Irish version of this remarkable book, made at the close of the 15th century, by an eminent
Irish chieftain, Finghin O'Mathgamhna, or O'Mahony. This is no
doubt the same Finghin, or Florence (as the name is generally angli-
cized) O'Mahony who died in the year 1496, according to the Chronology of the Four Masters, and who is described by them as Finghin
O'Mahony of Fonn-iartharach†, "general supporter of the humanity
and hospitality of West Munster, a wise man, learned in the Latin and
the English." The Annals of Ulster (Dublin MS.) called him "a man
of understanding, penetration, learning, and knowledge in the history of
the world, ᴄoıp ⁊ abap, "in the east and here."

This description agrees very well with what we may conceive to
have been the character of a man who had executed such a work as a
translation into Irish of Sir John Mandeville's Travels. The writer
then gives us the genealogy of this Fingin O'Mahony, up to Diarmait
Mór; and the Four Masters mention another Diarmait, "a truly hos-
pitable man, who never refused anything to any one," who died in 1427.
This was perhaps the father of Fingin, the translator of Sir John Mandeville. The early genealogy of Mathgamhain, son of Cian, who was a
contemporary of Brian Borumha, will be found in the Append. A. to

---

* Ivaugh or Iveagh, is an attempt to
soften for English pronunciation the Irish
Ibh [ablative plural of *Ui* or *Hy*] *Eoch-
adha.* See Wars of the Gael and the Gall,
p. 243, Table IV., No. 8, Intr., p. clviii.,
n. 5.

† *Fonn-iartharach,* i. e. the western
land; the name given to the territory of
Hy nEachadho, the patrimony of this
branch of the O'Mahonys. See Dr. O'Donovan's note on the Four Masters, at A. D
1496.

the Danish Wars, Table V., The generations between him and the
Fingin who translated Sir John Mandeville are as follows :—

```
Mathgamhain son of Cian
    |           a quo O'Mahony.
Diarmaid.
    |
Conchobhar.
    |
Diarmaid.
    |
Domhnach of the Ui n Eochad
    |
Conchobhar.
    |
† Diarmait Mór.
    |
† Fingin.
    |
† Dmhnall.
    |
Diarmait, ob. 1427.
†   |
† Fingin*, ob. 1496.
```

The Irish author of the memorandum just quoted further tells us that
Sir John Mandeville set out on his travels on Michaelmas day, 1332,
that he was thirty-four years "visiting the world;" that on his return to Rome "his book was confirmed by the Pope;" and that Fingin
O'Mahony "put it into Irish," in the year 1472.

The importance of this translation into Irish of the famous travels
of Sir John Mandeville can scarcely be exaggerated. If it were
transcribed and printed, it would probably add considerably to our
Irish vocabulary; and it would also establish the state of the text of
Sir John's work at the close of the 15th century, which is suspected
of having been corrupted by many interpolations of the monks, with
a view to promote pilgrimages to the Holy Land. That Sir John's book
was "confirmed by the Pope," is expressly stated by himself. See
Halliwell's edition, Lond. 1860, pp. 314, 315.

It is worthy of notice that the earliest printed edition of the work,
with a date, was that in Italian, by Pietra de Cornero, Milan, 1480,
4to. which was followed by the edition in English, printed at West-

---

* The names marked (†) are given in
the passage just quoted from the Rennes
MS. They will also be found, with the
earlier portion of the genealogy, in Cron-
nelly's Hist. of the Eoghanachts, in a note,
quoted from a Lambeth MS., p. 225.

minster, by Wynkyn de Worde, 1499, 8vo.; the Irish version of the work, written in 1472, was therefore earlier than any printed edition*.

Then we have a very curious and interesting list of the chieftains of the principal Irish tribes in this latter year. It speaks for itself, and cannot fail to be of great value to the genealogist. It will be seen that, although some preponderance is given to the southern tribes, yet the list extends to all Ireland.

It may be convenient to some readers to have here, in a tabular form, the names of the above-named chieftains under their respective clans or kingdoms :—

1. *Mac Carthy mòr.* TADHG [called *Liath*, the Grey], son of Domhnall óg, son of Tadhg na Mainistrech, son of Domhnall óg.

2. *O'Sullivan Beare,* or *Berre.* DIARMAIT, s. of Tadhg, s. of Amhlaibh [or Olaf].

3. *Uì Echach.* DONNCHAD, s. of Diarmait, s. of Domhnall, s. of Finghin, and DOMHNALL, with their brothers. [The family name, after surnames were established, was O'Mathgamhna, or O'Mahony. Book of Rights, p. 256, *n.,* Topograph. Poems of O'Dubhagain and O'Huidhrin, p. lxviii. *n.* (588)].

4. *Uì Cairpre.* CORMAC, s. of Donnchadh, s. of Domhnall Riabhach [or Reagh].

---

* According to some authorities there was a Latin version of Sir John Mandeville's travels, printed at Liége, in 1455; but others tell us that this edition is without date. The truth is, that this Latin version was made from the original French, in 1355, at Liége, but printed at Venice, perhaps about the year 1455, although the date of printing is not given. See the colophon at the end of it. A fine copy of this rare book is in the Library of Trinity College, Dublin. It forms one of a series of five Tracts, bound together, which were all evidently printed at the same time, and were probably issued in the same volume. The book has no pagination. The tracts it contains are (1) S. Bonaventuræ animæ et hominis interioris dialogus, *sign.* a—(in eights); (2) Proverbia in theutonico primo deinde in Latino sibi invicem consonantia, *sign.* a—d; (3) Liber cujus auctor fertur Joannes de Mandeville, *sign.* A—H; (4) Ludolphi de itinere ad terram sanctam (1336), *sign.* aa—hh; (5) Liber Marci Pauli de Veneciis, De Consuetudinibus et conditionibus orientalium regionum, *sign.* a—k.

Sir John Mandeville died at Liége, 17 Nov., 1372. Many MSS. of his Travels exist in our public libraries; but as Sir John died before the invention of printing, it is not wonderful that a century should have elapsed after his death before the book was printed.

5. *Mac Carthy Cairbrech.* DIARMAIT, s. of Domhnall Riabhach [or Reagh]. See the genealogy, *Life of Florence Mac Carthy*, by Daniel Mac Carthy, p. 453.

6. *Slioht Diarmada Remhair.* DOMHNALL, s. of Domhnall, s. of Domhnall Cluasach.

7. *O'Eidirsceoil* (or *O'Driscoll*) *mór.* FINGHIN, s. of Mac Con, s. of Mac Con, s. of Finghin.

8. *Musgraidhe* (or *Muskerry*). CORMAC, s. of Tadhg, s. of Cormac.

9. *The O'Brien.* DONNCHAD ÓG, s. of Tordealbach [or Turlogh], s. of Mathgamhain [or Mahon].

10. *The O'Neill.* HENRY, s. of Eoghan, s. of Niall óg.

11. *Trian Conghail,* or *Clann-Aedha-Buidhe* [now *Clanaboy*]. CONN, s. of Aedh Buidhe, s. of Brian Ballagh.

12. *O Neill Buidhe.* The brother of Aedh Buidhe (see No. 11).

13. *The O'Donnell* (with the power of lower Connacht). AEDH RUADH, s. of Niall Garbh, s. of Tordealbach an Fina.

14. *The O'Conchobhair* [or *O'Conor*]. FEIDHLIM, s. of Tordealbach, s. of Aedh, s. of Tordealbach.

15. *The O'Cellaigh* [or *O'Kelly*]. TADHG CAOCH, s. of William O'Cellaigh; but William, s. Aedh, s. of Brian, was opposed to him on the Eastern side of the river Suck [i. e. in Dealbhna Nuadhat].

16. *Sil Anmchada* [the *O'Madughain*, or *O'Madden*]. EOGHAN, s. of Murchad O'Madughain.

17. *King of Leinster.* MURCHADH, s. of Muircheartach, s. of Donchadh Caemhanach [Kavenagh].

18. *O'Conchobhar* [*Failghe*]. CATHAIR, s. of Con, s. of the Calbach.

19. *O'Duinn* (*O'Dunne*). TADHG, s. of Laighen, s. of Ruaidhri.

20. *King of Eile* [i. e. *Eile* or *Ely O Carroll*]. TADHG, s. of Tadhg.

21. *O'Meachair.* GILLA-NA-NAEMH, s. of Tadhg, s. of Gilla-na-naemh.

Fol. 69. a. col. 1.—Here follows a religious tract of no historical interest, to fol. 74 a.

Fol. 74. b.—was originally blank, but now contains the following note:—

> "Ambitiosus honos, luxus, turpisque voluptas
> Haec tria pro trino Numine mundus habet.

Miri Emainb óg o Ceallaig bo
rcriob an panb laibni ri ain baile
puirc an ribeni .i. anra Gleanb, an
reireb la bo mi Aubure, 1599, an
ceb bliabain bo cobab Muimneb a
naigaibi gall; ꝛ go ma leoran cneo-
óar rin ma ca coil bia [*read* Dé] linn
bocum na guigi rin bo benam.

" I am Edmond óg O'Kelly who wrote*
this Latin verse in Baile-Puirt-an-Rideri*,
i. e. in the Glenn, the sixth day of the
month of August, 1599; the first year of
the war of the Munstermen against the
Foreigners; and may this plundering fall
upon them, if the will of God be with us in
making this prayer.

The " Foreigners" here spoken of are of course the English. A
full account of the " war" alluded to will be found in the Four Masters
(1599, 1600), O'Sullevan Beare, *Hist. Catholicor. Ibern. Compend.* (tom.
iii. lib. 5. c. ix.), and other authorities. The unfortunate expedition of
the Earl of Essex in Munster is no doubt intended.

Fol. 75. a. col. 1.—The Life of St. Colman, son of Luachan, com-
mencing " Viriliter agite et confortetur cor vestrum omnes qui speratis
in Domino :" the rest is in Irish; it occupies fifteen leaves. I am not
aware of the existence of any copy of this Life in Ireland. Colgan does
not appear to have had it in his possession. He makes no mention of
it, and has made up a short life, compiled by himself, from the various
notices of St. Colman mac Luachain, and of his half brother, who was
also named Colman. *Acta SS.* 30 *Mart.*, p. 792.

There is great confusion between these two saints, in consequence
of their having had the same name, as well as from the similarity in the
names of their churches. Lassar, their common mother, had two
sons, both named Colman, but by different fathers. One of these, called
also *Mo-Colm-og* (with the diminutive affix *og*, little or beloved, and
the devotional prefix *mo*, my, that is to say, " my special saint or patron"), was venerated on the 30th March. He was of the tribe of Hua
Guala, whose territory was Gail-fhine in Ulster; his church was *Lann-
mocholmog* [church of St. Mocholmog] now Magheralin or Maralin, in
Dalaradia in Ulster. The other Colman, *mac Luachain*, or son of

---

* " The town of the Knight's port in
the Glenn." Dr. Reeves suggests that this
must be Glin, or Glenn-Corbraighe, in the
N. W. of the Co. of Limerick, where there
is a good harbour on the Shannon, where
the *Knight of Glin* resides, and from which
he takes his title; in Irish, *Ridire an Gle-*
anna. The castle of Glin was called Cloch-
Glenna. It was surprised and sacked, and
every soul within it put to death, including
some women and children, by Sir George
Carew, President of Munster, aided by the
Earl of Thomond, in 1600. See *Four*
Masters.

Luachan, was venerated on the 17th of June, at a place in Meath, called also *Lann*, and *Lann-mic-Luachain* [church of the son of Luachan], to distinguish it from the *Lann*, or church of his half-brother. This Luachan was son of Aedh, son of Maine, son of Fergus Cearbhaill, son of Conall Crimhthann, son of Niall of the Nine Hostages. Both the brothers Colman flourished at the close of the 7th century. See Colgan, *ubi supra*, and Four Masters, at A. D. 699.

It is probable that the Irish Life of St. Colman mac Luachain preserved in the Rennes MS., would effectually remove this confusion between the two brothers; and I regret very much, for that reason, that it was not in my power, during my stay at Rennes, to transcribe it; but it would have taken at least a fortnight's hard work to do so; and as I was ordered abroad for relaxation, and to escape hard work, this was to me impossible.

Fol. 90. a.—Here follows, in a most beautiful hand, a copy of the Dinnsenchus, or History of the Forts of Ireland. This part of the volume is certainly as old as the close of the 13th or beginning of the 14th century.

It commences thus :—

Senchair bind Erend mro bo   The history of the forts of Erinn begins
rigne amongein mac amhalga inpile here, which Amorgein, son of Amhalgaidh,
bona beirib cempach . . .   the Poet of the Deisi of Tara, wrote . .

Of this tract we have several copies—a very good one (although imperfect) in the book of Leinster in Trinity College, and others in the Library of this Academy. But the Rennes copy exceeds in beauty of penmanship almost any MS. of its date that I have ever seen.

With this the volume terminates.

It is unfortunately impossible, as I have been informed, consistently with the rules of the Rennes Library, to obtain a loan of this, to us, singularly interesting volume; but if any competent Irish scholar, who could spend some weeks at Rennes, would transcribe the Irish version of Sir John Mandeville's Travels, and the Life of St. Colman mac Luachain, he would confer a most important benefit on Irish literature.

DE QUIBUSDAM EPISCOPIS.

BODLEIAN MS.; RAWLINSON, No. 480.

[*See Proceedings of the Royal Irish Academy*, vol. ix. (1865) p. 184.]

ISU Cpırc, Mapıa, Pacpaıc, Cotum Cılle, bpıʒıb.—Cuımpe cuımnıʒce punna ap apoıle bo eapboccaıb Epenn ba naċ dıpmcep puıbe eappocba anopa, ʒé ʒombab dıpmeca ına puıbıb aʒup peıb ubepne.

Cuıʒ a léʒċóıp na púıbe ap copaċ, ıp na heappoıce ıapccaın.

Mıpı an Dubalcaċ mac pıpbıpıʒ eʒpap po 17 Mapċſſ anno Chpıpcı 1665 no 1666.

Aċab Caoın.—Caċbab mac Penʒupa eppcop Aċaıb caoın cencerrımo anno aecacıp puae obııc.

Noca: ʒo mab ıonann Aċub caoın aʒup cınn annpo.

Aċab Cınn.—Caċbub mac Penʒupa eppcop Aċaıb Cınn, anno Chpıpcı 554. Caoʒa ap céb blıabna apaoʒal.

Aċab Coʒapca.—bpıʒıb ınʒen Dallbponaıʒ, ⁊ Dıapmaıb, aʒup Aonʒup, aʒup Eppcop Eoʒan—bo Pocapcaıb bóıb. Icé pıl ın Achab Coʒapca ı ccpích Ua nDuach muıʒe hAıpʒebpoıp.

Aıpb Móıp—Deacclan Aıpbe Moıpe, eppcop aʒup conpeppóın; bo píól Pébleımıb peaċcmaıp pı Epenn. Dona heappoccaıb babap pıa bPacpaıc ın Epınn ın Declan pın.

---

[1] For the annotations the translator is indebted to W. M. Hennessy, M.R.I.A.

[2] *Achadh-Caoin* (or *Achadh-cinn*). This place has not been satisfactorily identified. Colgan (*Trias Thaum.*, p. 182) thought that it was the same place as Achadh-na-Cille (Aughnakilly, barony of Kilconway, county of Antrim). See Reeves's *Down and Connor*, p. 89, note ᵇ, and O'Donovan's *Four Masters*, A.D. 554, note °.

[3] *Cathbadh—Cathdubh*. Different names of the same person, who is called *Cathub* in the Martyrologies of Tallaght and Donegal, where his obit is entered under April 6. The Four Mast. (A. D. 554) also write the name *Cathub*; but the Chron. Scotorum (A. D. 555) has

ON SOME BISHOPS OF IRELAND,

BY DUALD MAC FIRBIS.[1]

TRANSLATED BY D. H. KELLY, M. R. I. A.

JESUS, MARY, PATRICK, COLUMB CILLE, BRIGIT.—Brief memorials here of certain Bishops of Erinn, for whom episcopal sees are not now reckoned; although they were reckoned in their own times and sees.

Take notice, reader, that the sees are placed first, and the bishops after.

I am Duald Mac Firbis who arranges this, the 17th March, Anno Christi 1665 or 1666.

ACHADH-CAOIN.[2] Cathbadh,[3] son of Fergus, bishop of Achadh-Caoin; in the one hundred and fiftieth year of his age he died.

NOTE: Haply Achad-Caoin and [Achadh]-Cinn are identical.

ACHADH-CINN.—Cathdubh,[3] son of Fergus, bishop of Achadh-Cinn, Anno Christi 554; fifty and one-hundred years his age.

ACHADH-TOGARTHA.—Brigid, daughter of Dallbronagh, and Diarmaid and Ængus, and Bishop Eoghan; they were of the Fotharta.[4] It is they who are in Achadh-Togartha,[5] in the territory of Hy Duach of the plain of Airgedros.[6]

ARDMORE.[7]—Declan of Ardmore, bishop and confessor, of the race of Fedhlimidh Rectmhar, king of Erinn. This Declan was of the bishops that were in Erinn before Patrick.

Cathbadh. The latter authority also gives his age as 150 years.

[4] *Fotharta:* now the barony of Forth, county of Carlow; called *Fothartha-Ui-Nolain*, or O'Nolan's Fothartha, to distinguish it from other districts called Fothartha.

[5] *Achadh-Togartha.* See next note.

[6] *Airgedros.* Ui-Duach, or Hy-Duach, is represented by the present parish of Odogh, barony of Fassadineen, county of Kilkenny. But, according to an Inquisition taken in the year 1635, the district of Ui-Duach was then considered co-extensive with the said barony. See O'Donovan's note, Four Masters, A. D. 850, note [e], and MS. 24, C. 6., R. I. A.

[7] Barony of Decies-within Drum, Co. Waterford.

Αιρεɣαl Mυαδαιn. .ι. Mυαδαn epϝcop ó διρεɣαl Mυαδαιn;
30 Αυɣυϝc.

Αιριυδ Ιonδυιɣ.—Διαρmαιδ epϝcop ó Οιριυδ Ιonδυιɣ.

Αιρɣιαll.—Αοδ Ο Ceαllαιδe epϝcop Αιρɣιαll, ιϝ cenn cαnαnαċ
Eϝenn, qυιευιc 1182.

Mαοlιoϝα Ο Ceϝδαιll, epϝcop Αιρɣιαll, qυιευιc 1187.

Mαοlιoϝα mαc αn epϝcoιp mιc Mαοιlċιαϝαιn, epϝcop Αιρɣιαll,
δο δcc 1195.

Νιocol mαc Cαcαϝαιɣ, epϝcop Αιρɣιαll, floruit anno 1356.

Ḃϝιαn mαc Cαċmαιl, epϝcop Αιρɣιαll, δο δcc 1358.

Αοδ Uα hEδċαιɣ, epϝcop Αιρɣιαll, qυιευιc 1369.

Αιρċeϝ αδαιδ.—Luɣαιδ epϝcop Αιρċeϝ αδαιδ.

Αιρċeϝ Lαιɣen.—Flαιċeṁ Uα Ḋυιδιδιϝ, epϝcop αιρċeϝ Lαιɣen,
δο ecc 1104.

Ḋαɣδαn ιnδιϝ Ḋαοιle, .ι. epϝcop, ιn αιρċeϝ Lαιɣen αcα ιn
Ιnδeϝ Ḋαοιle. 13 Sept.

Αιρċeϝ Mαιɣe.—Διαρmαιδ mαc Meċαιϝ epϝcop ó Αιρċeϝ
mαιɣe, ι cCυαιc ϝαċα ι ϝϝeϝαιδ Mαnαch.

Αolmαɣ.—Seċc neϝϝcoιϝ ó Αolmύιɣ .ι. ιn Ḋomnαch móϝ .ι.
υn. neϝϝcoιϝ Ḋomnαιɣ móιϝ Αolmυιɣe. Mάϝ ó αcα Αolmαɣ ι
mḃϝeιϝne Uι Rυαιϝc.

Ḋαllαn Αolmυιɣe epϝcop, 14 December.

Αonδϝυιm.—Cυιmιne epϝcop nΑonδϝomα, qυιευιc cιϝcα αn-
num 661.

Oeɣecċαιϝ epϝcop nΑonδϝomα, pausat 730.

Colmαn epϝcop nΑonδϝomα, qυιευιc 871.

Cϝonαn δeɣ, epϝcop nΑonδϝomα, anno Cϝιϝcι 642. Ɣo mαδ ó
ϝo le ccυιϝceϝ Cαenδϝυιm; ϝec Cαonδϝυιm.

Mochomα epϝcop nΑonδϝomα.

---

[1] Errigal, county of Monaghan.

[2] *Airiud-Ionduigh*, not identified.

[3] Airgiall (Oriel), i. e. bishopric of
Clogher.

[4] *O'Cellaigh*. The Four Mast. and the
Ann. L. Cé, &c., call him O'Caellaighi,
or O'Kealy; but in Ware's list of the
bishops of Clogher, he is called O'Kelly.

[5] Ann. L. Cé, and IV. M.

[6] IV. M.; but Ware says in 1184.

[7] Ware.

[8] Ob. 1356, Four Masters.

[9] IV. M.

[10] *Aedh O'Heothaigh* : i. e. Hugh
O'Hoey. His name is not in Ware's list
of the bishops of Clogher. The IV. M.
have the death of Aodh O'Neill, bishop
of Clogher, at the year 1369, as also the
Annals of Loch Cé; and the name Ua
Heothaigh is probably a mistake for

AIREGAL-MUADHAIN.[1] — Muadhan, bishop of Airegal-Muadhain, 30th August.

AIRIUD-IONDUIGH.[2]—Diarmaid, bishop of Airiud-Ionduigh.

AIRGIALL.[3]—Hugh O'Cellaigh,[4] bishop of Airghiall, and head of the canons of Erinn, quievit 1182.[5]

Maolisa O'Carroll, bishop of Airgiall, went to his rest 1187.[6]

Maolisa, son of the bishop Mac Maelchiaran, bishop of Airgiall, died 1195.[7]

Nicholas Mac Cathasaigh, bishop of Airgiall, flourished 1356.[8]

Brian Mac Cathmail, bishop of Airgiall, died 1358.[9]

Aodh O'Heothaigh,[10] bishop of Airgiall, quievit 1369.

AIRTHER-ACHAIDH.[11]—Lughaidh, bishop of Airther-achaidh.

AIRTHER-LAIGHEN.[12] — Flaithemh O'Dwyer, bishop of Airther-Laighen, died 1104.[13]

Dagdan of Inbher-Daile,[14] id est bishop; in Airther-Laighen he is, in Inbher-Daile, 13 Sep.[15]

AIRTHER-MAIGHE.[16]—Diarmaid, son of Mechar, bishop of Airther-Maighe, in Tuath-ratha[17] in Fermanagh.

AOLMAGH.[18]—Seven bishops from Aolmagh, id est in Domhnach-mor; viz., seven bishops of Domhnach-mor-Aolmaighe. If this be so, Aolmagh is in Breifne-O'Ruairc.

Dallan of Aolmagh, bishop, 14 December.[19]

AONDRUIM.[20]—Cummine, bishop of Aondruim, quievit circa annum 661.[21]

Oegetchair, bishop of Aondruim, pausat 730.[22]

Colman, bishop of Aondruim, quievit 871.[23]

Cronan Beg, bishop of Aondruim, anno Christi 642.[24] Perhaps this is he with whom Caendruim is placed. *See* Caendruim.

Mochoma, bishop of Aendruim.

---

that of O'Neill.

[11] *Airther-Achaidh*, not identified.

[12] *Airther-Laighen;* East Leinster.

[13] Four Masters.

[14] *Inbher-Daile;* Ennereilly, county of Wicklow.

[15] Mart. Taml. and Mart. Doneg.

[16] *Airther-Maighe.* Armoy, Co. Fermanagh.

[17] *Tuath-ratha.* Toorash in Fermanagh.

[18] *Aolmagh.* Donaghmore, barony of Dromahaire, county of Leitrim.

[19] Mart. Doneg.

[20] *Aondruim.* Mahee Island, in Strangford Lough.

[21] Four Masters, 658: Tig. and Chron. Scot. 659.

[22] IV. M.

[23] IV. M.

[24] Ob. IV. M.

Cᴘιοcαn eᴘſcop nᴀonᴅᴘoma, anno Cᴘιſcι 632.

Cuιmen eᴘſcop nᴀonᴅᴘoma, anno ᴅomιnι 698.

Aᴘa.—Ꮄccnech comaᴘᴃa Ꮄnna Aιᴘne, eᴘſcop aᵹuſ ancoιᴘe, anno 916.

Aelchu ᴃaᴘaᴃ aιnm pupa Aιᴘne, mac Ꝓaolᴄaιᴘ mιc Ꮄᴃᴅluιᵹ; aᵹuſ ſa ſí Oᴘᴘuιᵹe ιn Ꝓaolᴄaιᴘ ſιn. Aᴘ uaιᴅ ſíol Ꝓaolᴄaιᴘ la hOᴘᴘaιᵹe. Uιme aᴅᴃeᴘaᴘ ᴃo pupa .ι. papa; ó ᴘo ᵹaᴃ aᴃᴅaιne na Ꭱoṁa caᴘ éιᴘ nᵹᴘeᵹoιᴘ, aᵹuſ ſoᴘᴘacaιᴃ a aᴃᴅaιne aᵹuſ ᴅo luιᴅ ᴅo ιaᴘᴘuιᴅ a maιᵹιᴘᴅᴘech caιᴘιſ ᵹo hιaᴘᴄaᴘ Ꮄoᴘᴘa, aᵹuſ ᵹo hAᴘuιnn na·nᴅeṁ; ᵹonaᴅ í an cᴘeſ ᴘelιc aιnᵹιl Aιᴘne ᴘelιc Ꝓupa mιc Ꝓaelᴄaιᴘ mιc Ꮄaᴅaluᵹ.

ᴃᴘecan (nó ᴃᴘacan) eᴘſcop: ᵹo maᴅ ó ᴘo ᴃᴘecan Aιᴘne ι ccιll ᴃhᴘecᴅιn ι ncuaᴅ Muιnan.

Aᴘᴅ ᴃᴘecaιn.—Aelᵹnaᴅ eᴘſcop aιᴘᴅ ᴃᴘecaιn, moᴘcuuſ 776.

Maoluma eᴘſcop aιᴘᴅ ᴃᴘecaιn, oᴃ. 823.

ᴃᴘecan eᴘſcop (aιᴘᴅe ᴃᴘecaιn Mιᴅe), no aᴃᴃ Maιᵹe ᴃιle, 6 December.

Aᴘᴅ ᴄaᴘna.—ᴃeoaιᴅ eᴘſcop Aᴘᴅa ᴄaᴘna, quιeuιc 523. A ſéιl aᴘ an 8. lá ᴅo Maᴘca.

Aᴘᴅ ſᴘaᴄa.—Ꮄᴘſcop Ꮄoᵹan Aᴘᴅa ſᴘaᴄa.

Moᴘᴘ Maoιlſᴘoᵹaᴘcaιᵹ, eᴘſcop Aᴘᴅa ſᴘaᴄa, 678.

Coιᴃᴅen eᴘſcop Aᴘᴅa ſᴘaᴄa, quιeuιc 705. Ꭰoιᵹ ᵹuſ ιonann ιſ Coιᴃᴅenaᴄ eᴘſcop Aᴘᴅa ſᴘaᴄa, ceᴘᴅa anno Cᴘιſcι 706, ſa ſéιl aca aᴘ an 26 la ᴅo November.

Aᴄ-ᴃa-laaſᵹ.—Ꮄᴘſcop Coιnne ó aᴄh ᴃa laaſᵹ (1° Dec⸀.) ι ccaoᴅ chenannᴘa ι Mιᴅe.

---

1 638, Chron. Scot. and IV. M.

2 *Cuimen.* This Cuimen is not referred to in any of the Irish Annals; and the editor does not know where Mac Firbis found the date of his obit.

3 The Great island of Aran, in Galway Bay.

4 Four Masters.

5 *Pupa.* In the Life of S. Endeus, published by Colgan, a note occurs relative to this Pupa, or Papa, of which the following is a translation:—

"Three holy men went from Ireland into Britain, &c.; after some time they went to Rome. At this time the Roman pontiff died, and the people and clergy sought to make S. Pupeus, one of the three, pope, but which he refused to consent to, and St. Hilarius was made comarb of Peter. . . . At length the three return to Ireland, and go to Aran."—Act. SS. p. 708, cap. 19.

6 *Cill-Brecain;* now Kilbreckan, barony of Upper Bunratty, county of Clare.

Criotan, bishop of Aondruim, [ob.] anno Christi 632.[1]

Cuimen,[2] bishop of Aondruim, [ob.] anno Domini 698.

Ara.[3]—Eccnech, comarb of Enna of Ara, bishop and anchorite, [ob.] anno 916.[4]

Aelchu, who was named the Pope of Ara, the son of Faolchar, son of Edalach; the said Faolchar was king of Ossory, and from him descend the race of Faolchar in Ossory. The reason why he was called Pupa[5] (Pope), was because he obtained the abbacy of Rome after Gregory; and he vacated the abbacy, and went in search of his master (i. e. Gregory), across to the west of Europe, and to Ara of the saints; so that the third angelical cemetery of Ara is the cemetery of Pupa, son of Faolchar, son of Edalach.

Brecan, or Bracan, bishop. Perhaps this is Brecan of Ara, who is [venerated] in Cill-Brecain[6] in Thomond.

Ard-Brecain.[7]—Aelgnad, bishop of Ard-Brecan, died 776.[8]

Maoluma,[9] bishop of Ard-Brecain, ob. 823.

Brecan, bishop (of Ard-Brecain in Meath), or abbot of Magh-Bile,[10] 6 December.[11]

Ard-Charna.[12]—Beo Aedh [Aedus vivus], bishop of Ard-Carna, quievit 523.[13] His festival is on the eighth day of March.[14]

Ard-Sratha.[15]—Owen, bishop of Ard-Sratha.

Death of Maelfogharty, bishop of Ard-Sratha, 678.[16]

Coibden, bishop of Ard-Sratha, quievit 705. Probably this is the same as Coibdenach, bishop of Ard-Sratha, who died A. D. 706,[17] whose festival is on the 26th day of November.[18]

Ath-da-laarg.[19]—Bishop Coinne from Ath-da-laarg (1st December), near Cenannus, in Meath.

---

[7] *Ard-Brecain*, county of Meath.

[8] Four Masters.

[9] *Maeluma*. The Four Masters record, under A. D. 823, the death of a Maelrubha, bishop of Ard-Brecain.

[10] *Magh-Bile*. Moville, county of Down. The festival of Brecan, abbot or bishop of Magh-Bile, is set down in the Calendar at 29 April.

[11] Mart. Doneg.

[12] *Ard-Charna;* Ardcarne, barony of Boyle, county of Roscommon.

[13] Four Masters; 518, Chron. Scot.

[14] Mart. Doneg.

[15] *Ard-Sratha.* Ardstraw, county of Tyrone.

[16] IV. M. Chron. Scot.

[17] Ann. Ulster and Chron. Scot.

[18] Mart. Doneg.

[19] *Ath-da-laarg.* "Ford of two forks;" near Kells, county of Meath.

Αὁ ὁυιρη.—Ϝιηηέϲ ὁυιρη, ερρϲορ Cιʟʟe Ϝιηηϲe, ό Αϲh ὁυιρη ιη Ορραιξe 2 Feb.

Αϲh ραὁαϲ.—Ἰὁ ερρϲορ ο Αϲ ραὁαϲ ι Ἰαιξηιϐ, 14 Julii.

Αϲh ϲρυιm.—Ὁορmιϲαϲιο Ϲορmαιϲ ερρϲορ Αϲha ϲρυιm, 741.

Ϝοιρϲeρη ερρϲορ (ὁιρξιϐυʟ Ραϲραιϲϲ), ό Αϲ ϲρυιm α Ἰαοξαιρe, χι Οϲϲοϐερ.

Ϲeηηραeʟαὁ ερρϲορ Αϲha ϲρυιm, ϥυιeυιϲ 819.

Ἰοmαη, ερρϲορ ό αϲh ϲρυιm (ὁιρξιϐυʟ Ραϲραιϲ) χι Οϲϲοϐερ.

Ϻαοʟέϲιη ερρϲορ αξυρ αηξϲοιρe αϲha ϲρυιm, 929.

Ϲορmαϲ ερρϲορ Αϲα ϲρυιm, αξυρ ϲοmαρϐα Ραϲραιϲ; anno 496, 17 February.

Ορραιη ερρϲορ ο Ραιϲ Ορραιη ϝρι Αϲh ϲρυιm αηιαρ; anno Ϲριρϲι 686 ; February 17.

Ϲυιmeη ερρϲορ ιη Αϲ ϲρυιm; February 17.

Ἰαϲhϲαη ερρϲορ ιη Αϲ ϲρυιm; February 17.

ϐαιʟe Sʟαιηe.—Ϲαρϲ Sʟάιηe ερρϲορ Ἰιοʟϲαιξ, ιρ ό Ϝeρϲα ϝeρ ϝeξ ι ϲϲαοϐ Sιοϐα ϲρυιm αηαιρ ; anno 512 αη ϲαη ϲeρϐα, χϲ. α ὁοιρ. Αρ ό αϲα ιmϐαϊʟe Sʟαιηe et cetera.

ϐeηηϲορ.—Ὁυιϐιηρι, ραοϊ αξυρ ερρϲορ mυιηϲιρe ϐeηηϲαιρ, 951.

Ὁιαρmαιὁ Ο Ϻαοιʟϲeʟϲha, ϲοmαρϐα Ϲhοmξαιʟʟ, eαϲϲηυιὁ ϝοιρϲϲe, ρξριϐηιὁ αξυρ ερρϲορ, ὁο όξ 1016.

Ὁαηιeʟ ερρϲορ ϐeηὁϲαιρ, 11 Septembris.

Ϲeʟe Ὁαϐαιʟʟ mαϲ Sξαηὁαιʟ, ερρϲορ eϲ ϲeϲeρα, ὁο όϲ 927. Ϲeʟe Ραϐαιʟʟ mαϲ Sξαηὁυιʟ ὁο όυʟ ὁοη Ροϊϻ α haϐὁαιηe ϐeηὁϲαιρ, 926.

---

[1] *Ath-Duirn*, i. e. "the *Ford of Dorn*." The Mart. of Donegal adds that *Dorn* was the name of a hill in Magh-Raighne. It was probably near or at Cill-Finnche.

[2] *Cill-Finnche;* the church of Finnech, now Killinny, in the parish and barony of Kells, county of Kilkenny.

[3] *Ath-fadat;* Aghade, or Ahade, barony of Forth, county of Carlow.

[4] Mart. Doneg.

[5] *Ath-Truim;* Trim, county of Meath.

[6] Four Masters; 745, Ann. Ult.

[7] *Laoghaire*, or Ui-Laoghaire, the ancient name of a district comprising the greater part of the present baronies of Upper and Lower Navan, county of Meath.

[8] Mart. Doneg.

[9] IV. M.

[10] Mart. Doneg.

[11] *Maelécin.* This name is written Maeleoin (Malone) by the Four Masters. He was probably the same as Maeloin,

ATH-DUIRN.[1]—Finnech-Duirn, bishop of Cill-Finche[2] from Ath-duirn in Ossory, 2 Feb.

ATH-FADAT.[3]—Id, bishop of Ath-fadat, in Leinster, July 14.[4]

ATH-TRUIM.[5]—Dormitatio of Cormac, bishop of Ath-truim, 741.[6]

Fortchern, bishop (disciple of Patrick), from Ath-truim, in Laoghaire,[7] 11 October.[8]

Cennfaeladh, bishop of Ath-truim, quievit, 819.[9]

Loman, bishop, from Ath-truim, a disciple of Patrick, 11 October.[10]

Maolécin,[11] bishop and anchorite of Ath-Truim, ob. 929.[12]

Cormac, bishop of Ath-truim, and comarb of Patrick, [ob.] anno 496,[13] 17 Feb.[14]

Bishop Ossan, from Rath-Ossain,[15] to the west of Ath-truim, anno Christi 686,[16] 17 Feb.[17]

Cuimen, bishop in Ath-truim, 17 Feb.[18]

Lachtan, bishop in Ath-truim, 17 Feb.[19]

BAILE SLAINE.[20]—Erc of Slane, bishop of Liolcagh, and from Ferta-fer-feg, at the eastern side of Sidh-truim. It was the year 512[21] when he died: his age was 90. It is he that is (venerated) in the town of Slane, &c.

BENNCHOR.[22]—Duibhinsi, a most eminent man, and bishop of the community of Bennchar, 951.[23]

Diarmaid O'Maeltelcha, comarb of Comghall, a perfect wise man, scribe and bishop, died in 1016.[24]

Daniel, bishop of Benncha, 11 September.[25]

Ceile-Dabhaill, son of Scannall, went to Rome from the abbacy of Benncha, 926.[26]

---

bishop and anchorite, whose festival is given in the Mart. Dung. at the 20th of October.

[12] Four Masters.

[13] IV. M. and Chron. Scot.

[14] Mart. Doneg. and Mart. Taml.

[15] *Rath-Ossain.* This was the name of a place a little to the west of Trim. In the Annals of Ulster and of the Four Masters, Ossan, or Osseni, is called bishop of Monasterboice.

[16] Ann. Ult.

[17] Mart. Doneg. and Mart. Taml.

[18] Mart. Taml.

[19] Mart. Taml.

[20] *Baile Slaine.* Slane, county of Meath.

[21] Four Masters; 513, Chron. Scot.

[22] *Bennchor;* Bangor, county of Down

[23] IV. M.

[24] IV. M.; 1017, Chron. Scot.

[25] Mart. Taml. and Mart. Doneg.

[26] IV. M.

beᵹ Éρe.—Eρρcop luḃaρ baoı ın Eρınn na eρρcop ρuıl caınᵹ Þaóρaıᵹ na eρρcop ınce, bo óıcıᵹ ıρın ınıρ (aρ muıρ laıṁ le Laıᵹnıḃ) bana haınm beᵹ E'ρe. Ceρba anno Chρıρcı 500. A ρel 23 Clpρeıl.

Cρonnmael abb beᵹ Eρenn, eρρcop ıρ ρeρ leᵹınb Camlaċca, 964.

bıoρρa.—Ðobıu, eρρcop bıoρρa, 842.

Þlaıchnıa eρρcop bıoρρa, mortuus 851.

bó clúaın.—Þρaoċan eρρcop ó bó cluaın ı Laoıᵹıρ, ó chluaın óıóneċh ρaıρ, nó aρ ḃéulaıḃ Þlébe blaóma ım bó clúaın, nó ó Inıρ mıc Eaρca, no o Inρı mıc Eaρca.

boch ċonaıρ.—Céle Cρıρc, ó cıll Cele Cρıρc; ın Uıḃ Ðunchaba, ı ρρoċaρcuıḃ a Laıᵹnıb aca Cıll Cele Cρıρc ó bóıch ċonuıρ, 3 Marta.

bρecmuıᵹ.—Cıbḃċe eρρcop ıρ abb ċρe ba ᵹlaıρ.

Cıbḃe .ı. aoóbeó, uaıρ ba beó eρén a bþeaρcaıḃ aᵹuρ a míoρbuılıb. Cca a ceall ρρı hlṁleċ anbeρ, no ı mbρeċmuıᵹ a cCeρa ın ıaρċaρ Connachc.

bρeþne.—Cóó O Þínb, eρρcop na bρeþne, bo óᵹ ın Inıρ Cloċρaınn, 1136.

Þlann Ua Connachcaıᵹ eρρcop na bρeþne, quıeuıc 1132.

Síomon o ρuaıρc, eρρcop na bρeıþne, quıeuıc 1285.

Maċa maᵹ Ðuıḃne, eρρcop na bρeıþne, quıeuıc 1314.

Eρρcop na bρeıþne .ı. O. Cρıobacaın, quıeuıc 1328.

Conċóbaρ mac Connama, eρρcop na bρeıþne, quıeuıc 1355.

---

[1] *Beg-Eri;* Beggery Island, Wexford Harbour.

[2] Four Masters, and Chron. Scot.

[3] Mart. Doneg. and Mart. Taml.

[4] IV. M.

[5] *Biorra;* Birr, King's County.

[6] IV. M.

[7] IV. M.

[8] *Bo-chluain,* "Cow's lawn or (meadow)." From the description, it would appear that two places in Laighis (Leix, Queen's County,) were so called—one to the east of Clonenagh, and the other somewhat to the west of it, or in front of Sliabh-Bladhma. The one here re-ferred to is a couple of miles to the west of Maryborough.

[9] *Both-Chonais,* pronounced Bo-chonais. This establishment is now represented by the old grave-yard in the townland of Binnion, parish of Clonmany, barony of Inishowen, and county of Donegal.

[10] *Hy Dunchadha.* This was the name of the tract of land extending between the River Liffey and the Dublin mountains, the patrimony of the family of Mac Gilla Mocholmog, for an account of whom see Gilbert's "History of Dublin," vol. i. pp. 230, 403.

Beg-Eri.[1]—Bishop Ibhar, who was in Erinn as a bishop before Patrick came as a bishop into it, dwelt in an island (in the sea near to Leinster), which is named Beg-Eri. He died A. C. 500.[2] His festival is on the 23rd April.[3]

Cronmael, abbot of Beg-Eri, bishop and lector of Tamlacht; [died] 964.[4]

Biorra.[5]—Dodiu, bishop of Biorra, 842.[6]

Flaithnia, bishop of Biorra, mortuus 851.[7]

Bo-chluain.[8]—Fraechan, bishop of Bo-chluain, in Laighis, to the east of Cluain-eidhnech, or right before Sliabh-Bladhma, in Bo-chluain, or from Inis-mic-Erca, or from Insi-mic-Erca.

Both-Chonais.[9]—Cele-Christ, of Cill-Cele-Christ, 3 March; in Hy Dunchada,[10] in the Fotharts[11] of Leinster, is the church of Cele-Christ of Both-Chonais.

Brecmuigh.[12]—Aidhbche, bishop and abbot of Tir-da-glais.[13]

Aidbhe i. e. Aedh-beo (Aedus vivus), for he was active in prodigies and in miracles. His church is to the south of Imlech, or in Brechmagh, in Cera, in the west of Connaught.

Breifne.[14]—Aedh O'Finn, bishop of the Breifne, died in Inis-Clothrainn,[15] 1136.[16]

Flann O'Connaghty, bishop of the Breifne, quievit 1132.[17]

Simon O'Ruairc, bishop of the Breifne, quievit 1285.[18]

Matthew Mac Duibhne, bishop of the Breifne, quievit 1314.[19]

The bishop of the Breifne, i. e. O'Criodachan,[20] quievit 1328.[21]

Conor Mac Connamha, bishop of the Breifne, quievit, 1355.

---

[11] *In the Fotharts;* ı ꝼꝓoꝻꝛꝲ. This should probably be ı poꝛꝼuꝣꝲ, "in the Fortuathas (or border lands)," as the *Fortuatha* of Leinster included the southern part of the county of Dublin, and was not confined to the territory of Ui-Mail, in Wicklow, as O'Donovan thought. (*See* "Book of Rights," p. 250, *note.*)

[12] *Brecmuigh.* Breaffy, barony of Carra, county of Mayo.

[13] *Tir-da-glais.* Terryglass, barony of Lower Ormond, county of Tipperary.

[14] *Breifne,* i. e. the present diocese of Kilmore.

[15] *Inis-Clothrainn.* Now Iniscloghran, in Lough Ree.

[16] Ann. Loch Cé, and IV. M.

[17] 1231, Ann. Four Masters, Ult., and Loch Cé.

[18] IV. M., Ann. Loch Cé, and Ware.

[19] IV. M., Ann. Loch Cé, and W.

[20] *O'Criodachan.* This seems to have been the same as the bishop who is called "Patrick" in Ware's list of the bishops of Kilmore. (Harris's ed. of "Ware," vol. i. p. 227).

[21] IV. M.; Ann. Ult.

Riccarb O Raiჳilliჳ, eprcop na breipne, bo ecc 1369.

Tomar mac Ɑinbriu meჳ brᵭbuiჳ, eprcop aჳur eircinnec an bᵭ brepne re ré 30 bliaban, quieuic 1511.

Copmac maჳ Sampabain, bar ჳaireb eprcop ir in mbrepne, quieuic 1511.

bricania.—Teoborur eprcop bricanae, quieuic 689.

Cairiol Iorrae.—brón eprcop ó cairiol Iorrae in Ib Fiacrac muaibe, anno Domini 511; luin 8 la.

Caonbruim (Forte Ɑonbruim).—Quier Cronain eprcop Caonbroma, circa annum 639. Fec Ɑonbruim.

Carn Furbuibe.—Muaban eprcop o Carn Furbuibe, marca 6 morcuur.

Ceannanur.—Maelpinnen mac Neccain, eprcop Cenannra, comarba Ulcain aჳur Cairniჳ, 967.

Cillachaib, no aichib.—Reccabra, eprcop Cille hacaib, 952.

Cillachaib braiჳniჳe.—Dubarcac, eprcop Cille achaib, quieuic 869.

Eprcop Darrcac ó Cill achaibh braiჳniჳe.

Mac Erc Cille achaibh, eprcop.

Cill air.—Ɑeb mac bric, eprcop, ó Cill áir i Mibe, aჳur ó Sliab liaჳ i ccír bóჳuine i ccenel Conaill, quieuic anno Cpirci 588. Ɑ rel χᵒ Novemb.

Cill achaib broma Foca.—Sincell, abb Cille achaib broma Foca, .i. an ren Sincell, 548; 330 bliabna a aoir.

baccar 12 eprcop ir 12 oilicrec, ჳo niomab ele, a cCill achaib broma Foca, in Ib Failჳe, áic ambái Sincell roran raჳarc, aჳur Śincell rinrir eprcop.

---

[1] Four Masters.

[2] IV. M.

[3] IV. M.

[4] 690 Angl. Sax. Chron.

[5] *Caisiol-Iorra*; Killaspagbrone, barony of Carbury, county of Sligo.

[6] IV. M.; 510 Chron. Scot.

[7] Mart. Doneg. and Mart. Taml.

[8] *Caondruim ;* this was one of the ancient names of the hill of Tara. See next note.

[9] *Cronan.* This is apparently the Cronan mentioned under the head of Aondruim, for which Caondruim seems to be a mistake.

[10] *Carn-Furbaidhe.* It is stated in the Dinnsenchus, "Book of Lecan," fol. 231, that this was the name of a large carn on Sliabh-Cairbre, or the Carn mountain, in the north of the county of Longford ; and Colgan (AA. SS., p. 253) observes that Cill-Modani was "juxta Carn-fur-

Richard O'Reilly, bishop of the Breifne, died 1369.[1]

Thomas, son of Andrew Mac Brady, bishop and herenech of the two Breifnes during 30 years, quievit 1511.[2]

Cormac Mac Samhradhain, styled bishop in the Breifne, quievit 1511.[3]

BRITANNIA.—Theodorus, bishop of Britannia, quievit 689.[4]

CAISIOL-IORRA.[5]—Bron, bishop of Caisiol-Iorra, in Hy-Fiachrach of the Moy, anno Domini 511.[6] His festival is on the 8th of June.[7]

CAONDRUIM[8] (Forte Aondruim).—Quies of Cronan,[9] bishop of Caondruim, ob. circa annum 639. *See* Aondruim.

CARN-FURBAIDHE.[10]—Muadan, bishop of Carn-Furbaidhe, March 6 mortuus.[11]

CEANNANUS.[12]—Maolfinnen, son of Nechtan, bishop of Cennanus, comarb of Ultan[13] and of Cairneeh,[14] 967.[15]

CILL-ACHAIDH (or ACHIDH).[16]—Rechtabra, bishop of Cill-achaidh, 952.[17]

CILL-ACHAIDH-DRAIGHNIGHE.[18]—Dubhartach,[19] bishop of Cill-achaidh, quievit 869.[20]

Bishop Darrtach, from Cill-achaidh-draighnighe.

Mac Erca, bishop of Cill-achaidh.

CILL-AIR.[21]—Aedh Mac Bric, bishop of Cill-air in Meath, and from Sliabh-Liag in Tir-Boghuine, in Cinel-Conaill, quievit anno Christi 588.[22] His festival on 10th November.

CILL-ACHAIDH-DROMA-FOTA.[23]—Sinchell, abbot of Cill-achaidh-droma-fota, i. e. the Elder Sinchell, 548;[24] 330 years was his age.

There were 12 bishops and twelve pilgrims, with many others, in Cill-achaidh-droma-fota, in Ui-Failghe, where Sinchell junior was priest, and Sinchell senior bishop.

---

baidhe."

[11] Mart. Taml. and Mart. Doneg.

[12] Kells, county of Meath.

[13] *Ultan;* founder of Ard Brecan, in Meath.

[14] *Cairnech.* St. Cairnech of Tulen, or Dulane, near Kells, in Meath.

[15] Four Masters, Chron. Scot.

[16] *Cill-achaidh;* Killaghy, county of Fermanagh.

[17] IV. M.

[18] *Cill-achaidh-draighnighe,* the same as Cill-Achaidh of note [16].

[19] *Dubhartach.* This name is written Dubhtach by the Four Masters.

[20] IV. M.

[21] *Cill-air;* Killare, county of Westmeath.

[22] Chron. Scot.; IV. M.

[23] *Cill-achaidh-dromo-fota;* Killeigh, King's County.

[24] IV. M.; Chron. Scot. 551.

Cill (ƥopꞇe caiꞃbꞃe in) ᵹaiꞃe.—Ᵹomaꝺ Caiꞃꞃꞃe epꞃcop aꞇa **Nouembꞁiꞃ** 1, ꝺo beꞇ iꞃin cill ꞃin.

Cill aiꞃꞇeꞃ.—Ioain (.i. Ꝑóin) epꞃcop Cille aiꞃꞇeꞃ.

Cill ꝺaiꞃꞃinn, ꞃe hꝐꞃ ꞃuaiꝺ [aꞇuaiꝺ].—ꝺaiꞃꞃionn epꞃcop, 8 Mai.

Cill Chaꞃꞇuiᵹ.—1 ꞇíꞃ boᵹuine, 6 Maꞃꞇa; Caꞃꞇhach epꞃcop, mac Ꝺonᵹuꞃa mic Naꞇꞃꞃaic, ꞃiᵹ Ꝑoᵹanaꞯꞇa Ċaiꞃil.

Cill bia.—Neman epꞃcop ó ꝺill bia, 1 Sept.

Cill bꞃacain.—bꞃacan no bꞃecan, epꞃcop, Aiꞃꞃil 1.

Cill Cele Cꞃiꞃꞇ.—Cele Cꞃiꞃꞇ, epꞃcop ó cill Cele Cꞃiꞃꞇ in Ꞇꞃ Ꝺunꞯaꝺa il Laiᵹniꞯ.

Cill Cuanna.—Ꝑpꞃcop Ƥeꞇmeꞯ ó ꝺill Chuanna, .i. Ƥeꞇmeꞯ ó ꝺill Ꞇuama no Ꞇoama.

Cill-cuilinn.—Mac Ꞇail Cille cuilinn; epꞃcop eꞃiꝺe, aᵹuꞃ Ꝑoᵹan a ainm, 548. Maoi 11.

Suibne mac Seᵹonain, epꞃcop aᵹuꞃ ꞃiaᵹloiꞃ Cille cuilinn 962.

Ꞇuaꞯhal Ua Ᵹaꞃꝺain, epꞃcop Cille cuillinn, ꝺo ecc 1030.

Cill cunᵹa.—Ꝺabnan epꞃcop Cille cunᵹa, 11 Aꞃꞃil.

Cill ꝺa leꞃ.—Sancꞇan, epꞃcop, ó ꝺill ꝺa leꞃ, 9 IꝈaói.

Cill ꝺuma ᵹlinn.—Moᵹenoᵹ, epꞃcop, o Cill ꝺuma ᵹluinn i nꝺeꞃᵹiꞃꞇ bꞃeᵹ, Ꝺecemb. 26.

Cill eanᵹa.—Ꝑpꞃcop Ꝺiomba ó Cill eannᵹa. Cill eꞃᵹa, ꞃoꞃꞇe Cill ꞃoꞃᵹa.

Cill epꞃcop Sancꞇain.—Ꝑpꞃcop Sancꞇan mac Canꞇoin ꞃiᵹ bꞃeꞇan.

Cill epꞃcop Ꝺꞃonain.—Ꝑpꞃcop ꝺꞃonan i Cill eꞃꞃuic Ꝺꞃonain.

---

[1] Cill ... ingaire. The Compiler suggests that this might be "Cill-Cairbre." The Mart. Doneg. commemorates a bishop Cairbre at 1 November, and adds that there was a Cill-Cairbre near Assroe, in the county of Donegal.

[2] Cill-airther ; in Ulster.

[3] Kilbarron, county of Donegal.

[4] 7 May, Mart. Donegal and Mart. Taml.

[5] Kilcar, barony of Banagh, county Donegal.

[6] *Tir-Boghuine*. Now the barony of Banagh, county of Donegal.

[7] 5 Mar., Mart. Doneg. and Mart. Taml.

[8] *Cill-Bia* ; not identified.

[9] Mart. Donegal.

[10] 1 May, Mart. Doneg. and Mart. Taml. ; and see above under Ara.

[11] *Cill-Cele-Christ*. See under Both-chonais.

[12] *Hy Dunchadha*. See note [10], r. 90, supra.

Cill- (perhaps Cairbre) Ingaire.[1]—Perhaps it is Cairbre, the bishop, who is [commemorated] Nov. 1, that is in this church.

Cill-airther.[2]—Joain (i. e. John), bishop of Cill-airther.

Cill-Bairrinn.[3]—To the north of Es-ruadh. Bairrion, bishop, 8 May.[4]

Cill-Carthaigh.[5]—In Tir-Boghuine;[5] 6 March,[6] Carthach, bishop, the son of Aongus, son of Nathfraech, king of the Eoghanacht of Cashel.

Cill-Bia.[8]—Nemhan, bishop of Cill-Bia, 1 September.[9]

Cill Bracan.—Bracan, or Brecan, bishop, April 1.[10]

Cill-Cele-Christ.[11]—Cele-Christ, bishop of Cill Cele-Christ, in Hy Dunchadha,[12] in Leinster.

Cill-Cuana.[13]—Fethmech, bishop of Cill-Cuana, i. e. Fethmech, bishop of Cill-Tuama, or [Cill]-Toama.

Cill-Cuilinn.[14]—Mac Tail of Cill-Cuilinn: (he was a bishop, and his name was Eoghan); 548.[15] May 11.[16]

Suibhne, son of Segonan, bishop and ruler of Cill-Cuilinn, 962.[17]

Tuathal O'Garvan, bishop of Cill-Cuilinn, died, 1030.[18]

Cill-Cunga.[19]—Dadnan, bishop of Cill-Cunga, 11 April.[20]

Cill-da-les.[21]—Sanctan, bishop of Cill-da-les, 9 May.

Cill-duma-Glinn.[22]—Mogenog, bishop of Cill-duma-glinn, in the south of Bregia, December 26.[23]

Cill-Eanga.[24]—Bishop Dioma, from Cill-Eanga. Cill-Erga, forte Cill-Forga.

Cill-Espuc-Sanctan.[25]—Bishop Sanctan, son of Canton, king of Britain (i. e. Wales.)

Cill-Espuc-Dronan.[26] — Dronán, bishop of Cill-Espuc-Dronan.

---

[13] *Cill-Cuana. Cill-Tuama.* The former would now be written Kilquan, and the other Kiltoome. There are many places in Ireland bearing these names.

[14] *Cill-Cuilinn;* Old Kilcullen, county of Kildare.

[15] Four Masters; 551 Chron. Scot.

[16] May 11; *recte* June 11. Mart. Doneg. and Mart. Taml.

[17] IV. M.

[18] IV. M.

[19] *Cill-Cunga;* not identified.

[20] Mart. Doneg. and Mart. Taml.

[21] *Cill-da-les;* not identified.

[22] *Cill-Duma-Glinn;* Kilglynn, barony of Upper Decie, county of Meath.

[23] Mart. Doneg.

[24] *Cill-Eanga.* The Compiler adds, "Cill-erga, *forte* Cill-forga;" Killarga, barony of Dromahaire, county of Leitrim.

[25] *Cill-Espuc-Sanctan;* Kill-Saint-Anne, county of Dublin.

[26] *Cill-Espuc-Dronan;* not identified.

Cill Oᘁonain.   Oᘁonan eᴘᴘcop ó cill Oᴘohain, Oecemb. 12.

Cill Ƒinnċe.—Ƒinneċ buiᴘn, eᴘᴘcop Cille Ƒinnċe o aċ Ouiᴘn in Oᴘᴘaiᵹe, Ƒeb. 2.

Cill Ƒoiᴘċceᴘn, in Uiḃ Oᴘona.   Ƒoiᴘċceᴘn eᴘᴘcop, biᴘᵹibal Paċᴘaic, Occ. 11.

Cill ᴘoiċiᴘḃe.—Ƒec Cuil ᴘoiċiᴘḃe.

Cill ᴘoᴘᵹa no Cill eaᴘᵹa.—Ƒionnċaḃ eᴘᴘcop, Nouemb. 11.

Cill Ᵹᴘeallain.—Eᴘᴘcop ᵹᴘeallan (acaiḃ bá ċill Ᵹᴘeallain i ccíᴘ ᴘiachᴘach muaiḃe), Sepc. 7.

Cill Ian.—Eᴘᴘcop Aoḃ i Cill Ian.

Cill inᴘi.—Aillcín, eᴘᴘcop, aᵹuᴘ an óᵹ (no inᵹen óᵹ) o Cill inᴘi. Noca. — Cill Aillcin in iniᴘ Sᵹᴘeobuinn i ccíᴘ Ƒiaċᴘaċ Muaiḃe; maiᴘiḃ múᴘ na heaᵹlaiᴘi ᴘin ᴘoᴘ.   Nouemb. 1.

Cill maiᵹnenn.—Maiᵹnen eᴘᴘcop iᴘ abb cille Maiᵹnenn, la caob Aċa cliaċ, Oecemb. 18.

Cill Mainċin.—Eᴘᴘcop Manċan, no Mainċain, i cill. M.

Cill moiᴘ Eniᴘ.—Cᴘunnmael eᴘᴘcop, ab Cille moiᴘe Eniᴘ, quieuic 765.

Cill Muine.—Oauiḃ eᴘᴘcop, Cille Muine, iᴘ aiᴘḃ eᴘᴘcop iniᴘi bᴘecan uile, Maᴘ. 1.

Cill Mobiuic.—Simplex, eᴘᴘcop .i. Mobiuic ó Cill Mobiuic i Soᵹuin, Ƒeb. 12.

Cill ᴘaċain.—(Blank in original).

Cill ᴘiᵹmanaḃ in Albuin.   Cainneċ abb, Occ. 11.

Cill ᴘuaiḃe.—Colman mac Caċbaḃa, eᴘᴘcop Cille ᴘuaiḃe i nOailaᴘaiḃe, aᴘ bᴘú Loċa Laoiᵹ in Ulcoiḃ, Occob. 16.

---

[1] *Dronan.* The form Drunan is also suggested by the compiler.

[2] Mart. Doneg.

[3] Killinny, in the parish and barony of Kells, county of Kilkenny.

[4] Mart. Doneg. and Mart. Taml.

[5] Idrone, county of Carlow.

[6] Mart. Doneg. and Mart. Taml.

[7] Killarga, county of Leitrim.

[8] Nov. 11, *recte* 12; Mart. Doneg.

[9] *Tir-Fiachrach.* Now the barony of Tireragh, county of Sligo.

[10] 17, Mart. Doneg.

[11] *Cill Insi. See* text.

[12] *Inis-Sgreobuinn,* otherwise Eiscir-abhann, now Inishcrone, in the parish of Kilglass, barony of Tireragh, and county of Sligo.

[13] Mart. Doneg.

[14] Kilmainham, near Dublin.

[15] Mart. Doneg.

[16] Kilmanaghan, barony of Kilcoursey,

CILL-DRONAN. Dronan,[1] bishop, from Cill-Dronan, December 12.[2]

CILL-FHINNHCE.[3]—Finnech-Duirn,. bishop of Cill-Fhinnche, from Aith-duirn, in Ossory, Feb. 2.[4]

CILL-FORTCHERN IN UI-DRONA.[5]—Fortchern, bishop, disciple of Patrick, Oct. 11.[6]

CILL-FOITHIRBHE. *See* Cuil-Foithirbhe.

CILL-FORGA, or CILL-EARGA.[7]—Finnchad, bishop, Nov. 11.[8]

CILL-GREALLAN.—Greallan, bishop (there are two Cill-Greallans in Tir-Fiachra[9] of the Moy), Sept. 7.[10]

CILL-IAN.—Bishop Aedh, of Kill-Ian.

CILL-INSI.[11]—Ailltin, bishop, and the virgin (or the young maiden) of Cill-insi. Nov. 1.[12]

NOTE.—Ailltin's church is in Inis-Sgreobbhuinn,[13] in Tir-Fiachra of the Moy. The walls of that church are still in existence.

CILL-MAIGHNEN.[14]—Maighnen, bishop and abbot of Cill-Maighnenn near Dublin, Dec. 18.[15]

CILL-MAINCHIN.[16]—Bishop Manchan, or Mainchin, in Cill-Manchan.

CILL-MOR-ENIR.[17]—Crunnmael, bishop, abbot of Cill-mor-Enir, quievit 765.[18]

CILL-MUINE.[19]—David, bishop of Cill-Muine, and archbishop of the isle of Britain, Mar. 3.[20]

CILL-MODIUT.[21]—Simplex, bishop, i. e., Modiut of Kill-modiut in Soghan,[22] Feb. 12.[23]

CILL-RATHAIN.—(Blank in original.)

CILL-RIGHMANAD, IN ALBA.[24]—Cainnech,[25] abbot, October 11.[26]

CILL-RUADH.[27]—Colman, son of Cathbadh, bishop of Cill-ruadh in Dal-Araidhe, on the brink of Loch-Laegh[28] in Uladh, Oct. 16.[29]

King's Co.

[17] Kilmore, three miles east of Armagh.

[18] Four Masters.

[19] *Cill-Muine ;* St. David's, Wales.

[20] Mart. Doneg.

[21] Kilmude, in Hy-Many.

[22] *Soghan,* in Hy-Many, the district of the enslaved tribes, near the Suck.

[23] Mart. Doneg.

[24] *Cill-Righmanad, in Alba;* St. Andrew's, Scotland.

[25] *Cainnech.* St. Canice of Achadh-bo, Queen's County; also founder of Cill-Cainnigh, i. e. Kilkenny.

[26] Mart. Doneg. and Mart. Taml.

[27] Kilroot, barony of Lower Belfast, county of Antrim.

[28] *Loch-Laegh,* the ancient name of Belfast Lough, which Adamnan Latinizes *Stagnum Lacus Vituli.* See Reeves' "Adamnan."

[29] Mart. Doneg. and Taml.

Cill Sganbuil, no cill bian. Fergur eprcop Cille Sganbuil, no bian ; agur ir fíóp rin.

Cill Sgire. Robaptač (Fionnglairi), eprcop; Conull eprcop Cille rgire, 865.

Cill rlebe. Fiacc (eprcop Slebte) cille rlebe.

Cill Cibill. Eprcop Foircebal (i cill Cibil), mac Cail, mic Dega, mic Cuirc mic Luigbeč. Sečt nercop cille Cibil, no bproma Cibil, Nouemb. 1.

Cill cuama (no coama). Ninnib eprcop cille cuama. 1 Míbe. Nouemb. 13. Fec cill Cuanna.

Cill Uraille. Uuaraille, eprcop, mac ua Daipb. Aug. 27. Aca cill Uraille a Laignib.

Cenel Eogain. Catarač mac Ailche, eprcop cenel Eogain, 946. Fec tír Eogain.

Ua Cobčaig, apb eprcop cenel Eogain, quieuit, 1173.

Giolla an čoimbeb Ua Cerballain, eprcop tíre Eóguin, 1279.

Floirint Ua Cerballain, eprcop tíre hEeogain, quieuit, 1293.

Cinb Galapac. Iolan, eprcop Cinb galapac, quieuit, 687.

Cinb garab. Daniel eprcop, anno 659 ; Feb. 18. Aca Cill Garab anb, et cetera.

blaan eprcop ó cinb garab, i nGallgaoibelaib; Dubblaan a priom cacaoir ; ir be gaircer "blaan bliabač bpecan." Aug. 10.

Cinriolaig. Ant eprcop Ua Caeccain, i. apb eprcop Ua Cenrelaig, quieuit, 1135.

Iorep Ua hAeba, eprcop Ua cCinriolaig, 1183.

Clochor, Pilip, Mar. 4.

Ailill eprcop, quieuit, 867.

---

1 Not identified.

2 Killskeery, co. Meath.

3 Four Masters ; and 867, Chron. Scot.

4 *Cill-sleibhe.* This is apparently a mistake, for *Cill-slebhte*, or Slatey, in the Queen's Co., as *Cill-sleibhe* is Killeavy, Co. Armagh.

5 Probably Kilteel, barony of Salt, Co. Kildare.

6 Mart. Doneg.

7 Kiltome, barony of Fore, Co. Westmeath.

8 Mart. Doneg.

9 Killossey, near Naas, Co. Kildare.

10 Mart. Doneg.

11 *Cenel-Eoghain,* i. e. the diocese of Derry.

12 Four Masters.

13 O'Coffey, Ua Cobhthaigh. His Christian name was Murrough (Muiredhach).

14 IV. M.; and Ann. Loch-Cé.

15 *Gilla-an-Choimdedh.* This is Latinized Germanus by Ware.

Cill-Sgandail, or Cill-Bian.[1]—Fergus, bishop of Cill-Sgandail, or Cill-Bian, and that is true.

Cill-Sgire.[2]—Robhartach of Finglas, bishop; Conall, bishop of Cill-Sgire, ob. 865.[3]

Cill-Slebhe.[4]—Fiach (bishop of Sleibhte) of Cill-Slebhe.

Cill-Tidil.[5]—Bishop Foirceadal of Cill-Tidil, son of Tal, son of Dega, son of Corc, son of Lughaidh. The seven bishops of Cill-Tidil (or Druim Tidil), Nov. 1.[6]

Cill-Tuama (or Toma).[7]—Ninnidh, bishop of Cill-Tuama in Meath, Nov. 13.[8] See Cill-Cuanna.

Cill-Usaille.[9]—Usaille (Auxilius), bishop, son of Ua Baird, Aug. 27.[10] Cill-Usaille is in Leinster.

Cenel-Eoghain.—Cathasach, son of Ailche, bishop of Cenel-Eoghain,[11] 946.[12]

O'Coffey,[13] archbishop of Cenel-Eoghain, quievit 1173.[14]

Gilla-an-Choimdedh O'Carolan,[15] bishop of Tir-Eoghain, 1279.[16]

Florence O'Carolan, bishop of Tir-Eoghain, quievit 1293.[17]

Cind-Galarat.[18]—Iolan, bishop of Cinn-Galarat, went to his rest 687.[19]

Cind-Garad.[20]—Daniel, bishop of, A°. 659,[21] 18 Feb.[22] There is a Cill-Garad, &c.

Blaan, bishop, from Cinn-Garad in Gall Gaeidhela. Dunblane is its chief city. He is named Blaan the virtuous of Britain, Aug. 10.[23]

Cinzsiolaigh.[24]—The bishop O'Caettain, i. e., the chief bishop of Hy-Cinnsiolaigh, quievit 1135.[25]

Joseph O'Hea, bishop of Hy-Cinnsiolaigh, 1183.[26]

Clochor. Philip,[27] March 4.

Ailill, bishop, quievit 867.[28]

[16] Four Masters, and Ann. Loch-Ce.
[17] IV. M., and Ann. Loch-Cé.
[18] *Cind-galarat.* This is a mistake for Cind-garad, or Cenn-garad. It is written Cinngarad in the Chron. Scot., but Cindgalarat by Tigernach.
[19] 688, IV. M.; 685, Chron. Scot.
[20] Kingarth, Bute, Scotland.
[21] IV. M.; 656-660, Chron. Scot.
[22] Mart. Doneg. and Mart. Taml.
[23] Mart. Doneg. and Mart. Taml.
[24] *Cinnsiolaigh. Rectè* Hy-Cïnnsiolaigh. Now the diocese of Ferns.
[25] Four Masters.
[26] IV. M.; Ann. Loch-Cé.
[27] Philip. In the Mart. Doneg. he is Philip of Cluain-Bainb; and in the Mart. Taml. the place is called Clochar-Bainni.
[28] IV. M.

Cluain aiccen. Epᵳcop Luġaċ a ccluain Aiccen a Laiġioᵳ, Occ. 6.

Cluain bainḃ. Ρilip epᵳcop Cluana bainḃ, no naoiṁ epᵳcop ó Chloċoᵳ, Maᵳc. 4.

Cluain caoin. Aᵳuin epᵳcop Cluana caoin, Auġ. 4.

Cluain Conaiᵳe comain. Maoinenn epᵳcop i ccluain Conaiᵳe comaim, i ccuaiᵳʒeᵳc Ua ᵱᵱaolain, Sepc. 16.

Cluain cua. uii. nepᵳcop Cluana cua, Occ. 3.

Cluain cᵳema. Oᵳᵳbᵳan epᵳcop Cluana cᵳema, quieuic 747. Laeʒaiᵳe epᵳcop Cluana cᵳema, Nou. 10.

Cluain cióneċ. Cellaċ mac Eᵳoᵳain, epᵳcop Cluana heióneċ, 940.

Muiᵳeḋaċ Ua Concaḃaiᵳ, epᵳcop, aʒuᵳ comaᵳba ᵱionncain Cluana heióniċ, 970.

Ciobᵳaiḋe, epᵳcoᵳ Cluana heióniċ, 909.

ᵱioncan coᵳaċ, epᵳcop cluana ᵱeᵳca bᵳenainḃ, aʒuᵳ a ccluain heiónec beoᵳ, ᵱeb. 21.

Munḃa, epᵳcop aʒuᵳ ab Cluana heióniċ i Laoiʒiᵳ; anno Ḋo mini an can ceᵳba, 634. Occ. 21.

Cluain eoiᵳ. Ciʒeᵳnaċ mac Caiᵳᵳᵳi, ᵳanccuᵳ epiᵳcopuᵳ Cluana eoiᵳ, quieuic 548; Aᵳᵳil 4.

Caencompac mac Caᵳᵳain, ᵳui epᵳcop, aʒuᵳ ab Cluana heoaiᵳ, 961.

ᵱlaiċbeᵳcaċ Ua Cecnen, comaᵳba Ciʒeaᵳnaiʒ, ᵳenoiᵳ aʒuᵳ ᵳui epᵳcop, ḋo ʒoin ó ᵱeᵳaiḃ bᵳéʒ, aʒuᵳ a ḋcc iaᵳᵳin ina ḋill ᵱén a oCluain Eoaiᵳ, 1012..

Cluain eaṁuin. Ailill (epᵳcop Aᵳoṁaċa ä̈nno Cᵳiᵳci 535) ; aliceᵳ epᵳcop Cluana emuin.

Cluain ᵱoca. Epᵳcop Eḋen (ó cluain ᵱoca) mac Maine ecciᵳ ḋo ᵳiol Concoḃaiᵳ abᵳac ᵳuaiḋ.

---

1 Clonkeen, Queen's Co.
2 Mart. Doneg. and Mart. Taml.
3 *Cluain-bainbh.* Not identified.
4 Mart. Doneg. and Mart. Taml.
5 Clonkeen, Co. Louth.
6 August 1. Mart. Doneg. and Mart. Taml.
7 Cloncurry, Co. Kildare.
8 Mart. Doneg. and Mart. Taml.
9 *Cluain-Cua ;* in the Queen's Co.
10 Mart. Doneg. and Mart. Taml.
11 Clooncraff, near Elphin, Co. Roscommon.
12 Four Masters.
13 Mart. Doneg.
14 Cloncnagh, Queen's Co.
15 IV. M.
16 IV. M.

CLUAIN-AITCHENN.[1]—Bishop Lugach, in Cluain-Aitchenn in Leix, Oct. 6.[2]

CLUAIN-BAINBH.[3]—Philip, bishop of Cluain-bainbh, or holy bishop of Clogher, March 4.[4]

CLUAIN-CAIN.[5]—Aruin, bishop of Cluain-Cain, Aug. 4.[6]

CLUAIN-CONAIRE-TOMAIN.[7] — Maoinen, bishop in Cluain-Conaire-Tomain, in the north of Hy-Faolain, September 16.[8]

CLUAIN-CUA.[9]—Seven bishops of Cluain-Cua, Oct. 3.[10]

CLUAIN-CREMHA.[11]—Ossbran, bishop of Cluain-cremha, rested 747.[12]

Laeghaire, bishop of Cluain-cremha, Nov. 10.[13]

CLUAIN-EIDHNECH.[14]—Cellach, son of Eporan, bishop of Cluain-eidhnech, 940.[15]

Muiredhach O'Conchobhair, _bishop, and comarb of Finntan of Cluain-eidhnech, 970.[16]

Tiobraide, bishop of Cluain-eidhnech, 909.

Finntan Corach, bishop of Clonfert-Brendan, and at Cluain-eidnech also, Feb. 21.[17]

Munda, bishop and abbot of Cluain-eidnech, in Laighis; in A. D. 634[18] he died, Oct. 21:[19]

CLUAIN-EOIS.[20]—Tighernach, son of Cairbre, holy bishop of Cluain-eois, quievit 548,[21] April 4.[22]

Caencomrac, son of Carran, eminent bishop and abbot of Cluain-eois, 961.[23]

Flaithbhertach O'Cetnen, comarb of Tighernach, a senior, and distinguished bishop, was wounded by the men of Bregia,[24] and he died afterwards in his own church at Cluain-eois, 1012.[25]

CLUAIN-EAMHUIN.[26]—Aillill, bishop of Armagh, A. D. 535[27]; otherwise bishop of Cluain-Eamhuin.

CLUAIN-FOTA.[28]—Bishop Etchen (from Cluain-fota), son of Maine the poet, of the race of Conchobar Abrat-ruadh.

[17] Mart. Doneg. and Mart. Taml.
[18] Four Masters. Chron. Scot.
[19] Mart. Doneg. and Mart. Taml.
[20] Clones, Co. Monaghan.
[21] IV. M. 545 Chron. Scot.; 550 Keating.
[22] Mart Doneg. and Mart. Taml.
[23] Chron. Scot., IV. M., and Ann. Ult.

[24] *Bregia.* The Annals generally attribute this violence to the men of Breifne.
[25] Chron. Scot.; Ann. Ult.; and Four Masters.
[26] Cloonowen, Co. Roscommon.
[27] IV. M. Chron. Scot.
[28] Clonfad, bar. of Farbill, Co. Westmeath.

Nota. Etchen eprcop cluana pota baovain aba, floruit circa annum 576.

Cluain poba pepa bile. Etcen eprcop (Cluana poba pepa bile i Mīde); arē tug grāda ragairc ar Colum cīlle, Feb. 11.

Cluain poba pine. Senač eprcop ó Cluain poba pine a peraib tulach .i. Cluain poba Libren; comarba Pinnen cluana hepairb, agur a bergebul, in Senač eprcop ro.

Cluain mōr. Eprcop Colman ó Cluain mōr.

Cluain porta. berchan eprcop agur pāib ó Cluain porta, in tb Pailge, Dec. 4.

Cluain uair. Iorep eprcop cluana uair, 839.

Comann. Corgrač mac Maoilmocairge, eprcop tige Močua agur na cComann, 951.

Conmaicne. Maelpeačluinn ó Pergal, eprcor Conmaicne, quieuit 1307.

Craob Grellain, eprcop Grellan, rept. 7.

Cruačan bri Éle. Mac Caille, eprcop, agur i ccruacain bri Éle in tb Pailge ata a čell, 489.

Cūil benbčair. Eprcop Lugač i ccuil benbčair, oct. 6.

Cūil bracain. Marcain eprcop i ccūil bracain in tb Pailge .i. i ctuait ba maige.

Cuil copra. Senač mac Ecin, agur Srapan, agur Senčell agur bruibiuctin, u. eprcop agur Aitecaeni agur eprcop mac Cairčin, agur Conlaog agur brigib i cCuil copra.

Cuil (cill, no) cluain poičirbe no počairbe no puičirbe. Nati eprcop, aug. 1; mač Senuig.

---

1 The same place as the preceding.

2 Mart. Doneg. and Mart. Taml.

3 Clonfad, bar. of Fartullagh, Co. Westmeath.

4 *Senach.* His festival is set down in the Calendar at August 21.

5 *Cluain-mor.* There are so many places of this name, that it would be useless, without further evidence, attempting to identify the one here referred to.

6 Clonsost, King's County.

7 Mart. Doneg.

8 *Cluain-uais;* the same as Cluain-Eois, q. v.

9 Four Mast.; Chron. Scot.; Ann. Ult.

10 *Comann;* otherwise na tri Comann, the Three Comanns; three septs anciently settled in the district comprising the southern part of the Queen's Co., and the northern part of Kilkenny.

11 IV. M.

12 *Conmaiene;* i. e. the bishoprick of Ardagh.

NOTE: Etchen, bishop of Cluain-fota-Baodan-aba, floruit circa annum 576.

CLUAIN-FODA-FERA-BILE.[1]—Etchen, bishop (of Cluain-foda-Fera-bile, in Meath). It was he that conferred the grade of priest on Colum Cille, Feb. 11.[2]

CLUAIN-FODA-FINE.[3]—Senach, bishop, from Cluain-foda-fine, in Fera-tulach, i. e., Cluain-foda-Librein. The comarb of Finnen of Clonard, and his disciple, was this bishop Senach.[4]

CLUAIN-MÓR.[5]—Bishop Colman of Clonmore.

CLUAIN-SOSTA.[6]—Berchan, bishop and prophet, from Cluain-sosta in Offaly, Dec. 4.[7]

CLUAIN-UAIS.[8]—Joseph, bishop of Cluain-uais, 839.[9]

COMANN.[10]—Cosgrach, son of Maolcairge, bishop of Tech-Mochua (Timohoe), and the Comanns, 951.[11]

CONMAICNE.[12] — Maelseachluin O'Ferrall, bishop of Conmaicne, quievit 1307.[13]

CRAOBH-GRELLAIN.[14]—Bishop Grellan, 7 September.[15]

CRUACHAN-BRI-ELE.[16]—Mac Caille, bishop, (and in Cruachan-Bri-Ele in Offaly his church is), 489.[17]

CUIL-BENDCHAIR.[18]—Bishop Lugach of Cuil-Bendchair, Oct. 6.

CUIL-BRACAIN.[19]—Martin, bishop of Cuil-Bracan in Offaly, i. e. in Tuath-da-mhaighe.[20]

CUIL-CORRA.[21]—Senach, son of Ecin, and Srafan, and Senchell, and Brodigan—five bishops[22]—and Aitecaem, and Bishop Mac Cairthin, and Conlaogh, and Brigid, in Cuil-Corra.

CUIL-(Cill, or Cluain)-FOITHIRBE (or Fothairbe, or Fuithirbe[23]).—Nathi, bishop, Aug. 1 ; the son of Senagh.

---

[13] Four Masters; Ann. Loch Ce.

[14] *Craobh-Grellan;* probably Creeve, bar. of Ballymoe, Co. Roscommon.

[15] *Sept.* St. Grellan's festival is set down in Mart. Doneg. at Nov. 10.

[16] Croghan, in the bar. of Lower Philipstown, King's Co.

[17] IV. M. ; 487, Chron. Scot.

[18] *Cuil-Bendchair.* Probably Coolbanagher, in the barony of Portnahinch, and Queen's County. The Mart. Doneg. adds, that probably Lugach was either of this place or of another Coolbanaghar

"on the brink of Loch Erne."

[19] Coolbracken, King's Co.

[20] *Tuath-da-mhaighe* (Anglicè Tuomoy); i. e. "the district of the two plains." This district included the present barony of Warrenstown and a large portion of the adjoining district, in the north of the King's County.

[21] Coolarn, near Galtrim, Co. Meath.

[22] *Five bishops.* Only four are enumerated.

[23] *See* Cuil-Sacaille.

Cuil Ratain. Caippre, eprcop, ó Cuil patain, Nou. 11.

Cuil racaille. Nati eprcop cuile Potaipbe, no cuile Sacaille, aug. 1.

Daiṁinir. Siollan, eprcop Daiṁinpi.

Daipinir. Pachtna, eprcop agur ab Daipinpi, aug. 14.

Daipe Calgaig. Caoncompac mac Maoluiṁip, eprcop agur ab daipe Calgaig, 927.

Maolpinnen, rui eprcop daipe Calgaig, 948.

Daipe Lupain. Lupech (.i. Luipech), duanaipe ó daipe Lupain in Ultaiḃ, eprcop, peb. 17.

Lupan, eprcop, ó daipe Lupain, oct. 24.

Daipe mop. Colman, eprcop, 20 maoi ; July 31, Colman eprcop.

Daimliag. Cianan eprcop Daimliag i mbpegaiḃ; ar do tuc Patraic a foirceta; floruit, 488.

Pepgur eprcop Daimliag, quieuit, 772.

Colmam eprcop Daimliag agur Lurca, quieuit 902 (Colman rgpiḃniḃ).

Caoncompac, eprcop Daimliag, 941.

Pionchap, eprcop Daiṁliag, 918.

Giolla Mochua, mac Camtuapta, eprcop Daiṁliag, quieuit 1117.

Tuatal mac Oenecain, eprcop Daiṁliag, quieuit 927.

Cetet eprcop (ó domnach Saipige ag daiṁliag Cianain), June 16.

Darṁag. Copmac Ua Liatain, ab Darṁaige, agur eprcop, anno Cpirti 868 ; June 21.

Dealgae. Occipir hEgnaigi eprcoip dealgae, 837.

Depgept Epenn. Giolla na naeṁ Ua Muipteptaig, uaral eprcop depgept Epenn, renoip oig cpaibdech egne, deec 1149.

---

1 Coleraine, Co. Londonderry.
2 Mart. Doneg.
3 *Cuil-Sacaille ;* not identified.
4 Mart. Doneg. and Mart. Taml.
5 Devenish Island, in Loch Erne.
6 *Dairinis ;* Molana, Co. Waterford.
7 Mart. Doneg. and Mart. Taml.
8 Londonderry.
9 Four Masters.
10 Mart. Doneg. and Mart. Taml.
11 Oct. 28. Mart. Doneg.
12 Derrimore, in Eliogarty, Co. Tipperary.
13 Mart. Doneg. and Mart. Taml.
14 Duleek, Co. Meath.
15 Ob. 486 ; Chron. Scot.
16 Four Masters ; Ann. Ult. 782.
17 902, IV. M. ; 906, Chron. Scot.

Cuil-Rathain.[1]—Cairbre, bishop of Cuil-Rathain, Nov. 11.[2]

Cuil-Sacaille.[3]—Nathi, bishop of Cuil-Fothairbe, or Cuil-Sacaille, August 1.[4]

Daimhinis.[5]—Siollan, bishop of Daimhinis.

Dairinis.[6]—Fachtna, bishop and abbot of Dairinis, Aug. 14.[7]

Daire-Calgaigh.[8]—Caencomhrac, son of Maoluidhir, bishop and abbot of Daire-Calgaigh, 927.

Maolfinnen, distinguished bishop of Daire-Calgaigh, 948.[9]

Daire-Lurain.[10]—Lurech (i. e. Luirech), poet, from Daire-Lurain in Ulster, bishop, Feb. 17.[11]

Luran, bishop of Daire-Lurain, Oct. 24.

Doire-mor.[12]—Colman, bishop, 20 May ;[13] July 11, Colman, bishop.

Daimhliag.[14]—Cianan, bishop of Daimhliag in Bregia. It was to him Patrick gave his Gospel: floruit 488.[15]

Fergus, bishop of Daimhliag, quievit 772.[16]

Colman, bishop of Daimhliag, quievit 902.[17]   (Colman the scribe).

Caencomhrac, bishop of Daimhliag, 941.[18]

Fionnchar, bishop of Daimhliag, 918.[19]

Gilla-Mochua, son of Camchuairt, bishop of Daimhliag, quievit 1117.[20]

Tuathal, son of Aenacan,[21] bishop of Daimhliag, quievit 927.[22]

Cethech, bishop, (from Domnach-Sairighe[23] at Daimhliag-Cianain), June 16.[24]

Darmhagh.[25]—Cormac Ua Liathan, abbot of Darmhagh, bishop, anno Christi 865,[26] June 21.[27]

Delgae.[28]—The slaying of Egnach, bishop of Delga, 837.[29]

Desgert-Erenn.[30]—Giolla-na-naemh O'Muircheartaigh, the noble bishop of the south of Erinn, a virgin, pious, wise elder, died 1149.[31]

[18] Four Masters.

[19] 918, IV. M. ; Chron. Scot.

[20] IV. M.

[21] Son of Aenacan. He is called O'Enecain in the Chron. Scot.

[22] IV. M., and Chron. Scot.

[23] Domhnach-Sairighe. Donaghseery, near Duleek, Co. Meath.

[24] Mart. Doneg. and Mart. Taml.

[25] Darmhagh. Durrow, King's Co.

[26] Four Masters. 867, Chron. Scot.

[27] June 21. Mart. Doneg., Taml., and Mar. Gor.

[28] Dealgae. Kildalkey, Co. Meath.

[29] IV. M.

[30] Desgert-Erenn. South of Erinn, i.e. the diocese of Cloyne.

[31] IV. M.

Oιγιοpτ Oιαpmaɖa. Oιαpmaιɖ aua Ᾱeɖa poin), eppcop o
ɖιpιopτ Oιαpmaɖa ιn Uιɓ Mυιpeaɓaιᵹ, June 21.

Cυmpaɖ mac Oepepo aᵹυp Maonach mac Soιceɓaιᵹ, ɖa eppcop
Oιpιopτ Oιαpmaɖa, ɖo ecc 842.

Mυιpᵹep eppcop ɖιpιopτ Oιαpmaɖa, qυιeuιτ 895.

Ua Ᵹaɓaιɖ, pυι eppcop Oιpιopτ Oιαpmaɖa, ɖo ecc 1038.

Oιpιopτ Fυlapτaιᵹ.—Fυlapτaċ mac ɓpιc, eppcop cluana
hιpaιpɖ ι Mιɖe, ιp ó Oιpιopτ Fυlapτaιᵹ ιn Iɓ Faιlᵹe, anno 778,
Marta 29.

Oιpιopτ Cola.—Cola, eppcop ó Oιpιopτ Cola ιn Uaċτap Oaιl
cCaιp, Map. 30.

Oomnaċ mιc Laιċɓe; .ι. Oomnac móp mιc Laιċɓe; eppcop
Eċepn. May 27.

Oomnaċ Feɓe.—Eppcop τamlachτa ιnɖomnaċ Feɓe.

Oomnaċ mop Maιᵹe epé.—Oιanach eppcop Oomnaċ móιp
Maιᵹe epe, Jan. 16.

Oomnaċ móp Aolmaιᵹe. Seċτ neppcop Oomnaιɖ moιp Aol-
mυιᵹe, Aug. 23.

Oomnaċ mop mυιᵹe Oamaιpne. Eapc eppcop Oomnaιɖ moιp
Maιᵹe Oamaιpne, no Maιᵹe Coɓa, Sepτ. 17.

Oomnaċ móp Seċnaιll.— Seaċnall .ι. Secunɖιnυp, eppcóp,
Nov. 27.

Oomnaċ mop mυιᵹe Luaɓaɖ.—Eapc eppcop, Oct. 27.

O. Caoιɓe.—Caoτι eppcop, Oct. 24.

O. Mυιᵹe Coɓa.—Eapc eppcop, Oct. 27.

O. Saιpιᵹe.—Ceτech eppcop, June 16.

Opυιm aιpɓeulaιᵹ.—Uιι. Neppcop Opoma aιpɓeulaιᵹ, Jan. 15.

---

[1] Castledermot, Co. Kildare.

[2] Mart. Doneg. and Mart. Taml.

[3] Four Masters ; Ann. Ult.

[4] IV. M.

[5] IV. M.

[6] *Disert-Fulartaigh.* Dysart, barony of Carbury, county of Kildare.

[7] 774; IV. M.

[8] Mart. Doneg. and Mart. Taml.

[9] *Disert-Tola.* Dysart O'Dea, county of Clare.

[10] Mart. Doneg. and Mart. Taml.

[11] *Domhnach-mic-Laithbhe.* In the Mart. Doneg. it is stated that this church was in Mughdborna, now the barony of Cremorne, county of Monaghan; but Dr. O'Donovan suggests (IV. M. 1150, note) that it may be the Donaghmore near Slane.

[12] Mart. Doneg. and Mart. Taml.

[13] *Domhnach-Febe.* Not identified. The entry seems defective.

[14] *Domhnach-mor of Magh Ere.* Not identified.

[15] Mart. Doneg. and Mart. Taml.

[16] *See* under Aolmagh.

DISERT-DIARMADA.[1]—Diarmuid (descendant of Aedh Ron), bishop of Disert-Diarmada in Hy-Muiredhaigh, June 21.[2]

Cumsadh, son of Derer, and Maonach, son of Soitedach, two bishops of Disert-Diarmada, died 842.[3]

Maurice, bishop of Disert-Diarmada, quievit 895.[4]

O'Gabhaidh, a distinguished bishop of Disert-Diarmada, died 1038.[5]

DISERT-FULARTAIGH.[6]—Fulartach, son of Brec, bishop of Clonard, in Meath, and from Disert-Fulartaigh in Offaly,778,[7] March 29.[8]

DISERT-TOLA.[9]—Tola, bishop, from Disert-Tola, in upper Dal-Cais, March 30.[10]

DOMHNACH-MIC-LAITHBHE,[11] i.e. Domnach-mor-mic-Laithbhe. Bishop Ethern, May 27.[12]

DOMHNACH-FEBE.[13]—The Bishop of Tamhlacht (*sic*), in Domhnach-Febe.

DOMHNACH-MÓR OF MAGH-ERE.[14]—Dianach, bishop of Domhnach-mor of Magh-Ere, January 16.[15]

DOMHNACH-MÓR-AOLMAIGHE.[16]—The seven bishops of Domhnach-mór-Aolmaighe, August 23.[17]

DOMHNACH-MOR OF MAGH-DAMAIRNE.[18]—Earc, bishop of Domhnach-mor of Magh-Damhairne, or of Magh-Cobha, September 17.[19]

DOMHNACH-MOR-SECHNAILL.[20]—Sechnall, i. e. Secundinus, bishop, Nov. 27.[21]

DOMHNACH-MÓR OF MAGH-LUADADH.[22]—Earc, bishop, Oct. 27.[2]

DOMHNACH-CAOIDE.[24]—Caoite, bishop, Oct. 24.[25]

DOMHNACH-MAIGHE-COBHA.[26]—Earc, bishop, Oct. 27.[27]

DOMHNACH-SAIRIGHE.[28]—Cethech, bishop, June 16.[29]

DRUIM-AIRBHELAIGH.[30]—The seven bishops of Druim-Airbbelaigh, Jan. 15.[31]

---

[17] Mart. Doneg. and Mart. Taml.

[18] *Domhnach-mor o Magh-Damairne.* Magh-Damairne is now Magheramorne, county of Antrim. *See* under Domhnach-Maighe-Cobha.

[19] Mart. Doneg. and Mart. Taml.

[20] *Donach-mor-Sechnall.* Dunshauglin, county of Meath.

[21] Mart. Doneg.

[22] Donaghmore, barony of Salt, county of Kildare.

[23] Mart. Doneg. and Mart. Taml.

[24] Donaghady, county of Tyrone.

[25] Mart. Doneg. and Mart. Taml.

[26] Donaghmore, barony of Upper Iveagh, county of Down.

[27] See under Domhnach-mor of Magh-Damhairne.

[28] Near Duleek, county of Meath.

[29] See under Daimhliag.

[30] Drumreilly, county of Leitrim.

[31] Mart. Doneg. and Mart. Taml.

 Open_Druim bertach.—Nem erpcop Droma bertaiʒ, Feb. 18.
Gonʒur erpcop Droma bertaiʒ, Feb. 18.

D. Cuilinn.—Dairrionn erpcop, May 21.

D. Crema.—Dura (no Duran) erpcop, Feb. 6.

D. da letir.—Cuimin foba mac Fiaċna, erpcop, Nou. 12.

D. Dallain.—Nem erpcop, May 3.

D. eanuiʒ.—Fionnċan, erpcop May 17.

D. Fer, no Feri.—Fionnċan erpcop rempaite, May 17.

Druim ʒobla.—Fiacc Slebte, erpcop.

Druim Feartain. — Cartaċ erpcop; ler Druim Feartain.
marc. 5.

Druim inerʒlain. Tiʒernaċ mac Muirebaiʒ, erpcop Droma
inerʒlain, quieuit 875.

Druim Laiʒille.—Sanctan erpcop, Maoi. 9.

Druim Letʒlairi.—Ferʒur erpcop Droma letʒlairi, quieuit
583, Mar. 30.

Druim liar.—benen in abbaine i nDruimliar, Nov. 9.

Druim Cibil.—Uii. neprcoip Droma Cibil, no cille Cibil,
Nov. 1.

Druim urċaille.—Uii. neprcoip Droma urcaille.

Nota.—143 nuimir na cceall dá relbaiʒter reċt neprcoip ba
ʒac cill (no ait) aca, ʒonab e a lion rin uile, eðon 1001 earpoʒ mur
ro in naoiṁ renċar naoiṁ erenn, toraiʒar ler in lan reċt neprcoib
rin : reċt nerbuicc Droma urċoille, fecc nerbuicc cille Derc-
bain, ┐ araile.

Dún mbaile.—Caillin erpcop Fiobnaċa, Nov. 13.

eaċbruim.—Geliomarċain, erpcop eaċbroma, quieuit 746.

---

[1] Burt, barony of Inishowen West, county of Donegal.

[2] Mart. Doneg. and Mart. Taml.

[3] Drumcullen, barony of Eglish, King's County.

[4] Mart. Doneg. and Mart. Taml.

[5] Not identified.

[6] Mart. Doneg. and Mart. Taml.

[7] Mart. Doneg. Not known.

[9] Mart. Doneg. and Mart. Taml.

[10] Not known.

[11] Mart. Doneg. and Mart. Taml.

[12] Not known.

[13] Mart. Doneg. and Mart. Taml.

[14] *Drum-Gobhla.* Near Slatey, in the present Queen's County.

[15] *Drum-Feartan.* In Carbury, county of Kildare.

Druim-bertach.[1]—Nemh, bishop of Druim-Bertach, Feb. 18.[2] Aengus, bishop of Druim-Bertach, Feb. 18.

Druim-cuilinn.[3]—Bairrionn, bishop, May 21.[4]

Druim-crema.[5]—Dura, or Duran, bishop, Feb. 6.[6]

Druim-da-lethir.[7]—Cumin Foda, son of Fiachna, bishop, Nov. 12.

Druim-Dallain.[8]—Nemh, bishop, May 3.[9]

Druim-Eanuigh.[10]—Fionnchan, bishop, May 17.[11]

Druim-Fes, or Fesi.[12]—Fionnchan, bishop aforesaid, May 17.[13]

Druim-Gobhla.[14]—Fiach of Sletty, bishop.

Druim-Feartan.[15]—Carthach, bishop (Drum-Feartan belongs to him); March 5.[16]

Druim-inesglain.[17]—Tighernach, son of Muireadach, bishop of Druim-inesglain, quievit 875.[18]

Druim-laighille.[19]—Sanctan, bishop, May 9.[20]

Druim-lethglaisi.[21]—Fergus, bishop of Druim-lethglaisi, quievit 583, Mar. 30.[22]

Druim-lias.[23]—Benen, in the abbacy of Druim-lias, Nov. 9.[24]

Druim-Tidil.[25] — Seven bishops of Druim-Tidil, or Cill-Tidil, Nov. 1.[26]

Druim-urchaille.[27]—The seven bishops of Druim-urchaille.

Note.—143 was the number of the churches that possessed VII. bishops to each church or place ; so that the full number of them all is, viz., 1001 bishops. Thus it is in the "History of the Saints of Erinn," which commences with this number of VII. bishops, viz., VII. bishops of Druim-urchaille ; VII. bishops of Cill-Dercain, &c.

Dun-mbaile.[28]—Caillin, bishop of Fiodnacha, Nov. 13.[29]

Each-Druim.[30]—Aelimarchair,[31] bishop of Each-druim, quievit 746.[32]

[16] Mart. Doneg. and Mart. Taml.

[17] Drumiskin, county of Louth.

[18] 876 ; Four Masters.

[19] *Druim-laighille.* Not known.

[20] Mart. Doneg. and Mart. Taml.

[21] *Druim-lethglaisi.* Another name for Dun-lethghlaise, or Downpatrick.

[22] IV. M.; Chron. Scot.

[23] *Drum-leese.* County of Leitrim.

[24] Mart. Doneg.

[25] *See* under Cill-Tidil.

[26] Mart. Doneg.

[27] Drumurgill, county of Kildare ?

[28] Fenagh, county of Leitrim.

[29] Mart. Doneg.

[30] Aughrim, county of Galway.

[31] *Aelimarchair.* This name is written Maelimarchair by the Four Masters, which is probably the correct form.

[32] IV. M.

Θαnaċ ὄuin.—Muipcepτač O Ɍlaiτbéepταiʒ, eppcop Θanuiʒ, quieuiτ 1242.

Τomáp O Ɯeallaiʒ, eppcop Θanuiʒ, quieuiτ 1250.

Τomáp O Ɯeallaiʒ, eppcop Θanuiʒ ὄo ecc i ccuaipτ an papa, 1328.

Θὄnen.—Ɯaelpoil mac Ɑililla, eppcop, ancoipe, aʒup pʒpib-niὄ Leτe Cuinn, aʒup ab in Θὄnen, 920.

Θle.—Ipaac Ua Cuanain, eppcop Θle Roipp cpe, oʒ aʒup apὄ penoip ὄomain, quieuiτ 1161.

Θpe beʒ .i. beʒ Θpe.—Θppcop Ibap.

Cponnmaol. epὄcop beʒ Θpe, eppcop aʒup pep leʒinn Τam-lacτa, 964.

Θpe.—Θočaiὄ Ua Cellaiʒ, apὄ cenn pep Ɯiὄe, pui eppcop na hΘpenn uile, ὄéʒ in Ɗepmaʒ Coluim Cille, 1140.

Ɍaὄap.—Suaiplech, eppcop Ɍaὄaip, quieuiτ 745, Mart. 27.

Ɑeὄʒin, eppcop ip ab Ɍaὄaip, quieuiτ 766, Ɯaoi 1.

Ɍepτa Cepbain.— Cepban eppcop ó pepτa Cepbain, quieuiτ cipca annum 500.

Ɍepτa pep peic.—Θppcop Θapc Slaine.

Ɍioὄ cuilinn.—beoan mac Neppain, eppcop, Ɑuʒ. 6.

Ɍioὄ ὄuin.—Colman eppcop ip ab Ɍeὄa ὄuin, 948.

Ɯomaeὄoʒ eppcop Ɍeὄa ὄuin, Ɯaoi 18.

Ɍioὄnacha.—Caillin eppcop, Nov. 13.

Ɍionnabaip aὄa.—Ɍepʒil eppcop Ɍinnabaip aba, aʒup ab inὄ Θiὄnen, 902.

Ɍionnʒlaip.—Ɍlann eppcop Ɍionnʒlaipe, Jan. 21.

Ɍopʒnaiὄa.—Θppcop Ɯuinip, Ɗecemb. 18.

Ʒael.—Ʒaibpinn eppcop, June 24.

---

[1] Annaghdown, county of Galway.

[2] 1241; Ann. Loch-Cé, and Four Masters.

[3] Ann. Loch-Cé, and Four Masters.

[4] IV. M. and Ann. Loch-Cé.

[5] Not identified.

[6] IV. M.; 921 Chron. Scot.

[7] Eliogarty, county of Tipperary.

[8] IV. M.

[9] *Ere-beg*, i. e. Beg-Ere. *See* Beg-Ere.

[10] IV. M.

[11] *Ere.* Ireland.

[12] Four Masters.

[13] *Fore*, county of Westmeath.

[14] IV. M.; 749 Ann. Ult.

[15] Mart. Doneg. and Mart. Taml.

[16] IV. M.

[17] Mart. Doneg. and Mart. Taml.

[18] *Ferta-Cerbain.* Near Tara hill, in the county of Meath.

[19] 499, IV. M.; but 503–4 in the other annals.

EANACH-DUIN.[1]—Muirchertach O'Flaherty, bishop of Eanach-duin, quievit 1242.[2]

Thomas O'Mellaigh, bishop of Eanach-duin, quievit 1250.[3]

Thomas O'Mellaigh, bishop of Eanach-duin, died at the Papal court, 1328.[4]

EDHNEN.[5]—Maelpoil, son of Ailill, bishop, anchorite, and scribe of Leth-Chuinn, and abbot of the Edhnen, 920.[6]

ELE.[7]—Isaac O'Cuanain, bishop of Ele of Roscrea, virgin and chief elder of the world, quievit 1161.[8]

ERE-BEG, i. e. BEG-ERE.[9]—Bishop Ibar.

Cronmael, bishop of Beg-Ere, bishop and lector of Tallaght, 964.[10]

ERE.[11]—Eochaidh O'Cellaigh, chief head of the men of Meath, the eminent bishop of all Erinn, died in Dermagh of Colum-Cille, 1140.[12]

FABHAR.[13]—Suairlech, bishop of Fabhar, rested 745,[14] March 27.[15]

Aedgin, bishop and abbot of Fabhar, quievit 766,[16] May 1.[17]

FERTA-CERBAIN.[18] — Cerban, bishop, from Ferta-Cerbain, quievit circa annum 500.[19]

FERTA-FER-FEIC.[20]—Bishop Earc, of Slane.

FIODH-CUILINN.[21]—Beoan, son of Nessan, bishop, August 6.[22]

FIODH-DUIN.[23]—Colman, bishop and abbot of Fidh-duin, 948.[24]

Momhaedog, bishop of Fidh-duin, May 18.[25]

FIODHNACHA.[26]—Caillin, bishop, Nov. 13.

FIONNABAIR-ABHA.[27]—Fergil, bishop of Finnabhair-abha, and abbot of the Edhnen, 902.[28]

FINNGLAIS.[29]—Flann, bishop of Finnglais, January 21.[30]

FORGNAIDHE.[31]—Bishop Muinis, December 18.[32]

GAEL.[33] Gaibhrinn, bishop, June 24.[34]

---

[20] *Ferta-fer-Feic.* See under Baile-Slaine.

[21] Feighcullen, county of Kildare.

[22] August 8, Mart. Doneg. and Mart. Taml.

[23] *Fiodh-duin.* Fiddown, county of Kilkenny.

[24] Mart. Doneg. and Mart. Taml.

[25] Four Masters.

[26] *Fiodhnacha.* Fenagh, county of Leitrim. *See* under Dun-mbaile.

[27] Fennor, barony of Duleek, county of Meath.

[18] Four Masters; 906, Chron. Scot.

[29] Finglass, near Dublin.

[30] Mart. Doneg. and Mart. Taml.

[31] Forgney, county of Longford.

[32] Mart. Doneg.

[33] Gael. This place has not been identified.

[34] Mart. Doneg. and Mart. Taml.

Ᵹlairτimbeρ.—Pαὑραıᵹ eρρcop, Aug. 24.

Ᵹlenn ὑα lacha.—Caoimᵹin Ᵹlinne ὑα lacha.

Ɒαιρchill mac hɑıρıτα, eρρcop Ᵹlinne ὑα lacha, quieuiτ 676, May 3.

Eὑıρρᵹel mac Ceallaιᵹ, eρρcóp Ᵹlinne ὑα lacha, quieuıτ 809.

ɑmρuὑαn, no ɑmραὑαn, eρρcop ᵹlinne ὑα lacha, May 11.

ɑoὑ Ó Moὑαin, eρρcop Ᵹlinne ὑα lacha, quieuıτ 1126.

Coρmac Ua Maıl, eρρcop Ᵹlinne ὑα lacha, quieuıτ 1101.

Ᵹıolla na naeṁ Laıᵹen, uαραl eρρcop Ᵹlinne ὑα lacha, aᵹuρ cenn manach ıαρ ρın ın Uαıρıρbuρᵹ, ὑo 6c an ρeaττṁαὑ ıὑ ɑρρıl, 1085.

Maolbρıᵹıὑe Ua Maoilρınn, ραᵹαρτ, ancoıρe, aᵹuρ eρρcop Ᵹlinne ὑα lacha, quieuıτ 1041.

Nuαὑα eρρcop Ᵹlinne ὑα lacha, 928.

Cıonαoch Ua Ronαın, eρρcop Ᵹlinne ὑα lacha aᵹuρ τuαıρᵹeρτ Laıᵹen, quieuıτ 1173.

Molıoὑα mac Cholmαὑα ó Ᵹlenn ὑα lacha, eρρcop, Jan. 8.

Sıollan eρρcop Ᵹlinne ὑα lacha, Feb. 10.

Ruıρın eρρcop Ᵹlinne ὑα lacha aᵹuρ bennchαıρ, Apl. 22.

Ᵹlenn uıρen.—Ɒıαρmαıὑ eρρcop ᵹlinne hUıρρen, July 8.

Ᵹoὑuıl.—Ᵹuαıρe eρρcop ın Ᵹoὑuıl; ɑoὑ eρρcop ó Lıoρ Ᵹoὑuıl αρ loτ Eρne, 25 January.

Ᵹραnαρὑ.—Ᵹuαραττ eρρcop, January 24.

ıae.—Coeὑı eρρcop ıae, quieuıτ 710.

Fınᵹın, ancoıρe ıρ eρρcop ıae, 964.

Muᵹρon ab ıae, ρᵹρıbnıὑ aᵹuρ eρρcop aᵹuρ ρáı na ττρı ραnn, 978.

Feρᵹna bρıτ, eρρcop aᵹuρ ab ıae Coluım cılle, Mαρτα 2.

Imleτ bρoὑαὑα.—Eρρcop bρocαıὑ, luıl 9.

Inbeρ Ɒαoıle.—Ɒαᵹὑαn eρρcop, Mαρτα 12.

---

1 Glastonbury, England.

2 *Glenn-da-locha;* county of Wicklow.

3 Four Masters; 674, Chron. Scot.

4 Mart. Doneg. and Mart. Taml.

5 IV. M.; 814, Chron. Scot.

6 January 11, Mart. Doneg.

7 IV. M.

8 IV. M.

9 IV. M.

10 Four Masters.

11 IV. M.; 929, Chron. Scot.

12 IV. M.

13 Mart. Doneg. and Mart. Taml.

14 Mart. Doneg. and Mart. Taml.

15 Mart. Doneg.

16 Killeshin, barony of Slievemargy, Queen's County.

17 Mart. Doneg. and Mart. Taml.

GLAISTIMBER.[1]—Patrick, bishop, August 24.

GLENN-DA-LACHA.[2]—Caoimhghin of Glenn-da-locha.

Dairchill, son of Haireta, bishop of Glenn-da-locha, quievit 676,[3] May 3.[4]

Edirsgel, son of Cellach, bishop of Glenn-da-locha, quievit 809.[5]

Ampudan (or Anpadan), bishop of Glenn-da-locha, May 11.[6]

Aedh O'Modhain, bishop of Glenn-da-locha, quievit 1126.[7]

Cormac O'Mail, bishop of Glenn-da-locha, quievit 1101.[8]

Giolla-na-naomh of Leinster, noble bishop of Glenn-da-locha, and chief monk afterwards in Uarisburgh (Wurtzburg), died on the seventh of the ides of April, 1085.[9]

Maelbrighde O'Maelfinn, priest, anchorite, and bishop of Glenn-da-locha, quievit 1041.[10]

Nuada, bishop of Glenn-da-locha, 928.[11]

Cinaeth O'Ronain, bishop of Glenn-da-locha, and of the north of Leinster, quievit 1173.[12]

Molioba, son of Colmadh, from Glenn-da-locha, January 8.[13]

Siollan, bishop of Glenn-da-locha, Feb. 10.[14]

Ruifin, bishop of Glenn-da-locha, and of Bangor, April 22.[15]

GLENN-UISSEN.[16]—Diarmuid, bishop of Glenn-Uissen, July 8.[17]

GOBHUIL.[18]—Guaire, bishop of the Gobhuil.[19]

Hugh, bishop of Lis-gabhuil on Loch-Erne, 25 January.[20]

GRANARD.[21]—Guasacht, bishop, January 24.[22]

IAE.[23]—Coedi, bishop of Ia, quievit 710.[24]

Finghin, anchorite and bishop of Ia, 964.[25]

Mughron, abbot of Ia, scribe and bishop, and sage in the 3 divisions [of knowledge], 978.[26]

Fergna Brit, bishop and abbot of Ia-Coluim-Cille, March 2.[27]

IMLECH-BROCHADA.[28]—Bishop Brochad, July 9.[29]

INVER DAOILE.[30]—Dagdan, bishop, March 12.

---

[18] *Gobhuil. See* Lis-Gobhuil.

[19] 25 January; Mart. Taml.

[20] Mart. Doneg. and Mart. Taml.

[21] *Granard.* County of Longford.

[22] Mart. Doneg. and Mart. Taml.

[23] *Iae.* Iona, or Hy-Coluim-Cille.

[24] Four Masters; 711, Ann. Ult.

[25] IV. M.; Chron. Scot.

[26] Four Masters and Chron. Scot.

[27] Mart. Doneg. and Mart. Taml.

[28] Emlech. Barony of Costello, county of Mayo.

[29] Mart. Doneg. and Mart. Taml.

[30] Enerreilly. Barony of Arklow, county of Wicklow.

Iniṗ Alban.—Foċaḃ mac Ḃrain, ṗᵹrıḃnıḃ ⁊ eppcop ınṗı Alban, 961.

Iniṗ beᵹ Ere.—Feċ beᵹ Ere.

Iniṗ bo ṗınḃe.—Nauıᵹacıo Colmanı epıṗcop cum ṗelıquıṗ ṗcocoṗum aḃ Inṗolam uaccae albae, ın qua ṗunḃabac ecclerıam, 667.

Columban epıṗcopuṗ Inṗulae uaccae albae, pauṗac 674; ı cConmacnaıḃ maṗa, Auᵹ. 8.

Ḃaeḃan eppcop Inṗı bó ṗınḃı, quıeuıc 711.

Iniṗ bṗecan.—Feċ bṗıcanıa, ıṗ Cıll muıne.

Iniṗ Caoınḃeᵹa.—Ḃaıᵹ mac Caıṗıll, ceṗḃa 586, Auᵹ. 8.

Coṗᵹṗaċ mac Ḃunacaın, ṗuı eppcop ıṗ aıṗċınḃeċ Inṗı Caoın ḃeᵹa, 961.

Iniṗ Caṗċaıᵹ.—Caṗċach eppcop, mac Aonᵹuṗa, Maṗca 5.

Iniṗ Caċaıᵹ.—Senan eppcop Inṗı Caċaıᵹ, Mart. 1.

Aoḃan eppcop ó Inıṗ Caċaıᵹ, Auᵹ. 31.

Aeḃ Ua ḃechaın, eppcop Inṗı Caċaıᵹ, 1188.

Iniṗ Cealcṗa.—Ḃıaṗmaıḃ mac Caıchuıl eppcop ınṗı Cealcṗa, 951.

Iniṗ Cloċṗann.—Ḃıaṗmaıḃ eppcop ó Inıṗ Cloċṗann aṗ loċ Rıḃ, ḃo ṗíol Ḃachı ṗı Eṗenn, aᵹuṗ Ḃeḃı ınᵹen Cṗena mıc Ḃubċaıᵹ Ua Luᵹaıṗ, aṗḃ ṗıleḃ Eṗenn, maċaıṗ Ḃıaṗmaḃa, Enaıṗ 10.

Iniṗ eunḃaıṁ.—Caoncompac eppcop, Iuıl 23.

Iniṗ Faıċlenn no Faıᵹlenn.—Faıᵹlenn ó Inıṗ Faıċlenn (no Faıᵹlenn), mac Aeḃa ḃaṁaın, no mac Aeḃa ḃennaın, ḃo ṗlıoċc Cuıṗc mıc Luıᵹḃech.

Iniṗ maıc Eaṗca.—Fṗaeċan eppcop, Nov. 20.

Iniṗ muıᵹe ṗam.—Nınnıḃ eppcop, Enaıṗ 18.

Iniṗ maıc Ualaınᵹ.—Moṗıóce, eppcop Inṗı Ualaınᵹ, Auᵹ. 1.

---

1 *Inis-Alban.* Scotland.

2 Four Masters.

3 Bophin Island, off the coast of Mayo.

4 IV. M. ; 664, Chron. Scot.

5 IV. M.; Chron. Scot.

6 Mart. Doneg. and Mart. Taml.

7 IV. M.

8 Inishkeen, county of Louth.

9 Four Masters and Chron. Scot.

10 Mart. Doneg. and Mart. Taml.

11 IV. M.

12 *Inis-Carthaigh.* *See* Inis-Uachtar.

13 Mart. Doneg. and Mart. Taml.

14 Scattery Island, in the River Shannon.

15 Mart. Doneg. and Mart. Taml.

16 Mart. Doneg. and Mart. Taml.

INIS-ALBAN.[1]—Fothadh, son of Bran, scribe, and bishop of Inis-Alban, 961.[2]

INIS-BEG-ERE.—*See* Beg-Ere.

INIS-BO-FINDE.[3]—The navigation of Bishop Colman, with the remainder of the Scoti to Inis-bo-finde "the Isle of the White Cow," wherein he founded a church, 667.[4]

Columbanus, bishop of Insula-vaccæ-albæ, quievit 674;[5] in Con-maicne-mara, August 8.[6]

Baedan, bishop of Inis-bo-finne, quievit 711.[7]

INIS-BRETAN. *See* Britannia, and Cill-Muine.

INIS-CAINDEGHA.[8]—Daig, son of Cairell, died 586,[9] August 8.[10]

Cosgrach, son of Dunacan, eminent bishop, and herenach of Inis-Caindegha, 961.[11]

INIS-CARTHAIGH.[12]—Carthach, son of Aongus, bishop, March 5.[13]

INIS-CATHAIGH.[14]—Senan, bishop, from Inis-Cathaigh, March 1.[15]

Aedhan, bishop, from Inis-Cathaigh, August 31.[16]

Aedh O'Bechain bishop of Inis-Cathaigh, 1188.[17]

INIS-CEALTRA.[18]—Diarmaid, son of Caichel, bishop of Inis-Cealtra, 951.[19]

INIS-CLOTHRANN.[20]—Diarmaid, bishop, from Inis-Clothrann in Loch-Ribh, of the race of Dathy, king of Erin; and Dedi, daughter of Trian, son of Dubhthach Ua Lughair, chief bard of Erinn, was Diarmaid's mother; January 10.[21]

INIS-EUNDAIMH.[22]—Caoncomrac, bishop, July 23.[23]

INIS-FAITHLENN (OR FAIGHLENN).[24]—Faighlen [or Faighlenn], from Inis-Faighlen, son of Aedh Damhan, or son of Aedh Bennan, of the race of Corc Mac Luigdech.

INIS-MAIC-EARCA.[25]—Fraechan, bishop, Nov. 20.

INIS-MUIGHE-SAMH.[26]—Ninnid, bishop, January 18.[27]

INIS-MAIC-UALAING.[28]—Morioce, bishop of Inis-maic-Ualaing, Aug. 1.[29]

---

[17] Four Masters.

[18] Iniscatha, in Lough Dergdeirc.

[19] IV. M.

[20] Iniscloghren, or Quaker's Island, in Lough-Ree.

[21] Mart. Doneg. and Mart. Taml.

[22] Inishenagh, in Lough-Ree.

[23] Mart. Doneg. and Mart. Taml.

[24] Inisfallen, Killarney.

[25] *Inis-maic-Earca.* *See* under Bo-chluain.

[26] *Inis-mac-Saint*, in Lough - Erne, county of Fermanagh.

[27] Mart. Doneg. and Mart. Taml.

[28] *Inis-Bofin* in Loch-Ree.

[29] Mart. Doneg. and Mart. Taml.

Iniſ meḋċoiꞇ.—Aoḃan eprcop, Auᵹ. 31.

Iniſ.moiſ.—baoḃan eprcop, Enaiſ 14.

Iniſ uaċꞇaiſ.—Carꞇaċ eprcop, Marꞇ. 5.

Ionnlaċa Ċineoil Luᵹaiſ.—Conlaeḃ aᵹuſ uii neprcoiſ, aᵹuſ un ſaᵹaiſꞇ, aᵹuſ uii ninᵹena oᵹa, in Ionnlaċa ċineoil Luᵹaiſ.

Laiᵹen.—Fiacc ſleḃꞇa, ḃircioḃal Paḋraic, airḃeprcop Laiᵹen 6, aᵹuſ a comaſba ḃa éſ, Ocꞇoḃ. 12.

Cele mac Ḋonnacain, eprcop Laiᵹen, aᵹuſ arḃ ſenóiſ na nᵹaoiḃel, quieuiꞇ i nᵹlenn ḃa laċa, 1076.

Cormac Ua Caċaſaiᵹ, arḃeprcop Laiᵹen, quieuiꞇ 1146.

Flaiċeṁ Ua Ḋuiḃiḋiſ, eprcop aiſ ċeſ Laiᵹen, quieuiꞇ 1104.

Ᵹrene, arḃeprcop Ᵹall aᵹuſ Laiᵹen, quieuiꞇ 1162. (Lorcan O Cuaċail, comaſba Chaoimᵹin, ḃo oiſḃneḃ ina inaḃ la comaſba Paḋraiᵹ.)

Ᵹiolla na naoim Ua Muirceſꞇaiᵹ, uaſal eprcop ḃerᵹeſꞇ Erenn (ſaoilim ᵹoſ ḃon Mumain benuſ ſe), quieuiꞇ 1149.

Lorcan O Cuaċaill (.i. Laḃſaſ), arḃepſcop Laiᵹen aᵹuſ leᵹaiḃ na hErenn, quieuiꞇ i Saxanaiḃ 1180.

Lann Ᵹreallain.—Ᵹreallan eprcop ó Lainn, Sepꞇ. 17.

Lann Leſe.—Ᵹormᵹal mac Muiſeaḃaiᵹ, eprcop Lainn léſe, quieuiꞇ 843.

Maolciaſain mac Foiſꞇceſn, eprcop Lainne, quieuiꞇ 900.

Laċſaḃ ḃſuin.—Cormac, eprcop Laċſaiᵹ ḃſiuin, quieuiꞇ 854.

Leacain Míḋe.—Cſuimm eprcop, Ium 28.

Leaṁ ċoill.—Fionnꞇan coſaċ, Feb. 21.

Cuillenn, eprcop Leaṁcoille, April 22.

Moċonna eprcop ó Leamċoill, Enaiſ 13.

---

[1] *Inis-Medcoit.* Either Farne, or Lindisfarne, in England.

[2] *See* under Inis-Cathaigh.

[3] *Baedan.* In the Mart. of Donegal it is added that this Baedan died A. D. 712.

[4] Mart. Doneg. and Mart. Taml.

[5] *Inis - uachtar.* In Loch-Sheelin, county of Cavan.

[6] Mart. Doneg. and Mart. Taml.

[7] Not identified.

[8] *Laighen.* Leinster.

[9] Mart. Doneg. and Mart. Taml.

[10] Four Masters.

[11] IV. M.

[12] IV. M.

[13] *Grene.* He is called Gregorius by Ware, and others. *See* Harris's edition of Ware's Works, vol. i., p. 311.

[14] IV. M.

[15] *Munster.* He was bishop of Cloyne.

INIS-MEDCOIT.[1]—Aedan, bishop, August 31.[2]

INIS-MOR.—Baedan,[3] bishop, January 14.[4]

INIS-UACHTAR.[5]—Carthach, bishop, March 5.[6]

IONNLATHA-CINEOIL-LUGHAIR.[7]—Conlaed, and vii. bishops, and vii. priests, and vii. young virgins, in Innlatha-Cineoil-Lughair.

LAIGHEN.[8]—Fiac of Sletty, disciple of Patrick; he was archbishop of Leinster, and his comarb after him. October 12.[9]

Cele, son of Donnacan, bishop of Laighen, and arch-elder of the Gaidhel, quievit in Glenn-da-locha, 1076.[10]

Cormac O'Cathasaigh, archbishop of Laighen, quievit 1146.[11]

Flaithemh O'Duibhidhir, bishop of East Laighen, quievit 1104.[12]

Grene,[13] archbishop of the Gaill, and of Laighen, quievit 1162.[14]

(Lorcan O'Tuathail, comarb of Caemhghin, was ordained in his place by the comarb of Patrick.)

Gilla-na-naomh O'Muirchertaigh, noble bishop of the South of Erinn. (I think he belongs to Munster),[15] quievit 1149.

Lorcan[16] O'Tuathail (i. e. Lawrence) archbishop of Laighen, and Legate of Erinn, quievit in England,[17] 1180.

LANN GRELLAIN.[18]—Greallan, bishop, from Lann, September 17.[19]

LANN-LERE.[20]—Gormgal, son of Muireadach, bishop of Lann-Lere, quievit 843.[21]

Maol-Chiaran, son of Fortchern, bishop of Lann, quievit 900.[22]

LATHRACH-BRIUIN.[23]—Cormac, bishop of Lathrach-Briuin, quievit 854.[24]

LEACAN OF MEATH.[25]—Cruimin, bishop, June 28.[26]

LEAMH-CHOILL.[27]—Finntan Corach, February 21.[28]

Cuillenn, bishop of Leamh-choill, April 22.[29]

Mochonna, bishop of Leamh-choill, January 13.[30]

See Harris's "Ware," vol. i., p. 574.

[16] See note.

[17] England. Saxanaib. In the Annals of Boyle, Inisfallen, and Clonmacnoise, he is said to have died in France.

[18] Not identified.

[19] 18; Mart. Doneg. and Mart. Taml.

[20] Dunleer, county of Louth.

[21] Four Masters.

[22] IV. M.

[23] Laragh - Bryan, barony of North Salt, county of Kildare.

[24] Four Masters.

[25] Leckin, barony of Corkaree, county of Westmeath.

[26] Mart. Doneg. and Mart. Taml.

[27] Lowhill, Queen's County.

[28] Mart. Doneg. and Mart. Taml.

[29] Mart. Doneg. and Mart. Taml.

[30] Mart. Doneg. and Mart. Taml.

Leaṫ ċuinn.—Maolpoíl mac Aillella, eppcop, ancoipe, ṡṡpíḃníó Leiṫe Cuinn, aṡup ab inó Eḃnen, 920.

Liaṫ ḃpuim.—Mac Liaṡ, eppcop Liaṫ ḃpoma, Feb. 8.

Liaṫ móp (no Leṫmóip).—Naṡaip, eppcop, Iuil. 12.

Linn ḃuaċaill.—Comap eppcop aṡup ṡṡpíḃ, ab Linne ḃuaċaill, quieuic 803.

Liolcaċ.—Eapc Slaine, eppcop Liolcaiṡ, Nov. 2 ; quieuic 512.

Liop ṡoḃuil.—Aeḃ eppcop ó Liop ṡoḃuil ap Loċ Epne, Enaip 5.

Liop móp.—Moċuba eppcop, quieuic 636, Maoi 14.

Ronan eppcop Liop móip Moċuba, Feb. 9.

Capṫaċ eppcop, Mapṫa 3.

Loṫpa.—Ruaḃan eppcop Loṫpa.

Colum mac Faolṡupa, eppcop Loṫpa, quieuic 783.

Oinepṫaċ eppcop Loṫpa, quieuic 864.

Loċ Con.—Laoṡaipe, eppcop ó Loċ Con, Sepc. 30.

Luṡṁaḃ.—Moċca eppcop ó Luṡṁaḃ, 300 bliaḃan a paeṡal, Mapṫa 20.

Eochaiḃ mac Cuaṫail, eppcop Luṡṁaḃ, 820.

Maolcuile, eppcop Luṡṁaḃ, 871.

Caoncompaċ eppcop Luṡṁaḃ, 898.

Fionnaċca mac Ecciṡepn eppcop, ṡṡpíḃníó ip ab Luṡṁaḃ, 948.

Maolpacpaic mac ḃpoin, eppcop Luṡṁaḃ, 936.

Luiṡne, no cuaṫ Luiṡne.—Maolpinnia .i. Ua hAonuiṡ, fepleṡinó Faḃaip, aṡup eppcop cuaiṫ Luiṡne, 992.

Lupca.—Mac Cuilinn eppcop Lupca. Luacan mac Cuilinn

1 *Leath-Chuinn.* Ulster.
2 *Edhnen.* He died at Eu, in Normandy. *See* under Edhnen.
3 Leitrim.
4 Mart. Doneg. and Mart. Taml.
5 Leamakevoge, barony of Eliogarty, county of Tipperary.
6 Mart. Doneg. and Mart. Taml.
7 *Linn-duachaill.* Near Dundalk, county of Louth.
8 Four Masters.
9 Bective (?) county Meath.
10 *Earc of Slane.* *See* under Baile-Slaine.
11 Lisgoole, county Fermanagh.
12 25, Mart. Doneg.
13 Lismore, county Waterford.
14 Four Masters, and Chron. Scot. 637, Ann. Ult. Tig. and Clonmacnoise.
15 Mart. Doneg., and Mart. Taml.
16 *Carthach.* This is a mistake. The Carthach commemorated on March 5,

Leath-Chuinn.[1]—Maelpoil, son of Ailill, bishop, anchorite, and scribe of Leth-Chuinn, and abbot of the Edhnen,[2] 920.

Liath-Druim.[3]—Mac Liag, bishop of Liath-druim, Feb. 8.[4]

Liath-mor, or Leth-mor.[5]—Nazair, bishop, July 12.[6]

Linn-duachaill.[7]—Thomas, bishop, scribe, and abbot of Linn-Duachaill, quievit 803.[8]

Liolcach.[9]—Earc of Slane,[10] bishop of Liolcagh, quievit 512. November 2.

Lis-Gobhuil.[11]—Aedh, bishop, from Lis-Gobhuil on Loch-Erne, January 5.[12]

Lis-mor.[13]—Mochuda, bishop, quievit 636,[14] May 14.

Ronan, bishop of Lis-mór-Mochuda, Feb. 9.[15]

Carthach,[16] bishop, March 3.

Lothra.[17]—Ruadhan, bishop of Lorrha.

Colum, son of Faolgus, bishop of Lorrha, quievit 783.[18]

Dinertach, bishop of Lorrha, quievit 864.[19]

Loch-Conn.[20]—Laeghaire, bishop, from Loch-Conn, September 30.[21]

Lughmhagh.[22]—Mochta, bishop from Lughmhagh, 300 years was his age; March 20.[23]

Eochaidh, son of Tuathal, bishop of Lughmhagh, 820.[24]

Maoltuile, bishop of Lughmhagh, 871.[25]

Caencomrach, bishop of Lughmhagh, 898.[26]

Finnachta, son of Echtigern, bishop, scribe, and abbot of Lughmhagh, 948.[27]

Maolpatrick, son of Bran, bishop of Lughmhadh, 936.[28]

Luighne.[29] Maelfinnia (i. e. O'hAenaigh), lector of Fabhar, and bishop of Tuath-Luighne, 992.[30]

Lusca.[31]—Mac Cuilinn, bishop of Lusca. Luachan mac Cuilinn,

is the same whose name appears under Druim-fertain and Inis-Uachtar above.

[17] Lorrha, barony of Lower Ormond, county Tipperary.

[18] Four Masters.

[19] IV. M.

[20] i. e., Errew, near Loch-Conn, county Mayo.

[21] Mart. Doneg.

[22] Louth, county of Louth.

[23] March 20. Partly effaced. August 19, Mart. Doneg. and Mart. Taml.

[24] Four Masters; 822, Chron. Scot.

[25] IV. M.

[26] IV. M.; 903, Chron. Scot.

[27] IV. M.

[28] IV. M.; 737, Chron. Scot.

[29] Luighne, or Tuath-Luighne; the barony of Lune, county Meath.

[30] IV. M.

[31] Lusca. Lusk, county Louth.

a aınm bıleŗ, aᵹuŗ Caınnıᵹ, Cuınbıᵹ no Cuınbeb a ceb aınm, quıeuıc 497.

Aŗéó abeŗ Mac Fıŗbıŗıᵹ quıeŗ Cuınbeba maıc Caᶀbaóa .ı. Mac Cuılınn, epŗcop Luŗca, ec cecepa, Sepc. 6.

Ᵹuın Colmaın, epŗcop Luŗc, la .h. Cuıŗcŗe, 739.

Foŗbaŗaᶀ epŗcop Luŗca, 835.

Seᶀnaŗaᶀ epŗcop Luŗcan quıeuıc 887.

Maolŗuanaıb epŗcop Luŗca, quıeuıc, 880.

Colman ŗᵹŗıbnıb, epŗcop Baımlıaᵹ aᵹuŗ Luŗcaın, quıeuıc 902.

Aılıll mac Maonaıᵹ, epŗcop Suıŗb aᵹuŗ Luŗcaın, 965.

Ruaban epŗcop Luŗcan, 904.

Cuaᶀal mac Oenacaın, epŗcop Baımlıaᵹ aᵹuŗ Luŗcca, maoŗ muıncıŗe Paóŗaıᵹ, 927.

Maᵹ aı, no eó.—Fec Maᵹeo.

Maᵹ bıle.—Fınnıan Muıᵹe bıle, epŗcop, nó Fınıa epŗcop Maıᵹe bıle, Feb. 11.

Fınnen epŗcop Maıᵹe bıle.

Fınnıa mac Uı Fıacaᶀ a aınm aıle. aᵹuŗ Fıonnbaŗŗ Maıᵹe bıle a aınm ele; ó Fıacaᶀ fınb, ŗí Eŗenb, caínıc ŗé. Sepc. 10.

Sınell Maıᵹe bıle, epŗcop, cıŗca annum 600, no 602, quıeuıc.

bŗecan epŗcop ıŗ ab Maıᵹe bıle, Apŗıl 24.

Maolaıᶀᵹın, epŗcop Maıᵹe bıle, Sepc. 9.

Sıollan (mac Fıonnchaın), epŗcop aᵹuŗ ab Maıᵹe bıle, anno bomını 618; Auᵹ. 25.

Caıŗboe, epŗcop Maıᵹe bıle, Maoı 1.

Maᵹ bolᵹ.—Sıŗıc epŗcop ó Maıᵹ bolc, Nou. 26.

Maᵹ bŗeᵹ.—Oubbabaıŗenn mac Conŗuı, ŗuı epŗcop Maıᵹe bŗeᵹ, comaŗba buıce aᵹuŗ eᵹnuıb Laıᵹen, 964.

---

[1] 544, Chron. Scot.

[2] Mart. Doneg. and Mart. Taml.

[3] Four Masters; and 743, Ann. Ult.

[4] IV. M.

[5] IV. M.

[6] IV. M.; 883, Chron. Scot.

[7] *Lusca.* The Four Masters, under 739, record the death of a Colman, scribe and bishop of Leasan, now the parish of Lissan, situated partly in the counties of Donegal and Londonderry, adjoining the territory of Hy-Tuirtre.

[8] Four Masters; and Chron. Scot.

[9] IV. M.

[10] IV. M.; 928, Chron. Scot.

[11] Magh-Ai. Mayo.

[12] Movilla, barony of Lower Ards, county Down.

[13] Mart. Doneg. and Mart. Taml.

was his proper name, and Cainnigh, Cuindigh, or Cuindedh, his first name. He went to his rest in 497.[1]

What Mac Firbis says is " quies of Cuindid, son of Cathbadh, i. e. Mac Cuilind, bishop of Lusca, &c., September 6."[2]

The mortal wounding of Colman, bishop of Lusca, by the Hy-Tuirtre, 739.[3]

Forbasach, bishop of Lusca, 835.[4]

Sechnusach, bishop of Lusca, quievit 887.[5]

Maolruanaidh, bishop of Lusca, quievit 880.[6]

Colman, the scribe, bishop of Daimhliag and Lusca,[7] quievit 902.[8]

Ailill, son of Maenach, bishop of Sord and Lusca, 965.

Ruadan, bishop of Lusca, 904.[9]

Tuathal, son of Aenacan, bishop of Daimhliag and Lusca, steward of the people[10] of Patrick, 927.[11]

MAGH-AI (or Eo).—See Magh-Eo.

MAGH-BILE.[12]—Finnian of Magh-Bile ; or Finnia, bishop of Magh-Bile, February 11.[13]

Finnen,[14] bishop of Magh-Bile. Finnia Mac-Ui-Fiatach was his other name, and Fionnbar of Magh-Bile was another name of his. From Fiatach Finn, King of Erinn, he descended. September 10.[15]

Sinell of Magh-Bile, bishop, circa annum 600, vel 602, quievit.[16]

Brecan, bishop and abbot of Magh-Bile, April 24.[17]

Maelaithghin, bishop of Magh-Bile, Sept. 9.[18]

Siollan, son of Fionchan, bishop and abbot of Magh-Bile, A°. D¹. 618,[19] August 25.[20]

Cairbre, bishop of Magh-Bile, May 1.[21]

MAGH-BOLG.[22]—Siric, bishop, from Magh-Bolc, November 26.[23]

MAGH-BREGH.[24]—Dubhdabhairen, son of Curoi, eminent bishop of Magh-Bregh, comarb of Bute,[25] and sage of Leinster, 964.[26]

---

[14] *Finnen.* The same as Finnian, or Finnia.

[15] Mart. Doneg.

[16] 602, Four M. ; 603, Chron. Scot.

[17] 29 Mart. Doneg. and Mart. Taml.

[18] Mart. Doneg. and Mart. Taml.

[19] IV. M. ; 619, Chron. Scot.

[20] Mart. Doneg. and Mart. Taml.

[21] 3, Mart. Doneg. and Mart. Taml.

[22] Moybolgue ; partly situated in the counties of Cavan and Meath.

[23] Mart. Doneg.

[24] Bregia ; a district comprising a large part of the counties of Dublin and Meath.

[25] *Bute.* Patron and founder of Mainister-Buite, or Monasterboice, county Louth.

[26] Ann. Ult. and Four Masters.

Maġ cremhcoille.—Eoġan eprcop aġur eġnuiḋ Maiġe cremh-coille, Maoi 31.

Máġ eó.—Pontipex Maiġe eó Saxanum, Ġapailt, obiit 726; Mapta 13.

bpocaiḋ Imliġ bpoċaḋa, i Muiġ Eo (no Ḋói), Iuil 9.

Ḋoḋan, eprcop Maiġe eó, 768.

Mac an bpeṫemain, eprcop Maiġe eó; biḋpir mac Uilliam bupc .i. ant ab caoḋ 6.

Patpaic O hEliḋe, eprcop Maiġe eó; bo bapuiġeḋ 6 i ccill Mocelloġ, 1579, ap pon an cpebiṁ catoilcḋe.

Mainirḋir ḃhuicte.—buite .i. boeċiur, eprcop Mainirḋreḋ, quieuit 521. Dec. 7.

buitte (.i. buaḃaċ mac bpónaiġ).

Nt.—Ġin ċaóin Choluim ap cclépiġ,
Ḋniu ór Epinḋ óluiġ.
Por aon líṫ ní páḋ nuaḃaip
báp ḃán ḃhuaḃaiġ mec bpónaiġ.

Domnall mac Máicniaḋa, ab mainirḋreḋ buitte, eprcop aġur penoir naoṁ, 1004.

Maicnia, eprcop aġur comapba mainirḋreḋ buitte, bo 6c 1039.

Mainirḋir ṫuama.—Capṫaċ .i. an pen eprcop; pec Ṁoċúba Maoi 14.

Meaṫur tpuim.—Porannan, eprcop Metiur tpuim, 751.

Muġna.—Maolpoil, eprcop Muġna, 992.

Oipġiall, no Ḋipġiall.—Ḋoḋ ua hEoṫaiġ eprcop Ḋipġialla, quieuit 1369.

Orraiġe.—Ḋuṅċaḋ, ḃalta Diapmaḋa, eprcop 7 Saoi, aġur ollaṁ Orraiġe, 9 * *

---

1 *Magh-cremhchoille.* Not identified. The name Magh-cremhchoille signifies "the plain of the wild-garlic wood." Cremhchoill was the ancient name of the parish of Cranfield, barony of Upper Torme, county of Antrim. *See* Reeves' "Down and Connor," p. 8.

2 Mart. Doneg. and Mart. Taml.

3 Mayo, barony of Clanmorris, county Mayo.

4 Four M.; 781, Ann. Ult.; 731 Tig.

5 Mart. Doneg.

6 *See* under Imleach-Brochadha.

7 Ann. Ult., and IV. M.

8 Monasterboice, county Louth,

9 IV. M.; 518, Chron. Scot.

MAGH-CREMHCHOILLE.[1] — Eoghan, bishop and sage of Magh-Cremhchoille, May 31.[2]

MAGH-EO.[3]—The Pontiff of Magh-Eó of the Saxons, Gerald, obiit 726,[4] March 13.[5]

Brocaidh of Imlech-Brochada, in Magh-Eo (or Magh-Ai), July 9[6].

Aedhan, bishop of Magh-Eo, 768.[7]

Mac-an-Brehon, bishop of Magh-Eo; Mac William Burk, i. e. the Blind Abbot, expelled him.

Patrick O'Helidhe, bishop of Magh-Eo, who was put to death in Cill-Mochellog, 1579, for the Catholic faith.

MANISTER-BUTE.[8]—Bute, i. e. Boetius, bishop of Manister, quievit 521,[9] December 7.[10]

Buite (i. e. Buadach, son of Bronach).

NOTE.—" The gentle birth of Colum, our cleric,
          To-day over noble Erinn;
          On the same festival, it is no vaunting saying,
          [Is commemorated] the death of fair Buadach, son of
              Bronach."

Domhnall, son of Macniadh, abbot of Manister-Bute, a bishop and holy elder, 1004.[11]

Macnia, bishop and comarb of Manister-Buite, died 1039.

MANISTER-THUAMA.[12]—Carthach, i. e. the old bishop. See Mochuda, May 14.

MEATHUS-TRUIM.[13]—Forannan, bishop of Meathus-truim, 751.[14]

MUGHNA.[15]—Maolpoil, bishop of Mughna, 992.[16]

OIRGHIALL (or Airghiall).[17]—Aedh O'hEothaigh,[18] bishop of Airghiall, quievit 1369.[19]

OSRAIGHE.[20]—Dunchadh, foster-son of Diarmaid, bishop and sage, and ollave of Ossory, 9.[21]

---

[10] Mart. Mart.

[11] IV. M.; and Chron. Scot.

[12] *Manistir-Thuama.* Not identified. St. Carthach the Elder was the preceptor of St. Mochada, who is called Carthach Junior. *See* Lanigan's " Eccles. History," vol. 2., pp. 88, 9.

[13] *Meathus-truim.* Not identified.

[14] Four Masters.

[15] Dunnamanoge, county Kildare.

[16] Four Masters.

[17] Diocese of Clogher.

[18] *O'hEothaigh : O'Hoey.* The IV. M., and Ware call him Aedh O'Neill.

[19] IV. M.; Ann. Loch-Cé.

[20] Ossory.

[21] 971, IV. M.

Domnall Ua Fogaptaig, eppcop Oppaige, quieuic 1178.

Raic (no pac) aonaig; Raic muige aonaig (no eanaig). bpu-gaᵭ eppcop, Nou. 1.

Rac baptaige (no beptaige).—Cachchan (no gomab Cachóu), eppcop; Mapc. 20.

Rac Libcen.—Iollaban ua Eachach, epptcop, Iuin 10.

Rac muipbuilg.—Domangapc mac Eachaᵭ, pui epptcop, Mapca 24.

Raic Oppain.—Oppan epptcop. Feb. 17.

Racain.—Ceban Racain, [ɲ] Ceban ua Concumba, epipcopi, ec milicep Cpipci, in pace quieuepunc, agup Saepmug Eanaig buib, 787.

Rac Colpa.—Epptcop Cappach (a Raic Colpa), cepb Pacpaic; (ap ó cuc comaoin bo Pacpaic pe nécc); Appil 14.

Rac móp Muige cuaipgipc.—Lugaib epptcop, Occob. 6.

Rac na neptcop.—Cob glap, Congup. Feb. 16.

Rac Ronain.—Ronan, epptcop i Raic Ronain, in uib Cellaig Cualann.

Rac pfche.—Eogan epptcop Racha pfche, quieuic cipca annum 615.

Reachpa.—Flann mac Ceallaigh, mic Cpunnbmáil, epptcop Rechpaibe, quieuic 734.

Roṁ.—Gpigoip Roṁa, Mapca 12.

Pupa Cipne po gab abbaine Róma capép Gpigóip, ec cecepa.

Rop-ailicpe.—Faccna epptcop, .i. mac Mongaig a Rop ailicpe. Cug. 14.

---

1 Four Masters.

2 Raymochy, barony of Raphoe, county of Donegal.

3 Not identified.

4 Mart. Doneg., and Mart. Taml.

5 Rathlihen, barony of Balliboy, King's County.

6 Mart. Doneg. and Mart. Taml.

7 Maghera, county Down.

8 Mart. Doneg. and Mart. Taml.

9 *Rath-Ossain.* *See* under Ath-Truim.

10 Rahin, King's County.

11 *Eanach-dubh*, i.e. "the black marsh," now Annagh-duff, near Drumana, county Leitrim.

12 Four Masters.

13 Raholp, barony of Lecale Lower, county Down.

Domhnall O'Fogarty, bishop of Ossory, quievit 1178.[1]

RAITH- (or Rath) -aenaigh ; Rath-Maighe-aenaigh, (or Eanaigh).[2]— Brugach, bishop. November 1.

RATH-DARTHAIGHE (or Derthaighe).[3]—Cathchan (or perhaps Cath-chu), bishop ; March 20.[4]

RATH-LIBHTHEN.[5]—Iolladan, descendant of Eochaidh, bishop, June 10.[6]

RATH-MUIRBUILG.[7]—Domangart, son of Eochaidh, an eminent bishop, March 24.[8]

RATH-OSSAIN.[9]—Ossan, bishop, February 17.

RATHAIN.—[10]Aedhan of Rathain, [and] Aedhan, son of Cucumba, episcopi et milites Christi, quieverunt, and Saermugh of Eanach-dubh,[11] 787.[12]

RATH-COLPA.[13]—Bishop Tassach (in Rath-Colpa), Patrick's artist ; (it was he that gave the communion to Patrick before his death); April 14.[14]

RATH-MOR-MUIGHE-TUAISCAIRT.[15]—Lughaidh, bishop, October 6.[16]

RATH-NA-NEPSCOB.[17]—Aodh Glas, and Aongus, February 16.[18]

RATH-RONAIN.[19]—Ronan, bishop, in Rath-Ronain in Ui-Cellaigh-Cualann.

RATH-SITHE.[20]—Eoghan, bishop of Rath-sithe, quievit circa annum 615.[21]

REACHRA.[22]—Flann, son of Cellach, son of Crundmael, bishop of Reachra, went to his rest 734.[23]

ROME.—Gregory of Rome, March 12.

The Pope of Ara[24] got the abbacy of Rome after Gregory, &c.

ROS-AILITRE.[25]—Fachtna, bishop, i. e. the son of Mongach, of Ros-Ailitre,[26] August 14.[27]

---

[14] Mart. Doneg. and Mart. Taml.

[15] Rattoo, county Kerry.

[16] Mart. Doneg. and Mart. Taml.

[17] Not known.

[18] Mart. Doneg. and Mart. Taml.

[19] *Rath-Ronain*, county Wicklow.

[20] Rashee, barony and county of Antrim.

[21] 617, Four Masters.

[22] Lambay, county Dublin.

[23] Four Masters.

[24] *Pope of Ara*. *See* under Ara- (Aelchu, son of Faelchu).

[25] *Ros-Ailitre*. Rosscarbery, county Cork.

[26] *Ros-Ailitre*. The Mart. Doneg. describes this Fachtna, whose festival occurs on the 14th of August, as of Dairinis-Maelanfaidh, county Waterford.

[27] Mart. Doneg.

Rop baipenn.—Cuipican (no) Cipiac eppcop aʒup ab Ruip
menn, no Ruip baipenn. Mapca 16.

Rop menn.—peć Rop baipenn.

Rop Comain.—Siabal eppcop ip ab puip Comain, quieuic, 813.

Ceʼb mac Pianʒupa, eppcop Ruip Comain, 872.

Rop cpe.—Ipaac Ua Cuanain, eppcop Éle Ruip cpe, óʒ aʒup
ápʼb pénóip aipćep Mumhan, quieuic 1161.

Rop beala.—Sen Pacpaic, eppcop ip ab Ruip beala i Muiʒ
Lacha, Cuʒ. 24.

Saiʒip.—Ciapan Saiʒpe, eppcop baoi in Epinn pia Pacpaic,
Mapca 5.

Mebpan eppcop, Iuin 6.

Copmac eppcop Saiʒpe, 907.

Saxan.—Coban eppcop Saxan, quieuic cipca annum 650.

Siʼb cpuim.—Eppcop Cape, Nou. 2.

Slaine.—Eppcop Cape, Nou. 2.

Niallan, eppcop Slaine quieuic 867.

Copmac mac Clabaiʒ, eppcop Slaine, 867.

Maelbpiʒce, eppcop Slaine, 875.

Slebce.—Piacc, eppcop Slebce, Occob. 12; bipʒiobal Pacpaic.
Coʼb, eppcop Sleibce, 699; Peb. 7.

Sliab liaʒ.—Eppcop Ceʼb mac bpic ó pliab Liaʒ; Nou. 10;
quieuic 588.

Sopb.—Maolmuipe Ua Cainén, eʒnaiʼb aʒup eppcop Suipʼb
Coluim cille, quieuic 1023.

Siol Muipebaiʒ.—Ʒaʼb aic imbí eppcop piol Muipebaiʒ (éʼb ap
mian bapoile ap) eppcop Oilepin; ʒiʼbeʼb ni pilimpi lan biler bepin
in ʒaʼb aen aimpip.

---

1 *Ros-Bairenn.* Not identified.

2 Mart. Doneg. and Mart. Taml.

3 Roscommon.

4 813, Four Masters.

5 IV. M.; 873, Ann. Ult.

6 Roscrea, county Tipperary.

7 Cipćep Mumhan, i. e. Ormond.

8 IV. M.

9 Rosdalla, county Westmeath.

10 Mart. Taml.

11 Seirkeeran, in the King's County.

12 Mart. Doneg. and Mart. Taml.

13 Mart. Doneg. and Mart. Taml.

14 Four Masters.

15 Saxan. England.

16 648 = 651, Chron. Scot.

17 Near Trim, county Meath.

18 *See* under Baile-Slaine.

Ros-BAIRENN.[1]—Cuiritan, or Ciriac, bishop and abbot of Ros-menn, or Ros-Bairenn, March 16.[2]

Ros-MENN. See Ros-Bairenn.

Ros-COMAIN.[3]—Siadhal, bishop and abbot of Ros-Comain, quievit 813.[4]

Aedh, son of Fiangus, bishop of Ros-Comain 872.[5]

Ros-CRÈ.[6]—Isaac O'Cuanain, bishop of Ele of Ros-cre, virgin, and arch-elder of East Munster,[7] quievit 1161.[8]

Ros-DELA.[9]—Old Patrick, bishop and abbot of Ros-dela, in Magh-Lacha, August 24.[10]

SAIGHIR.[11]—Ciaran of Saighir, a bishop who was in Erinn before Patrick; March 5.[12]

Medran, bishop, June 6.[13]

Cormac, bishop of Saighir 907.[14]

SAXAN.[15]—Aedhan bishop of the Saxons, quievit circa annum 650.[16]

SIDH-TRUIM.[17]—Bishop Erc, Nov. 2.[18]

SLAINE.[19]—Bishop Erc, Nov. 2.

Niallan, bishop of Slane, quievit 867.[20]

Cormac, son of Eladach, bishop of Slane,[21] 867.

Maelbrighte, bishop of Slane, 875.[22]

SLEBHTE.[23]—Fiacc, bishop of Slebhte, October 12.[24]

Aedh, a disciple of Patrick, bishop of Slebhte, 699;[25] Feb. 7.

SLIABH-LIAG.[26]—Bishop Aedh Mac Bric, from Sliabh-Liag, Nov. 10;[27] quievit 588.[28]

SORD.[29]—Maelmuire O'Cainén, sage and bishop of Sord-Coluim-Cille, quievit 1023.[30]

SIOL-MUIREDHAIGH.[31]—Wherever a bishop of the Siol-Muiredhaigh may be, some are of opinion he is bishop of Elphin. However, I am not fully sure of this at all times.

---

[19] Slane, in the county Meath.

[20] Four Masters.

[21] Slane. The Ann. of the Four Mast. (867), and Ann. Ult. (861), state that Cormac, son of Eladach, was bishop and abbot of Saighir, or Seirkieran.

[22] 847, IV. M.; 876, Ann. Ult.

[23] Slebhte. Slatey, in the Queen's County.

[24] Mart. Doneg. and Mart. Taml.

[25] 698, Four Masters; 696 = 699 Chron. Scot.

[26] Slieve-League, county Donegal.

[27] Mart. Doneg.

[28] IV. M.; and Chron. Scot.

[29] Swords, county of Dublin.

[30] IV. M.; 1021, Chron. Scot.

[31] Diocese of Elphin.

Camlaċta.—Maolruain eprcop Camlaċta, 787: nír hiċeaḋ reóil aġur nír hiḃeḋ lionn aġ manċaiḃ Maoilruain re a ré rén; Iuil 7.

Eoċaiḋ eprcop Camlaċta, quieuit 807.

Corra eprcop Camlaċta, quieuit 872.

Cormac eprcop Camlaċta, 962.

Cronnmaol ab beġ Erenn, aġur eprcop aġur rerleġinn Camlaċta, 964.

Sġanḃlain eprcop aġur ab Camlaċta, 913.

Iorep eprcop Camlaċta Maoilruain, Enair 5.

Eoċaiḋ, eprcop aġur ab Camlaċta, Enair 28.

Airennán (no Erennán), eprcop Camlaċta, Feb. 10.

Camlaċt Menainn. Crıúr do ḃretnaiḃ annro .ı. Narad, beoan eprcop, ır Meallan ó Camlaċt Menain, aġ Loċ ḃricrenn in Uiḃ Eċhaċ Ulaḋ [n]ó o Camlaċta Uı Mail.

Camnaċ buaḋa.—Uiı nerrcoir ó Camnaċ buaḋa, Iuil. 21.

Ceaġ baoiċin.—baoiċin eprcop, Feb. 19.

Ceaġ Callain.—Ceċernaċ eprcop ó ċiġ Collain, quieuit in hl ına oiliċrı, 1047.

Ceaġ Connain.—Connan, eprcop o ċiġ Connain ı cCremċannuıḃ, Iuin 29.

Ceaġ bá ċua.—Eprcop Cen mac Maine, a cciġ Dácua mic Nemain.

Ceaġ Dioma.—Eprcop Dioma mac Senaiġ, do roċarcuıḃ a cciġ (no ó ċiġ) Dioma.

Ceaċ Moċua.—Corġraċ mac Maoilmoċeirġe, eprcop ciġe Moċua aġur na Comann, 931.

Ceaċ Moling.—Moling Luaċra, eprcop, 696, Iuin 17:

1 Tallaght, county Dublin.
2 Four Masters.
3 Mart. Doneg. and Mart. Taml.
4 IV. M.
5 IV. M.; Ann. Ult.
6 IV. M.
7 IV. M.; 914, Chron. Scot.
8 Mart. Doneg. and Mart. Taml.
9 Mart. Doneg. and Mart. Taml.
10 Mart. Doneg. and Mart. Taml.

11 *Tamlacht-Menainn ;* this was in the parish of Ahaderg, county Down, where there is a townland now called *Meenan. See* Reeves's " Down and Connor," p. 113.
12 *Loch-Bricrenn.* Lough Brickland, Co. Down.
13 *Ui-Echadh-Uladh.* Iveagh, county Down.

TAMLACHT.[1]—Maolruain, bishop of Tamlacht 789.[2] Meat was not eaten, nor ale drunk, by Maelruain's monks during his own time: July 7.[3]

Eochaidh, bishop of Tamlacht, quievit 807.[4]

Torpa, bishop of Tamlacht, quievit 872.[5]

Cormac, bishop of Tamlacht, 962.[6]

Cronmael, abbot of Beg-Eri, and bishop and lector of Tamlacht, 964. *See* under Beg-Ere.

Sgandlan, bishop and abbot of Tamlacht, 913.[7]

Joseph, bishop of Tamlacht-Maolruain, Jan. 5.[8]

Eochaidh, bishop and abbot of Tamlacht, Jan. 28.[9]

Airennán, or Erennán, bishop of Tamlacht, Feb. 10.[10]

TAMHLACHT-MENAINN.[11]—Three of the Britons here, viz., Nasad, Beoan, a bishop, and Meallan, from Tamlacht-Menainn at Loch-Bricrenn,[12] in Ui-Echach-Uladh,[13] or from Tamlacht-Ui-Maille.

TAMHNACH-BUADHA.[14]—Seven bishops from Tamhnach-buadha, July 21.[15]

TEACH-BAITHIN.[16]—Baothin, bishop, February 19.[17]

TEACH-CALLAIN.[18]—Cethernach, bishop, from Tech-Collain, quievit at Hy, during his pilgrimage, 1047.[19]

TEACH-CONNAIN.[20]—Connan, bishop, from Tech-Connain in Crimthann, June 29.[21]

TEACH-DACUA.[22]—Bishop Cén, son of Maine, from Tech-Dachua mic Nemain.

TEACH-DIOMA.—Bishop Dioma, son of Senach, of the Fotharta, in Tech-(or from Tech)-Dioma.

TEACH-MOCHUA.[23]—Cosgrach, son of Maelmocheirghe, bishop of Tech-Mochua and the Comauns, 931.[24]

TEACH-MOLING.[25]—Moling Luachra, bishop, 696,[26] June 17.[27]

---

[14] Not identified.

[15] Mart. Taml. and Mart. Doneg.

[16] Tibohine, county Roscommon.

[17] Mart. Doneg. and Mart. Taml.

[18] Stackallan, county Meath.

[19] Four Masters; 1045, Chron. Scot.

[20] *Teach-Connain.* Locality uncertain; but it was probably situated in *Crimthann*, in Meath.

[21] Mart. Doneg. and Mart. Taml.

[22] Ticknevin, barony of Carbery, county Kildare.

[23] Timahoe, Queen's County.

[24] Four Masters.

[25] St. Mullin's, county Carlow.

[26] IV. M.; 693, Chron. Scot.

[27] Mart. Doneg. and Mart. Taml.

Ceaḋ na comaince.—Uıı. nepꞃcoıp ó ṫıg na comaınce, Maoı 27.

Ceach Calláın.—Cıllín, epꞃcop ó ṫıg Caláın ın Aıꞃgıall, Maoı 27.

Cíꞃ Ċonaıll.—Epꞃcop ṫíꞃe Chonuıll .ı. Mag Ḋungaı(le), ḃecc 1366.

Cíꞃ ḃa glaꞃ.—Aıḃḃe, epꞃcop ıꞃ aḃ ṫíꞃe ḃa glaıꞃ, Maoı 24.

Ḋunċaḋ mac Ceallaıg, epꞃcop ıꞃ aḃ Cıꞃe ḃa glaıꞃ, 963.

Cıꞃ Eoġaın.—Ġıolla an coımḃeḋ O Ceaꞃḃallaın, epꞃcop ṫíꞃe hEoġaın, 1279.

Flıoꞃınc ó Ceaꞃḃallaın, epꞃcop, ṫíꞃe hEoġaın, quıeuıc 1293.

Cıꞃ poıꞃ.—Caıꞃeall epꞃcop, ı Cíꞃ poıꞃ, luín 13.

Coḃaꞃ ḃhíꞃın, ı ccíꞃ Fıacꞃaḋ Muaıḋe ıaꞃ nıaꞃgaıg. ḃıꞃın epꞃcop, Ḋecem. 3.

Colan.—Cıaꞃan, epꞃcop Colaın, 919.

Cꞃeḟoḋ.—Fꞃꞃannan, ꞃcꞃıḃa, epꞃcop Cꞃéoıḋ, quıeuıc 769.

Aoḋ, feꞃleġınḋ aguꞃ aḃ Cꞃeḟoıḋe, epꞃcop, eccnaıg, aguꞃ oılıcꞃeḋ, 1004.

Cuaḋ Múṁa.—Caḃg ua Longaꞃcaın, epꞃcop Cuaḋ Ṁúṁan, quıeuıc 1161.

Cuaım ḃa ualann.—Feꞃḃomnaċ (.ı. mac Caoṁaın), epꞃcop Cuama ḃa ualann, anno Ḋomını 781; luín 10.

Cuaım Muꞃgꞃaıge.—Ḋoṁaıngın (no Ḋaṁaıngın), epꞃcop, ó Cuaım Muꞃgꞃaıg, ḃeꞃḃꞃaṫaıꞃ ḃꞃennuınn, Aptil 29.

Cuaıꞃgıꞃc Laıgen.—Cıonaoc Ua Ronaın, epꞃcop Ġlınne ḃa lacha aguꞃ cuaıꞃgıꞃc Laıgen, quıeuıc 1173.

---

1 _Teach-na-comairce._ Parish of Clon-leigh, county Donegal.
2 Mart. Taml.; 28 March, Mart. Doneg.
3 Tyhallen, county Monaghan.
4 Mart. Doneg. and Mart. Taml.
5 _Tir-Conaill;_ i. e. the diocese of Raphoe.
6 Four Masters; Ware.
7 Terryglass, county Tipperary.
8 Mart. Doneg. and Mart. Taml.
9 Four Masters.
10 _Tir-Eoghain;_ i. e. the diocese of Derry.
11 Ann. Loch-Cé; and IV. M.
12 Ann. Loch-Cé; and IV. M.
13 In the county Monaghan.
14 Mart. Doneg. and Mart. Taml.

TEACH-NA-COMAIRCE.[1]—The seven bishops from Tech-na-comairce, May 28.[2]

TEACH-TALAIN.[3]—Cillin, bishop, from Tech-Tallain in Airghiall, May 27.[4]

TIR-CONAILL.[5]—The bishop of Tirconnell, i. e. Mac Dunghaile, died 1366.[6]

TIR-DA-GLAS.[7]—Aidhbhe, bishop and abbot of Tir-da-glas, May 24.[8]

Dunchadh, son of Cellach, bishop and abbot of Tir-da-glas, 963.[9]

TIR-EOGHAIN.[10] — Gilla-an-Coimdedh O'Carolan, bishop of Tir-Eoghain, 1279.[11]

Florence O'Carolan, bishop of Tir-Eoghain, quievit 1293.[12]

TIR-ROIS.[13]—Carell, bishop in Tir-Rois, June 13.[14]

TOBAR-BIRIN, in Tir-Fiachrach of the Moy, behind Iaskagh (Easky, Co. Sligo). Birin, bishop, December 3.[15]

TOLAN.[16]—Ciaran, bishop of Tolan, 919.[17]

TREFOD.[18]—Forannan, scribe, bishop of Treoid, went to his rest 769.[19]

Aedh, lector and abbot of Treoid, a bishop and learned man, and pilgrim, 1004.[20]

TUADH-MUMHA.[21]—Tadhg O'Lonergan, bishop of Thomond, went to his rest 1161.

TUAIM-DA-UALANN.[22]—Ferdomhnach (i. e. son of Caomhan), bishop of Tuaim-da-ualann, anno Domini 781,[23] June 10.[24]

TUAIM-MUSCRAIGHE.[25]—Domhainghin, or Damhainghin, bishop of Tuaim-Muscraighe, brother of Brenainn, April 29.[26]

TUAISGERT-LAIGHEN.[27]—Cionaoth O'Ronan, bishop of Glenn-da-locha, and of North Leinster, quievit 1173.[28]

---

[15] Mart. Doneg.

[16] Dulane, near Kells, county Meath.

[17] Four Masters ; 920.

[18] Trevet, barony of Skreen, county Meath.

[19] IV. M.

[20] IV. M.; 1003, Chron. Scot.

[21] *Tuadh-Mumha ;* i. e. the diocese of Kilfenora.

[22] Tuam, county Galway.

[23] Mart. Doneg.; 777, IV. M.

[24] Mart. Doneg. and Mart. Taml.

[25] Tomes, barony of West Muskerry, county Cork.

[26] Mart. Doneg. and Mart. Taml.

[27] North Leinster, i. e. the diocese of Glendalough.

[28] Four Masters.

Culuiʒ ċaɼbuiꝺ.—Eɼcop Calꝺ, ó Culaiʒ ċaɼbuiꝺ ı menna Cıɼe ın Iꝺ Méꞇ, Enaıɼ 26.

Ua bɼıuın.—Cuaꞇal O Connaċꞇaıʒ, epɼcop Ua mbɼıuın, quıeuıꞇ 1179.

Ua Cennɼelaıʒ.—Anꞇ epɼcop Ua Caꞇꞇaın, .ı. aıɼꝺ epɼcop Ua cCennɼıolaıʒ, quıeuıꞇ 1135.

Ua ċonʒbaıl.—Pachꞇna epɼcop on ua conʒbaıl, Enaıɼ 19.

Ua ꝼꝼıacɼaċ.—Iomaɼ Ua Ruaꝺaın, epɼcop ó ꝼꝼıacɼaċ, quıeuıꞇ 1176.

Anꞇ epɼcop O Ceallaıʒ, .ı. epɼcop O ꝼꝼıacɼaċ, quıeuıꞇ 1216.

Ʒıolla ceallaıʒ O Ruaıꝺín, epɼcop O ꝼꝼıaċɼaċ, quıeuıꞇ 1254.

Maolmaıɼe O Conmaıc, epɼcop O ꝼꝼıaċɼaċ ıɼ cınel Aeꝺa, quıeuıꞇ 1225.

Ua Maıne.—Maolıoɼa mac an ꝺaıɼꝺ, epɼcop Ua Maıne, quıeuıꞇ 1174.

Ua Neıll.—Moċꞇa epɼcop Ua Neıll, aʒuɼ ɼaʒaɼꞇ Aɼꝺa Macha, 924.

Ulaꝺ.—Maolıoɼa mac an ċléɼıʒ ċuıɼɼ, epɼcop Ulaꝺ, quıeuıꞇ 1175.

Ʒıolla ꝺomnaıʒ mac Coɼmaıc, epɼcop Ulaꝺ, quıeuıꞇ 1175.

---

[1] Tullycorbet, county Monaghan.
[2] Mart. Taml.
[3] *Ui-Briuin*; i. e. the diocese of Kilmore.
[4] Four Masters.
[5] Diocese of Ferns.
[6] IV. M.; Ann. Loch-Cé.

[7] Supposed by some to be Navan, county Meath.
[8] Mart. Doneg. and Mart. Taml.
[9] Diocese of Kilmacduagh.
[10] Four Masters.
[11] IV. M.

TULAGH-CARBUID.[1] — Bishop Calbh, from Tulach-Carbaid, in Menna-tire in Ui-Meith, January 26.[2]

UI-BRIUIN.[3]—Tuathal O'Connachty, bishop of the Hy-Briuin, went to his rest 1179.[4]

UI-CENNSELAIGH.[5]—The bishop O'Cattan, i. e. the arch-bishop of Ui-Cennselaigh, quievit 1135.[6]

UA-CONGBHAIL.[7]—Fachtna, bishop, from Ua-Congbhail, Jan. 19.[8]

UI-FIACHRACH.[9]—Iomhar O'Ruadhain, bishop of Ui-Fiachrach, quievit 1176.[10]

Bishop O'Cellaigh, i. e. bishop of the Ui-Fiachrach, quievit 1216.[11]

Gilla-Cellaigh O'Ruaidhin, bishop of the Ui-Fiachrach, quievit 1254.[12]

Maolmuire O'Conmaic, bishop of Ui-Fiachrach and Cenel-Aedha, quievit 1225.[13]

UA-MAINE.[14]—Mael-Isa Mac-a-Ward, bishop of Ui-Maine, quievit 1174.[15]

UA NEILL.[16]—Mochta, bishop of the O'Neills, and priest of Ard-Macha, 924[17].

ULADH.[18] — Maoliosa Mac-an-Clerigh-chuirr, bishop of Uladh quievit 1175.[19]

Gilla-domnaigh Mac Cormaic, bishop of Uladh, quievit 1175.[20]

---

[12] 1253, Four Masters.

[13] Ib.

[14] *Ua-Maine;* i. e. the diocese of Clon-fert.

[15] 1173, Four Masters.

[16] The O'Neills.

[17] Four Masters.

[18] Ulster, or the diocese of Down.

[19] Four Masters ; Ann. Loch-Cé.

[20] Ib.

IV.—TAIN BO FRAICH.

From MS. H. 2, 18 (*fol.* 183, *et seqq.*), *in the Library of Trinity College,*
Dublin.

TRANSLATED AND EDITED BY

J. O'BEIRNE CROWE, A.B.

THE following hitherto inedited romantic specimen of Irish life in the
first century is taken from the oldest portion of the "Book of Leinster,"
a compilation of the twelfth. The subject is this :—

Froech, son of Idath (a chieftain of Eirros Domno, in the present
county of Mayo), and of Befind, a *Sidè* lady, has come to learn that he
is loved by Find-abair, daughter of Ailill and Medb, king and queen of
the Connachta. He accordingly resolves to visit her parents in their
palace of Cruachu, now Rathcroghan, in the county of Roscommon,
and formally demand her hand in marriage. Before, however, proceeding on his journey, his friends say to him that, as Boand, the *Sidè*
governess of the Boyne, was his mother's sister, it would be well for
him to call on her at her palace in Mag Breg, and request her to fit
him out suitably for the occasion. He does so, and, with his request
fully granted, sets out for Cruachu.

The equipment of Froech's cavalcade was grand in the extreme.
Gold and silver, carbuncle and other precious stones, glittered on man
and horse; but the most curious beings in this train were the three *Sidè*
harpers, the sons of Uaithne and Boand. Their origin, name, form,
and dress are fully described, and in note (12) I have endeavoured
to give an interpretation of this figurative description. The approach
of Froech and his suite was duly announced by the watchman in Dun
Cruachan; and as these visitors from the *Sidè* approached, such was
the delicious odour which perfumed the air around, that several of the
family of Cruachu died of the effect.

Among all nations, the presence of divinities was accompanied and
attested by a supernatural perfume : and in our ancient tale, the *Sidè*
are always thus introduced. In tropical lands, in India, for example,
the deities when appearing to mortals exhibit also other characteristics,
such as garlands of flowers, blooming and erect, as a symbol of immor-

tality; this symbol with our *Sidé* is the never-fading, green tunic or head-dress.

Froech enjoyed the hospitality of his sovereigns for some weeks, and then preferred his suit in due form; the dowry, however, asked of him he deems too much, and so takes his leave abruptly. Meantime he had arranged everything with Find-abair; and though Ailill tried to have him drowned in the Brei, a river adjoining the palace, the kindness of his lady-love and the power of his divine mother saved him. The king and queen, finding him thus favoured, express regret for their conduct towards him, make their peace with him, and offer him their daughter, as soon as he should come back and join them in their intended spoil of the cows of Cualnge. He accepts the offer, and bids farewell.

On arriving at his mother's house, Froech learns that plunderers from the Alps had carried off his wife, his three sons, and his cows, and this is the origin of the title of our tale—"The Spoil of the Cows of Froech." The reader must not be surprised to find that our hero, though a suitor for the hand of Find-abair, had already a wife and family. To understand this, he must study life in ancient Eriu.

Froech consulted his mother in his present difficulty. She tried to dissuade him from the attempt to recover the stolen property, but he declined to take her advice. Accompanied, accordingly, by Conall Cernach, one of the three great champions of the Ulaid, he sets off for the Alps, brings back his wife, his children, and his cows; and then, agreeably to promise, joins in the Tain Bo Cualnge, in which expedition he perishes by the hands of his brother demigod, Cu Chulaind.

·τάιν bó ꝼꞃɑιch.

Fꞃoeᴄ̇ mac Iḃaιᴄh ḃo Chonnachᴄaιḃ—mac ꞃιḃe ḃo ḃéꝼιnḃ a Sꝺoιḃ: ḃeꞃḃ-ṁuꞃ ꞃιḃe ḃo ḃoιnḃ. Iꞅ hé Lаеᴄ̇ ιꞅ áιlḃem ꞃoḃúι ḃo ꝼeꞃaιḃ hEꞃenḃ ꞁ Alḃan, aᴄᴄ nι ḃa ꞃuᴄ̇aιn. Ḃoḃeꞃᴄ a maᴄaιꞃ ḃí ḃa ḃéᴄ ḃó aꞃꞅ·ιnᴄ Sꝺo: ιᴄ ó ꝼιnḃa, óι-ḃeꞃᴈa. ḃóι ᴄꞃeḃaḃ maιᴄ oca co cenḃ oᴄᴄṁ ḃlιaḃna cen ᴄaḃaιꞃᴄ mna ċuca. Cóιca maιᴄ ꞃíᴈ ꞃoꞃ ó lín a ᴄeᴈlaιᴄ̇: comáιꞃ, comcuᴄ-ꞃumma ꝼꞃιꞅ ule eᴄeꞃ ċꞃuᴄh ꞁ ċoꞃc. Capᴄhaι Ꝼιnḃ-aḃaιꞃ, ιnᴈen Aιlella ꞁ Meḃḃa, aꞃ a ιꞃꞅélaιḃ. Aḃꞃιaḃaꞃ ḃoꞃum oc a ᴄaιᴈ. Ropu Lán hEꞃιu ꞁ Alḃu ḃι a alluḃ ꞁ ḃι a ꞃꞅélaιḃ.

Iaꞃ ꞃuιḃιu ḃoᴄoꞃaꞃᴄaꞃ ꝼaιꞃ ḃul ḃo acallaιm na hιnᴈιne: ιm-maꞃoꞃaιḃ ꝼꞃι a munᴄιꞃ anꝼ ꞃιn. " Ꞇιaᴈaꞃ uaιᴄ ḃιn co ꝼιaꞃ ḃo maᴄhaꞃ co ᴄuᴄᴄhaꞃ ní ḃo éᴄuᴄ̇ ιnᴈanᴄaᴄ̇ ꞁ ḃe aꞃceḃaιḃ Sꝺḃe ḃuιᴄ uaḃι." Luιḃ ιaꞃum co ꝼιaꞃ .ι. co ḃóιnḃ, com ḃúι ιm Maᴈ ḃꞃeᴈ, ꞁ ḃoḃeꞃᴄ coιcaιᴄṁ ḃꞃaᴄᴄ̇ᴈoꞃm ꞁ ḃa coꞃmaιl ᴄeᴄ̇ ae ꞃι ꝼιn-ḃꞃuιheꞃ ḃóιle, ꞁ ceᴄheoꞃa oa ḃuḃ-ᴈlaꞃꞃa ꞃoꞃ ᴄeᴄ̇ ḃꞃuᴄᴄ, ꞁ mιleᴄ̇ ḃeꞃᴈᴈ-óιꞃ la ᴄeᴄ̇ṁ ḃꞃaᴄᴄ: ꞁ lénᴄι ḃán-ᴈela co ᴄuaᴈ-mílaιḃ óιꞃ ιmpu. Ocuꞃ ᴄóιca ꞃᴄꞅaᴄhn aꞃᴈḃιḃe con ꞅṁlιḃ, eᴄ caιnḃel ꞃíᴈ-chιᴈι ιl Laιm ᴄeᴄ̇ ae: ꞁ coꞃca ꞃemmanḃ ꝼιn-ḃꞃuιne aꞃ ᴄeᴄ̇n ae. Coꞅca ᴄoꞃaᴄᴄ ḃι óꞃ ꞃoꞃloιꞃᴄhι ιn ᴄeᴄ̇n ae: eꞃmιᴄιuḃa ḃι chaꞃꞃ-mocul ꞃoιḃ anꝼꞃ, ꞁ ιꞃ ḃι leᴄaιḃ loᴈmaιꞃιḃ an aιꞃꝼaꞃn: nolaꞃᴄaιꞃ ιn aιḃche amaιl ḃeᴄ̇ꞃ ꞃuιchnι ᴈꞃénι.

Ocuꞃ coιca claιḃeḃn óꞃ-ḃuιꞃn leo, ꞁ ᴈaḃaꞃ ḃoc-ᴈlaꞃ ꝼó ꝼuιḃι ᴄeᴄ̇ ꝼιꞃ, ꞁ ḃeιlᴈe óιꞃ ꝼꞃιu ; maellanḃ aꞃᴈᴈaιᴄ co clucιnιu óιꞃ ꝼo ḃꞃaᴈιᴄ ᴄeᴄ̇ eιch. Cóιca acꞃann coꞃcꞃa co ꞃꞃaᴄhιḃ aꞃᴈaιᴄ eꞃᴄιḃ, co ꞃꝺḃlaιḃ óιꞃ ꞁ aꞃᴈaιᴄ ꞁ co cenḃ-mιlaιḃ. Cóιca eᴄ̇laꞃᴄ ꝼιn-ḃꞃuιne com ḃaᴄᴄán oꞃḃa ꝼoꞃ cιnn ᴄeᴄ̇ ae. Ocuꞃ ꞃeᴄ̇ mιl-ᴄ̇oιn ι ꞃlaḃꞃaḃaιḃ aꞃᴈaιᴄ, ꞁ uḃulln óιꞃ eᴄeꞃ ᴄeᴄ̇n ae. ḃꞃoca cꞃeḃumaι

THE SPOIL OF THE COWS OF FROECH.

FROECH[1], son of Idath of the Connachta—a son he to Befind from the *Sidè*[2]: a sister she to Boand[3]. He is the hero, who is the most beautiful that was of the men of Eriu and of Alba, but he was not long-lived. His mother gave him twelve cows out of the Sid : they are white-eared. He had a good residence till the end of eight years without the bringing of a woman to him. Fifty sons of kings—it was the number of his household, co-aged, cosimilar to him all between form and dress. Find-abair[4], daughter of Ailill and Medb, loves him for the great stories about him. It is declared to him at his house. Eriu and Alba were full of his renown and of stories about him.

After this going to a dialogue with the daughter fell upon him : he discussed that matter with his people. "Let there be a message then sent to thy mother's sister, so that a portion of wondrous robing and of gifts of *Sidè* be given thee from her." He goes accordingly to sister, that is, to Boand, until he was in Mag Breg[5], and he carried away fifty blue cloaks, and each of them was like to the *findruine*[6] of a work of art, and four black-grey ears on each cloak, and a brooch of red gold with each cloak ; and pale-white shirts with loop-animals of gold around them. And fifty silver shields with edges, and a candle of a king-house in the hand of each of them [the men] : and fifty studs of *findruine* on each of them [the shields] : fifty knobs of thoroughly burned gold in each of them : pins of car-buncle under them from beneath, and their point of precious stones. They used to light the night as if they were sun's rays.

And fifty swords of gold-hilt with them, and a soft-grey mare under the seat of each man, and bits of gold to them : bands of silver with a little bell of gold around the throat of each horse. Fifty horse-robes of purple with threads of silver out of them, with drops of gold and of silver, and with head-animals. Fifty whips of *findruine*, with a golden hook on the end of each of them. And seven chase-hounds in

---

[1] This and the subsequent figures refer to the appended notes.

ιmpu : no co ꞃaƄι ᴅaᴄ naᴅ bech ιnᴄιb. Moꞃꝼeꞃꞃeꞃ coꞃnaιꞃe leo
co coꞃnaιb óꞃᴅaιb ⁊ aꞃᵹᴅιᴅιb, con eᴄaιᵹιb ιᴌ-ᴅaᴄhaᴅaιb, co mon-
ᵹaιb óꞃᴅáιb, ꞃíᴅbuᴅιb, co ᴌennaιb eᴄꞃaᴄᴄaιb.

Ƅaᴄιꞃ ᴄꞃι ᴅꞃúιch ꞃemιb co mιnᴅaιb aꞃᵹᴅιᴅιb ꝼo ᴅιóꞃ. Sceιᴄ
co ꞃeᴄhuᴌ ᴄonᴅuaᴌa ᴌa ceᴄn ae, co cíꞃ-bachᴌaιb con eꞃnaᴅaιb
cꞃeᴅumaι ιaꞃn a ᴄoebaιb. Cꞃιaꞃ cꞃuιᴄᴄιꞃe con óᴄoꞃc ꞃιᵹ ιm
ceᴄn ae. Ꝺocumᴌáᴄ aꞃꞃ ᴅo Chꞃuaᴄnaιb coꞃꞃ ιnᴅ ecuꞃc ꞃιn ᴌeu.

Ꝺoꞃnᴅéᴄᴄaι ιn ᴅeꞃᴄᴄaιᴅ ᴅι'n ᴅún ιn ᴄan ᴅobeᴅaᴄaꞃ ιm Maᵹ
Cꞃuaᴄan. "Ꝺιꞃιmm aᴄᴄιu-ꞃa," oᴌ ꞃe, "ᴅo'n ᴅún ιnn a ᴌín. O
ᵹabꞃaᴄ Aιᴌeᴌᴌ ⁊ Meᴅb ꝼᴌaιᴄ, nι coꞃᴄáιnιc ꞃιam ⁊ nι coꞃᴄιcꞃa ᴅí-
ꞃιmm baꞃ chóιmιu, na beꞃ ꞃáιnιu. Iꞃ cumma ᴌemm beᴅ ι ᴄauᴌ-
chubu ꝼιna nobech mo ᴄenᴅ ᴌaꞃ ιn ᵹaéch ᴅochaeᴄ ᴄaιꞃꞃιu. A
bꞃaꞃ ⁊ abaιꞃᴄ ᴅoᵹní ιnᴄ óc-ᴌᴅeᴄ ꝼιᴌ anᴅ, no ᴄonacca-ꞃa ꞃιam a
ᴄuᴄꞃumma. Ꝼoᴄeιꞃᴅ a bunꞃaιᵹ ꞃouᴄn auꞃchoꞃa uaᴅ : ꞃιu
coᴄꞃí ꞃι ᴄaᴌmaιn, noꞃᵹaιbeᴄ na ꞃeᴄᴄ mιᴌ-ᴄoιn con a ꞃeᴄᴄ ꞃᴌabꞃa-
ᴅιb·aꞃᵹᴅιᴅιb."

La ꞃoᴅaιn ᴅochιaᵹaᴄ ιnᴄ ꝼᴌuaιᵹ a Ꝺún Chꞃúaᴄan ᴅι án ᴅéᴄꞃιn.
Immuꞃmuᴄaᴄ ιn ᴅóιnι ιꞃꞃ ιn Ꝺún con aꞃᴄaᴄaꞃ ꞃé ꝼιꞃ ᴅéc oc on
ᴅeιᴄꞃιn. Caιꞃᴌenᵹaιᴄ ιn ᴅoꞃuꞃ ιn ᴅúιne. Scoιꞃιᴄ an eoᴄu ⁊ ᴌéᴄιᴄ
a míᴌ-ᴄona. Ꝺoꞃennaᴄ na ꞃeᴄᴄn aιᵹe ᴅo Ráιch Chꞃuaᴄan, ⁊
ꞃeᴄᴄ ꞃιnᴅu ⁊ ꞃeᴄᴄ mιᴌa maιᵹe, ⁊ ꞃeᴄᴄ ᴄoꞃcu aᴌᴄa, conᴅaꞃubaᴄaꞃ
ιnᴅ óιc ιꞃꞃ ιnᴅ auꞃᴌaιnᴅ ιn ᴅúιne. Iaꞃ ꞃaιn ꝼocheꞃbaᴄ ιn mιᴌ-
ᴄoιn beᴅᵹ ιm ᴅꞃeι : ᵹabaιᴄ ꞃeᴄᴄn ᴅoboꞃ-ᴄona. Ꝺoꞃbeꞃᴄaᴄaꞃ
ᴅoᴄum na aꞃᴅᴅa ιn ᴅoꞃuꞃ na ꞃꞃím-ꞃáᴄha. Ꝺeιꞃꞃιᴄeꞃ ιꞃ ꞃuιᴅιu.

Ꝺoᴄιaᵹaꞃ o'nᴅ ꞃíᵹ ᴅι an acaᴌᴌaιm. Imchomaꞃᴄaꞃ cιa bu ᴄan
ᴅóιb : noᴅaꞃᴌoιnᴅeᴄ ιaꞃum ιaꞃn a ꞃᴌonᴄιb ꝼíꞃaιb : "Ꝼꞃóeᴄ Mac
Iᴅaιᴄh ιnꞃo," oᴌ ꞃeaᴄ. Ráιᴄe ιn ꞃeᴄᴄaιꞃe ꝼꞃιꞃ ιn ꞃíᵹ ⁊ ιn ꞃíᵹnaι
(recte ꞃιᵹaιn). "Ꝼochen ᴅóιb," oᴌ Aιᴌeᴌᴌ ⁊ Meᴅb. "Iꞃ óᴄᴌáᴄ án ꝼιᴌ
anᴅ," oᴌ Aιᴌeᴌᴌ : "ᴄaéᴄ ιꞃꞃ ιn ᴌeꞃꞃ." Ꝺoᴌᴌeιᴄᴄheꞃ ᴅóιb ceᴄꞃamᴄhu
ιn ᴄaιᵹe. Eᴅ a óᴄoꞃc ιn ᴄaιᵹe—ꞃeᴄᴄ-oꞃᴅᴅ anᴅ ; ꞃechᴄn ιmᴅáι
o cheιn co ꝼꞃaιᵹ ιꞃ ιn ᴄaιᵹ ιmmecuaιꞃᴅ. Aιꞃιneᴄ ᴅι ᴄꞃeᴅumu ꝼoꞃ
ceᴄ ιmᴅáι : auꞃꞃcaꞃᴅaᴅ ᴅeꞃᵹᵹ-ιbaιꞃ ꝼó mꞃeᴄᴄ-ꞃuncaιn uιᴌe.
Cꞃí ꞃᴄéιᴌᴌ ᴄꞃeᴅumaι ιn auᴌaιch ceᴄa ιmᴅaι. Seᴄᴄ ꞃᴄιaᴌᴌa umaι

chains of silver, and an apple of gold between each of them. Greaves of bronze about them: by no means was there any colour which was not in them. Seven trumpeters with them with golden and silver trumpets, with many-coloured garments, with golden, silken heads of hair, with shining cloaks.

There were three jesters' before them with silver diadems under gilding. Shields with a cover of embroidery with each of them, with black staffs with filigrees of bronze along their sides. Three harpers with a king's appearance about each of them. They depart for Cruachna' with that appearance with them.

The watchman sees them from the dun when they had come into the Plain of Cruachu. "A multitude I see," he says, "towards the dun in their fulness. Since Ailill and Medb assumed sovereignty, there came not to them before, and there shall come not to them a multitude, which is more beautiful or which is more distinguished. It is the same with me that it were in a vat of wine my head should be, with the breeze that goes over them. The activity and play the young hero who is in it makes—I have not before seen its likeness. He shoots his pole a shot's discharge from him: before it reaches to earth the seven chase-hounds with their seven silver chains catch it.

At this the hosts come from the dun of Cruachu to view them. The people in the dun hide themselves, so that sixteen men die while viewing them. They alight in the door of the dun. They tent their steeds and they loose the chase-hounds. They (the hounds) chase the seven deer to Rath Cruachan, and seven foxes, and seven hares, and seven wild boars, until the youths kill them in the lawn of the dun. After that the chase-hounds dart a leap into Brei'; they catch seven water-dogs. They brought them to the elevation in the door of the chief-rath. They (Froech and his suite) sit down there.

A message comes from the king for a parley with them. It is asked what was their whence: they name themselves then according to their true names: "Froech, son of Idath, this," say they. The steward tells it to the king and to the queen. "Welcome to them," say Ailill and Medb; "It is a noble youth who is in it," says Ailill; "let him come into the *Less*[10]. The fourth of the house is allowed to them[10]. It is the array of the house[10]—a septi-range in it; seven apartments from fire to side-wall in the house all round. A rail of bronze to each apartment; a partitioning of red yew under variegated planeing all.

o 'n ᴅαmbαbαιᴄ ᴄo ᴄleιᴄe ιꝛꝛ ιn ᴄιʒ. Ɖe ʒιúꝛ boʒních α
ᴄeó: bα ᴄuʒα ꝝlιnneᴅ bóι ꝼαιꝛ ᴅιαneᴄᴄαιꝛ. bαᴄαꝛ ꝛé ꝛenιꝛᴄꝛι
béc ιꝛꝛ ιn ᴄιʒ, eᴄ ᴄomlαe humαe αꝛ ᴄeón ᴅι: ᴄuιḋ umαι ᴅαꝛꝛ α
ꝛoꝛléꝛ. Ceᴄheoꝛ oᴄᴄʒα humαι ꝼoꝛ ιmᴅáι Ɑιlellα ⁊ ᵯebbα,
ιmmᴅeꝛnιᴅe ᴅe ᴄhꝛeᴅumu uιlι, ιꝛꝛ ꝼ ι ᴄeꝛᴄ-meᴅón ιn ᴄαιʒe. Ɖα
αuꝛαιneᴄ αꝛʒʒαιᴄ ιmꝝe ꝼo ᴅιóꝛ. Ꝑleꝛᴄ αꝛʒαιᴄ ιꝛ ιnᴅ αιꝛιnnιuᴄ
ꝛoꝛαιʒeᴅ mιᴅ-lιꝛꝛιu ιn ᴄαιʒe. ᴄιmᴄellαᴅ α ᴄeᴄ ιmmeᴄuαιꝛᴅ o 'n
ᴅoꝛuꝛ ᴅι αlαιlιu. Ɑꝛꝛoᴄbαᴄ αꝛ ʒαιꝛᴄebα ιꝛꝛ ιn ᴄαιʒ ꝛιn eᴄ
ꝛebαιᴄ, ⁊ ꝼeꝛᴄhαιꝛ ꝼαιlᴄe ꝛιu.

"Ꝑoᴄen ᴅuιb," ol Ɑιlell ⁊ ᵯebb. "Iꝛꝛ eᴅ ᴅoꝛᴅαᴄᴄαmαꝛ," ol
Ꝑꝛóeᴄ. "Nι bα ᴅuꝛαιꝛ αꝛ αιʒ-bαιʒ on," ol ᵯebb, ⁊ eᴄꝛαιᴄ ᵯebb
⁊ Ɑιlell ꝝιᴅchell ιαꝛ ꝛιn. Ʒαιbιᴅ Ꝑꝛoeᴄh ιαꝛum ιmbeꝛᴄ ꝝιᴅchιlle
ꝛι ꝼeꝛ ᴅι α munᴄιꝛ. bα ᴄáιmᴅe ꝝιᴅᴄellα. Cláꝛ ꝝιnᴅ-ꝛuιne αnᴅ
ᴄo ᴄeᴄheoꝛαιb αuαιb ⁊ uιlneιb ꝼoꝛꝛι. Cαιnᴅel ᴅe líᴄ loʒmαιꝛ oᴄ
ꝼuꝛꝛunnuᴅ ᴅoιb. O'ꝛ ⁊ αꝛʒʒαιᴄ ιnᴅ ꝼuιꝛenᴅ bóι ꝼoꝛꝛ ιn ᴄhláꝛ.
"Ɑuꝛʒnαιᴅ bιαᴅ ᴅo nαιb oᴄαιb," ol Ɑιlell. "Ní heᴅ ιꝛ αᴄᴄoboꝛ
lιmm," ol ᵯebb, "αᴄᴄ ᴅul ᴅo ιmbeꝛᴄ nα ꝝιᴅchιlle ᴄhαll ꝼꝛι
Ꝑꝛoeᴄ." "Eιꝛʒ ᴅó: ιꝛ mαιᴄ lιm-ꝛα," ol Ɑιlιll. Imbeꝛαᴄ ιn
ꝝιᴅchιll ιαꝛum ⁊ Ꝑꝛóeᴄ.

bóι α munᴄeꝛ ᴄolléιᴄ oᴄ ꝼuιnιu nα ꝼιαᴅ-mίl. "Sennαᴄ
ᴅo ᴄꝛuιᴄᴄιꝛι ᴅún," ol Ɑιlιll ꝛι Ꝑꝛαéᴄ. "Sennαᴄ émm," ol Ꝑꝛáeᴄ.
Cꝛoᴄᴄ-bolʒ ᴅι ᴄꝛoᴄnιb ᴅoboꝛ-ᴄon ιmꝝu, ᴄon αn ιmbenαm ᴅo
ꝼαꝛᴄαιḋ ꝼo αn ιmbenαm ᴅι óꝛ ⁊ αꝛʒʒαᴄ. bιαnn-neꝛbbαᴅ
ιmꝝu αmmeᴅón: bα ʒιlιᴅιꝛ ꝛneᴄᴄα: ꝛellα ᴅub-ʒlαꝛꝛα ιnn
αm meᴅonαιᴅe. bꝛuιᴄ lίn ʒιlιᴅιꝛ ꝼuαṁ ʒeꝛꝛα ιm nα ᴄéᴄα ꝛιn.
Imꝝeιᴄhιᴄίꝛ nα ᴅelbα ꝛιn ιαꝛum ιnnα ꝛιꝛu ιmmeᴄuαιꝛᴅ.
Sennαιᴄ ᴅóιb ιαꝛum, ᴄonιᴅ αꝛᴄαᴄαꝛ ᴅα ꝼeꝛ béᴄ ᴅι α munᴄιꝛ lα ᴄóι
⁊ ᴄoꝛꝛι. bα ᴄáιn ⁊ bα bιnᴅ ιn ᴄꝛιαꝛ-ꝛα, ⁊ bαᴄαꝛ Cáιnι U'αιᴄnι
ιnꝛeιn. Iꝛ hé ιn ᴄꝛιαꝛ ιꝛᴅαιꝛᴄᴄ ᴄꝛι beꝛbꝛαᴄhιꝛ .ι. Ʒol-ᴄꝛαιʒeꝛ, Ʒen-
ᴄꝛαιʒeꝛ ⁊ Suαn-ᴄꝛαιʒeꝛ. boιnᴅ αꝛ Sίoιb αm mαᴄhαιꝛ α ᴄꝛιuꝛ.
Iꝛ ᴅι 'n ᴄeol ꝛeꝼhαιnn Uáιᴄne ᴄꝛuιᴄᴄ ιn Ɖαʒᴅαι, αιnmnιʒᴄheꝛ α
ᴄꝛιuꝛ. In ᴄαn bóe ιn ben oᴄ lαmnαᴅ, bα ʒol mαιꝛʒʒ lee lα ʒúꝛι
nαn ιᴅαn ι ᴄoꝛꝛuᴄ, bα ʒen ⁊ ꝼáιlᴄe αꝛbίᴄ αꝛmeᴅón αꝛ ιmᴄholᴄαιn
ιn ᴅα mαᴄ; bα ꝛúαn αlʒιne αꝛαbeιᴄᴄe ιn mαᴄ ᴅeᴅenαᴄ αꝛ ᴄꝛumme
ιnnα bꝛιᴄhe; ᴄonιᴅ ᴅe ꝛoαιnmnιʒeᴅ ᴄꝛιαn ιn ᴄhιúιl. Ɖoꝛιúꝛꝛιʒ

Three plates of bronze in the skirting of each apartment. Seven plates of brass from the ceiling to the roof-tree in the house. Of deal the house was made; it is a covering of shingle it had externally. There were sixteen windows in the house and a shutting of brass to each of them; a tie of brass across the roof-light. Four tester-poles of brass on the apartment of Ailill and of Medb, adorned all with bronze, and it in the exact centre of the house. Two rails of silver around it under gilding. In the front a wand of silver that reached the girders of the house. The house was encircled all round from the door to the other. They hang up their arms in that house, and they sit, and welcome is given to them.

"Welcome to you," say Ailill and Medb. "It is it we have come for," says Froech. "It shall not be a habitation for begging contention[11] this," says Medb, and Medb and Ailill arrange the chess-board after that. Froech then takes to the playing of chess with a man of their people. It was a beauty of a chess-board. A board of *findruine* in it, with four ears and elbows on it. A candle of precious stone at illuminating for them. Gold and silver the party that were on the table. "Prepare ye food for the youths," says Ailill. "Not it is my desire," says Medb, "but to go to play the chess yonder against Froech." "Get to it; I am pleased," says Ailill. They play the chess then and Froech[12].

His people were all at cooking of the wild animals. "Let thy harpers play for us," says Ailill to Froech. "Let them play indeed," says Froech. A harp-bag of the skins of water-dogs about them with their adornment of ruby beneath their adornment of gold and silver. The skin of a roe about them in the middle; it was whiter than snow; black-grey eyes in their centre. Cloaks of linen whiter than a swan's tunic around these ties. These figures accordingly used to run about the men all round. They play for them then, so that twelve men of their family die with weeping and sadness. Gentle were and melodious were this triad; and they were the Chants of Uaithne[13]. The illustrious triad are three brothers, namely, *Gol-traiges*, and *Gen-traiges* and *Suan-traiges*. Boand from the *Side* is the mother of the triad. It is from the music which Uaithne, the Dagda's harp played, the triad are named. The time the woman was at parturition, it had a cry of sorrow with the soreness of the pangs at first: it was smile and joy it played in the middle for the

aꝛum aꝛꝛ ınc ꝼúan ın boınb. "Auꝛꝺóım-ꝛıu," ol ꝛı, "bo chꝛı
maccu, a Uachnı lan-bꝛoca: ꝼobıch ꝼıle ꝛuan-cꝛaıbe ⁊ ꝣen-
cꝛaıbe ⁊ ꝣol-cꝛaıbe aꝛ budıb ꝛceo mnáıb bocoecꝛac la Meıbb
⁊ Aılıll, acbelac ꝼıꝛ la cluáıꝛꝼṁ ꝣléꝛꝛa bóıb."

Anaıc b'ınc ꝼenmaım ıaꝛ ꝛaın ıꝛꝛ ınb ꝛíꝣ-caıꝣ. "Iꝛ ꝛéꝣonb
boꝛanıc," ol Ꝼeꝛꝣuꝛ. "Ꝼobıb bún," ol Ꝼꝛóeb ꝼꝛı a munciꝛ,
"am bıab: cucaıb ıꝛ a ceb." Ꝺoꝺınꝣ Lochuꝛ ꝼoꝛ láꝛ ın caıꝣe:
ꝼobáıle bóıb am bıab: ꝼoꝛ a beꝛnaınb noꝛannab cecn áꝣe con a
ꝺlaınnıub ⁊ nı aıblech comaılc na ꝼeóıl (recte ꝼeóla): o ꝣabaıꝛ
ꝛannaıꝛecc nı aꝛchıúıꝛ bíab ꝼo a láım ꝛıam.

bacaꝛ cꝛı laa ⁊ ceoꝛa aıbche oc ımbeꝛc na ꝼıbchılle la ımmeb
nal ⰾıac loꝣmaꝛ ı ceꝣlub Ꝼꝛóıb. Iaꝛ ꝛın aꝣlabaꝛ Ꝼꝛóeb Meıbb:
"Iꝛ maıch ꝛonꝣabuꝛ ꝼꝛıcc," ol ꝛe: "ní bıuꝛ bo cóꝺaıll bı'nb
ꝼıchıll, na ꝛaıb mechn eınıc beıc anb." "O cú-ꝛa ıꝛꝛ ın bún-ꝛa,
ıꝛ eb laıche ınꝛo aꝛ ꝛam lımm," ol Mebb. "Ꝺeıbchıꝛ ón," ol
Ꝼꝛaeb: "acaac cꝛı laa ⁊ ceoꝛa áıbcı anb." La ꝛobaın acꝛaıꝣ
Mebb. ba mmebul lee buıch bo naıb ócaıb cen bíab. Luıb co
Aılıll: ꝛaıbcı ꝼꝛıꝛꝛ: "Móꝛ-ꝣním boꝛınꝣenꝛam," ol ꝛı, "ınb óıc
anneccaıꝛ bonnáncacaꝛ bo bıc cen bíab." "Ꝺılıu buıc ımbeꝛc ꝼıbchılle," ol Aılıll. "Nı beꝛban ın ꝼobaıl bı a munciꝛ
ꝛeom ꝛecnu ın caıꝣe. Acaac cꝛı laa ⁊ ceoꝛa aıbcı anb,"
ol ꝛıꝛı, "aoc naꝛánaıꝛıꝣmeꝛ ınn aıbchı la bán-ꝛuılꝛı ınb
ⰾıac loꝣmaꝛ íꝛꝛ ın caꝣ." "Aꝛꝛaıb ꝛıu," ol Aılıll, "anac
bı na cúmıb co ꝼobaılceꝛ bóıb." Ꝼobaılceꝛ bóıb ꝼaꝛum ⁊ ba
maıc ꝛombob ꝛꝛıu, ⁊ anꝛaıc cꝛı laa ⁊ ceoꝛa aıbce anb ıaꝛ ꝛın
ꝛoꝛꝛ ın ꝛlebuꝣub.

Iꝛ ıaꝛum conacꝛab Ꝼꝛáech ıꝛꝛ a cech ımmacallamae, ⁊
ımchoemꝛaꝛ bó cıb bobnucaı. "Iꝛ maıch," ol ꝛe, "lımm céⰾıbe
ⰾıb-ꝛı." "Nı holc óm laꝛꝛ a ceꝣlab ꝼoꝛṁ ꝣnáꝛ, ol Aılıll: "ıꝛ ꝼeꝛꝛ
ꝼoꝛ coꝛmab olbáꝛ ꝼoꝛ bıꝣbáıl." "Anꝛım-nı bın," ol Ꝼꝛaech "naꝛ
ꝛechcmaın." Anaıc ıaꝛ ꝛın co cenb coıccıꝣıꝛ ıꝛꝛ ın bún, ⁊

pleasure of the two sons : a sleep of soothingness which it played was
the last son, on account of the heaviness of the birth ; so that it is from it
the third of the music has been named. The Boand awoke afterwards
out of the sleep. " I accept," she says, " thy three sons, O Uaithne,
of full ardour: since there is *Suan-traide*, and *Gen-traide*, and *Gol-*
traide on cows and women, who shall fall by Medb and Ailill, men
shall perish by the hearing of art from them."

They cease from the playing after that in the palace. " It is
rushing it has come," says Fergus. " Divide ye to us," says Froech
to his people, " the food: bring ye it into the house." Lothar went
upon the floor of the house : he divides to them the food. On his
haunches he used to divide each joint with his cleaver, and he used
not touch the eating of the meats: since he assumed dividing, food
never failed beneath his hand.

They were three days and three nights at playing of the chess, on
account of the abundance of precious stones in the household of
Froech. After that Froech addresses Medb : " It is well we have
been entertained with thee," he says: " I take not away thy stake from
the chess-board that there be not a decay of hospitality for thee in it."
" Since I am in this dun, this is the day which I deem quiet,"
says Medb. " This is reasonable," says Froech: " they are three
days and three nights¹⁴ in it." At this Medb starts up. It was a
shame with her that the youths were without food. She goes to
Ailill: she tells it to him. " A great deed we have done," she says ;
" the extern youths who have come to us, to be without food."
" Dearer to thee is playing of chess," says Ailill. " It hinders not
the distribution to his suite throughout the house. They are three
days and three nights in it," she says, " but that we perceived not the
night with the white light of the precious stones in the house." " Tell
them," says Ailill, " to cease from the chanting until distribution is made to them." Distribution is then made to them, and things
are pleasing to them; and they stayed three days and three nights in it
after that over the feasting.

It is after that Froech was called into the house of conversation,
and it is asked of him what had brought him. " A visit with you," he
says, " is pleasing to me." " Your company indeed is not displeasing
with the household," says Ailill: " your addition is better than your
diminution." " We shall stay then," says Froech, " another week."

torrunḋ ḋóib ceċ oen-lá ḋoċum in ḋúine. Ḋoraiʒtir Connaċta ḃi an ḋécrin. ba imneḋ la Fraeċ cen acallaim na inʒine, reċ ba hé lerr notṁbert.

Laιchen anḋ atraiʒ ḋeuḋ aiḋċe ḋo inlut ḋo'nḋ abainḋ. Ir hé tan ḋolluiḋ rón ⁊ a hinailt ḋo inḋlut. Ʒaibiḋ-rom al láim-ri. "An ꝼi m'acallaim," ol re: "ir tú ḋo roaċtamar." "Ir ꝼoċen limra ém," ol inḋ inʒen : "ma ċotírrinḋ, ni ċumʒaim ní ḋuitt." Ceirt, in eláꝶa lim?" ol re. "Ni élub," ol ri, "or iram inʒen ríʒ ⁊ ríʒna. Ni ꝼil ḋo t'ḋaiḋbri-riu naċ immeta-ra o m' muntir; ⁊ biḋ hé mo ċhoʒa-ra ban ḋul ċucut-ra: ir tu roċharur. Ocur beir-riu lat inḋ or-nairc-re," ol inḋ inʒen, "⁊ biḋ etronḋ ḋo ċomarċhu. Ḋorrat mo maċhair bam-ra," ol ri, "ḋi a tairciḋ, ⁊ arbeir ir corroḋallḋur im muḋu." Ceit ban ceċtar ḋe aleċ iar rain.

"Attaʒur-ra," ol Ailill, "eluḋ inna hinʒine ucut la Fróeċ, ce ḋoberċhá bó 'n inmaiḋe ⁊ ḋo táireḋ arṁ ḋoċum con a ċeċrai ḋo ċobair ḋún oc on Taín." Ḋoċaet Froeċ cuccu irr a teċn immacaḋmae. "In cocur ꝼil liḃ ?" ol Fraeċ. "Ḋotallꝼa-ru inḋi," ol Ailill. "In tiberaiḋ bam-ra ꝼorn inʒin ?" ol Fraeċ. "Immanaiccet inc ꝼlúaiʒ ḋoberċhar," ol Ailill, "ḋia tuca tinnrcra amail arberċhar." "Rotbia," ol Fráeċ, "Trí ꝼichit eċn ḋuḃ-ʒlarr bam-ra," ol Ailill "con am beilʒiḃ óir ꝼriu, ⁊ ḃi laulʒaiċ ḋeec cummbleʒitar óln airr o ceċ ae, ⁊ laéʒ ꝼinḋ, ói-ḋerʒ la ceċn ae ; ⁊ tuiḃeċt ḋuit limm co t'lín uile ⁊ co t' aer chíúil ḋo ċhaḃair innam bó a Cuailnʒiu ; ⁊ ḋoḃerċhar mo inʒen-ra ḋuit áct cocír." "Ḋoċhonʒu-ra tar mo rciaċ ⁊ tar mo ċlaiḃeḃ ⁊ oar m' ꝼrelam, ni ċhibrinḋ i tinḋrcra ciḃ Meiḃi inrin." Ḋoċinʒ uaḋaiḃ ar a taiʒ iarum. Immornacaillet iarum Ailill ⁊ Meḃb. "Foarbbiba roċaiḃen immunḋ ḋe riʒaiḃ hErenḋ ḋia ruca rom inn inʒin. Aní ir maiċ—ꝼuairrem inn a ḃeʒaiḋ ⁊ marḃam roċetoir reriu rorruma ḃine rornn." "Ir liaċ ón," ol Meḃb ⁊ ir meċhn einiċ ḋúnn." "Ni ba meċn einiʒ ḋúnn : ni ba meċn eniċ ḋún," ol Ailill, "tuċt aranḃalꝼar-ra."

They stay after that till the end of a fortnight in the dun, and they have a hunt every single day towards the dun. The Connachta used to come to view them. It was a trouble with Froech not to have a conversation with the daughter: besides, it was the benefit which brought him.

A certain day he starts up at the end of night for washing to the river[15]. It is the time she had gone and her maid for washing. He takes her hand. "Stay for my conversing," he says: "it is thou we have come for." "I am delighted truly," says the daughter: "if I were to come, I can do nothing for thee." "Query, would'st thou elope with me?" he says. "I will not elope," she says, "for I am a king and a queen's daughter. There is nothing of thy display that I have not learned from my family: and it shall be my choice accordingly to go to thee: it is thou I have loved. And take thou with thee this ring," says the daughter, "and it shall be between us for a token. My mother gave it to me to put it by, and I shall say it is that I put it astray." Each of them accordingly goes apart after that.

"I very much fear," says Ailill, "the eloping of yon daughter with Froech, though she would be given to him on solemn pledge that he would come towards us with his cattle for aid to us at the Spoil.[16]" Froech goes to them into the house of conversation. "Is it a whisper ye have?" says Froech. "Thou would'st fit in it," says Ailill. "Will ye give me your daughter?" says Froech. "The hosts will clearly see she shall be given," says Ailill, "if thou would'st give a dowry as shall be named." "Thou shalt have it," says Froech. "Sixty black-grey steeds to me, with their bits of gold to them, and twelve milch cows, so that there be milked liquor of milk from each of them, and an ear-red, white calf with each of them: and thou to come with me with all thy force and with thy musicians for bringing of the cows from Cuailnge: and my daughter shall be given thee provided thou shouldst come." "I swear by my shield and by my sword, and by my accoutrement, I would not give that in dowry even of Medb." He went from them out of the house then. Ailill and Medb then hold a conversation. "It shall drive at us several of the kings of Eriu around us if he should carry off the daughter. What is good—let us dash after him, and let us slay him forthwith, before he may inflict destruction upon us." "It is a pity this," says Medb, "and it is a decay of hospitality for us." "It shall not be a decay of hospitality for us, it shall not be a decay of hospitality for us, the way that I shall prepare it."

Doċaeꞇ Ailill ⁊ Meḋḃ iꞃ aꞃ ꞃꞁꞃ-ċeċ. "Ꞇiaꞃam aꞃꞃ," ol
Ailill, "con accamaꞃ na mmil-chona oc coꞃꞃunꝺ, com meꝺón lái
⁊ ꝺombꞇaꞃ ꞃoꞇcha. Ꞇiaꞃaiꞇ aꞃꞃ uili iaꞃum ꝺo'nꝺ abainn ḃi a
poꞇhꞃucuꝺ. "Aꝺꞃiaꝺaꞃ ꝺam," ol Ailill, "aꞇ maich in uꞃꞁu.
Ꞇaiꞃ iꞃꞃ inꝺ linn iꞃea, con accamaꞃ ꝺo ꝼnám." "C'inꝺaꞃ na
linꝺi-ꞃe?" ol ꞃe. "Ní ꝼecamaꞃ naċn ꝺoꝺainꞃ inꞇi," ol Ailill, "⁊
iꞃ comꞇiꞃ poꞇhꞃucuꝺ inꞇi." Ꞃaꞇaiꝺ a éꞇaċ ꝺe iaꞃum ⁊ ꞇeiꞇ inꞇi, ⁊
ꝼacbaiꝺ a cꞃiꞃꞃ ꞇúaꞃ. Oꞃlaiꞃiꝺ Ailill iaꞃum a boꞃꞃán ḃi a óiꞃ, ⁊ bói
inꝺ oꞃꝺ-naꞃc anꝺ. Aꞇaꞃeuin Ailill iaꞃum. "Ꞇaiꞃchi, a Meḋḃ,"
ol Ailill. Ꝺocháeꞇ Meḋḃ iaꞃum. "Inn aiꞇhċein ꞃin?" ol Ailill.
"Aiꞇꞃen," ol ꞃi. Foꞃceiꞃꝺ Ailill iꞃꞃ inn abainꝺ ꞃíꞃ. Ꞃoaiꞃiꞃeꞃꞇaꞃ
Fꞃáeċ anꞁ ꞃin. Conaccai ní ꝺolleblainꞃ inꞇ écne aꞃ a ꝺenꝺ ⁊
ꞃabꞃuꞃ inn a beulu. Foċeiꞃꝺ beꝺꞃ cucai ⁊ ꞃaibiꝺ a óileꝺ, ⁊
ꝺoꞇháeꞇ ꝺoꞇum ꞇíꞃi, ⁊ ꝺombeiꞃ im maꞃin ꝺiamaiꞃ im bꞃúꞃ na
habanꝺ. Ꝺocháeꞇ ꝺo ꞇuiꝺeċꞇ aꞃꞃ inꝺ uꞃꞁi iaꞃum. "Na ꞇaiꞃ,"
ol Ailill, "co ꞇuoa ꞃꞃóꞃb ꝺam ḃi'n ċaiꞃꞇenꝺ ꞇall ꝼil im bꞃuuꝺ na
habanꝺ: iꞇ ailꝺi lim a ꝺaeꞃa." Ꞇeiꞇ ꞃum aꞃꞃ iaꞃum, ⁊ bꞃiꞃꞃiꞃ
ꞃeꞃca ḃi'n ċꞃunꝺ ⁊ ꝺambeiꞃ ꞃi a aiꞃꞃ ꞇaꞃꞃ inn uꞃꞁi. Ba heꝺ
iaꞃum aꞇeꞃe Finꝺ-abꞃaꝺ: "Naċ álainꝺ aꞇċiꝺ?" Ba haibiu lee
Fꞃóech ꝺo acꞃin ꞇaꞃ ꝺub-linꝺ: in coꞃꞃ ꝺo ꞃoꞃꞁi, ⁊ in ꞃolc ꝺo
ꞃoꝺilli, inꝺ aiꞃeꝺ ꝺo ċumꞇachꞇai, inꞇ ꝼúil ꝺo ꞃoꞃlaꞃꞃi: iꞃꞃ he
móeꞇ-óꞃlaċ cen loċꞇ, cen anim, con aꞃaiꝺ ꝼoꝺael, ꝼoꞃleꞇhain:
iꞃ hé ḃiꞃiuꝺ, ḃianim: in ċꞃaeb coꞃ na caeꞃaiḃ ḃeꞃꞃaiḃ eꞇeꞃ inꝺ
bꞃaꞃiꞇ ⁊ inn aꞃiꝺń ꞃil. Iꞃꞃ eꝺ aꞇḃeꞃeꝺ Finꝺ-abaiꞃ no conꝼacca
ní ꞃoꞃaiꞃꞃeꝺ leꞃ ná ꞇꞃian ꝺo cꞃuꞇ.

Iaꞃ ꞃain ꝺocuiꞃeꝺaꞃ na cꞃaeba ꝺóiḃ aꞃꞃ inꝺ uꞃꞁiu. "Iꞇ
ꞃéꞃꝺái ⁊ iꞇ áilꝺi na caeꞃa: ꞇuc ꞇóꞃmac ḃún ꝺíḃ." Ꞇéiꞇ aꞃꞃ
aꞇeꞃꞃuċ combúi im meꝺón inꝺ uꞃꞁi. Ꞃaibꞇi in beiꞃꞇ aꞃꞃ inꝺ
uꞃꞁi. "Ꝺomiceꝺ claiꝺeb uaiḃ," ol ꞃe, ⁊ ní ꞃabai poꞃꞃ in ꞇíꞃ
peꞃ nolamaꝺ a ꞇabaiꞃꞇ ꝺó aꞃ omun Ailella ⁊ Meḋba. Iaꞃ ꞃin
ꞃaꞇaiꝺ Finꝺ-abaiꞃ a heꞇaċ, ⁊ poċeiꞃꝺ beꝺꞃ iꞃꞃ inn uꞃꞁe coꞃꞃ in
chlaiꝺiuḃ. Ꝺolleici a haꞇhaiꞃ ꞃleꞃ cóiꞃ-ꝼinꝺ ḃi anuaꞃ ꞃouꞇn
auꞃchoꞃa, col luiꝺ ꞇꞃe ꝺꝺ ꞇꞃꞁiꞃꞃ ⁊ con ḃoꞃaꞃaiḃ Fꞃóech inn a
láim in ꞃꞁꞃ. Foꞃceiꞃꝺ ꞃibe iꞃꞃ a ꞇíꞃ ꞃúaꞃ in ꞃꞁꞃ, ⁊ am mꞁꞁ in a

Ailill and Medb go into the palace. "Let us go away," says
ill, "that we may see the chase-hounds at hunting till the middle
the day, and until they are tired." They all go off afterwards to
river to bathe themselves. "It is declared to me," says Ailill,
hat thou art good in water[17]. Come into this flood, that we may see
y swimming." "What is the quality of this flood?" he says.
We know not anything dangerous in it," says Ailill, "and bathing in
is frequent." He strips his clothes off him then, and goes into it, and
e leaves his girdle above. Ailill then opens his purse behind him, and
ie ring was in it. Ailill recognises it then. "Come here, O Medb,"
ays Ailill. Medb goes then. "Dost thou recognise that?" says
.ilill. "I do recognise," she says. Ailill flings it into the river
.own. Froech perceived that matter. He sees something—the
almon leaped to meet it, and caught it into its mouth. He (Froech)
gives a bound to it, and he catches its jole, and he goes to land, and
ie brings it to a lonely spot on the brink of the river. He proceeds to
come out of the water then. "Do not come," says Ailill, "until thou
shalt bring me a branch of the rowan-tree yonder, which is on the brink
of the river: beautiful I deem its berries." He then goes away and
breaks a branch off the tree and brings it at his back over the water.
The remark of Find-abair then was: "Is it not beautiful he looks?"
Exceedingly beautiful she thought it to see Froech over a black pool:
the body of great whiteness, and the hair of great loveliness, the face of
beauty, the eye of great greyness: and he a soft youth without fault,
without blemish, with a below-narrow, above-broad face: and he
straight, blemishless: the branch with the red berries between the
throat and the white face. It is what Find-abair used to say, that by
no means had she seen any thing that could come up to him half or
third for beauty.

After that he throws the branches to them out of the water. "The
berries are mellow and are beautiful; bring us an addition of them."
He goes off again until he was in the middle of the water. The serpent catches him out of the water. "Let a sword come to me from
you," he says; and there was not on the land a man who would dare
to give it to him through fear of Ailill and of Medb. After that Find-
abair strips off her clothes, and gives a leap into the water with the
sword. Her father lets fly a sharp-point spear at her from above, a shot's
throw, so that it passes through her two tresses, and that Froech

chάeb. Lecuιb όn cὸ poṅξabaιl ceneleṅ ιmbeṗcα ξaιṗcιb, col
luιb cαṗṗ ιn clαċc coṗcṗa ⁊ cṗeṗ ιn léιne bάι ιm αιlιll. Lαṗṗιn
coceιṗξec ιnb όιc lα αιlιll. Dοċάec Fιnb-αbaιṗ aṗṗ ιnb uιṗcιu, ec
ṗacbaιb ιn clαιbeb ιl lάιm Fṗaeċ; ⁊ comben a chenb be'n mίl com
baι poṗ a chόιeb, ⁊ bobeṗc am mίl leιṗṗ bοċum cίṗe. Iṗ be acά
Dub-lιnb Fṗaeċ ιm bṗeιb, ι cίṗιb Connaċc. Ceιc αιlιll ⁊ Mebb
ιn an bύn ιaṗum.

"Mόṗ ξnίm boṗιṅξenṗam," ol Mebb. "Iṗṗ ιnnaιċṗeċ." ol
αιlιll, "an boṗιṅξenṗam ṗιṗ ιn ṗeṗ: ιnb ιnξen, ιmmoṗo," ol ṗe,
"acbélαc a béoιl ṗιbe ιm baṗaċ babaιξ, ⁊ nι ba cιnṁ bṗeιċe ιn
chlaιbιb beιċιṗ bι. Dencaṗ ṗoċṗucub lιb bo'nb [ṗ]ιṗ-ṗa .ι. en-
bṗuιċen úṗṗaιlle ⁊ cάṗnα ṗamaιṗcι bo ιnbaṗξξaιn ṗo ċάl ⁊ beúιl
⁊ a chabaιṗc ιṗṗ ιn ṗoċṗucub." Dοξnίc uιle anί ṗιn amaιl
aṗbeṗc ṗom. α choṗnaιṗι ιaṗum ṗemι ṗιum bochum ιn bύιne.
Sennaιc bι[n] conιb abbab cṗιcha ṗeṗ bι ṗaιn-chaemaιb αιlellα aṗ.
ṁṗeċcaι. Dοċaec ιaṗum ιṗ ιn bύn ⁊ ceίc ιṗṗ ιn ṗoċṗucub. Cone-
ṗaιξ ιn ban-ċuιṗe ιmbι oc on babaιξ bι amblιch ⁊ bια ṗolcub a
chιnb. Dobṗech aṗṗ ιaṗum ⁊ boξnίc beṗξuċ.

Cocualacaṗ nί an ξol-ξaιṗe ṗoṗ Cṗuaċnaιb. Conaccaṗ na cṗί
cόιcαc ban con ιnaṗaιb coṗcṗaιb, co cenbaṗṗaιb uanιbιb, co
mιlechaιb aṗξξaιc ṗoṗ an bόιcιb. Cιαξaιṗ ċuccu bo ṗιṗ-ṗcél
bύṗ cιb ṗoċάιnṗec. "Fṗaeċ mac Ibaιch," ol ιn ben, "mac-
bṗeιccel ṗιξ Sίben hEṗenb." Lα ṗιn ṗoċluιnecaṗ Fṗaech aṅ
ξol-ξaιṗe. "Doméόcbaιb aṗṗ," ol ṗe, ṗι a muncιṗ. "Ξol mo
maċaṗ-ṗa ιnṗo ⁊ bancṗochca boιnnι." Cocabaιṗ ιmmaċ lα
ṗobaιn ⁊ beṗaιṗ cucu. Dοċιaξaιc na mnά ιmmι ⁊ beṗbaιc uabιb
ιṗ Sίb Cṗuaċan.

Conaccacaṗ nί ιn cṗάch nόna aṗn a bάṗach; bochάec ⁊
coιca ban ιmme, ιṗṗ é uάξ-ṗlάn cen όn, cen anιm; comaeṗa,
combelba, comaιllι, comċάιnι, comchόṗaι, comċṗocha, con ecoṗc
ban Sίbe ιmpu, con na bάι aιchξne neιċ ṗeċ alaιle bίb.
bec nab muċċά bόιne ιmpu. Scaṗṗac ιn boṗuṗ ιnb lιṗṗ. αcnα-
ξac aṅ ξol oc bul úab, co coṗaṗcaṗ na bάιnι bacaṗ ιṗ ιnb lιṗṗ
caṗ cenb. Iṗ be acά ξol-ξaιṗe ban Sίbe lα aéṗ cίuιl hEṗenb.

caught the spear in his hand. He shoots the spear into the land up, and the monster in his side. He lets it fly with a charge of the methods of playing of championship, so that it goes over the purple robe and through the shirt that was about Ailill. At this the youths who were with Ailill rise to him. Findabair goes out of the water and leaves the sword in Froech's hand; and he cuts his head of the monster, so that it was on its side, and he brought the monster with him to land. It is from it is Dub-lind Froech in Brei, in the lands of the Connachta. Ailill and Medb go into their dun afterwards.

"A great deed is what we have done," says Medb. "It is lamentable," says Ailill, "what we have done to the man; the daughter, however, he says—her flesh shall perish to-morrow at once, and it shall not be the guilt of bringing of the sword that shall be for her. Let a bath be made by you for this man, namely, broth of fresh bacon and the flesh of a heifer[18] to be minced in it, under adze and axe, and he to be brought into the bath." All that thing was done as he said. His trumpeters then before him to the dun. They play then until thirty men of the special friends of Ailill die for pleasureableness. He goes then into the dun and he goes into the bath. The female company rise around him at the vat for ablution and for washing of his head. He was brought out of it then and a bed was made.

They heard something—the lament-cry on Cruachu. There were seen the three fifty women with purple tunics, with green head-dresses, with pins of silver on their wrists. A messenger is sent to them to learn to know what they had bewailed. "Froech, son of Idath," says the woman, "boy-pet of the king of the *Sidè* of Eriu." At this Froech heard their lament-cry. "Lift me out of it," he says to his people. "This is the cry of my mother and of the women of Boand." He is lifted out at this, and he is brought to them. The women come around him and bring him from them into the Sid of Cruachu[19].

They saw something—the time of none on the morrow he comes and fifty women around him, and he quite whole, without stain and without blemish; of equal age (the women), of equal figure, of equal beauty, of equal fairness, of equal symmetry, of equal form, with the dress of women of the *Sidè* about them, so that there was no knowing of one beyond the other of them. Little but persons were suffocated around them. They separate in the door of the *Less*. They give forth their lament on going from him, so that they moved the persons who were in the *Less* excessively. It is from it is the lament-cry of the women of the *Sidè*[20] with the musicians of Eriu.

Ceic ꞃeom ιaꞃum ιꞃ ιn ḃún. Aᴛaꞃeᴣaᴛ ιnᴛ ꝼluaɪᴣ húιlι aꞃ a
chenꝺ ⁊ ꝼeꞃaιᴛ ꝼaιlᴛι ꝼꞃιꞃꞃ, amaιl ʙaꝺ a ꝺomun aιle chιꞃꞃaꝺ.
Aᴛꞃaιᴣ Aιlιll ⁊ Meꝺꝺ ⁊ ꝺoᴣnιaᴛ aιᴛhꞃιᴣıṅ ꝺó ꝺo'nꝺ eꞃ ꝺoꞃıṅᴣenꞃaᴛ
ꝼꞃιꞃ, ⁊ ꝺoᴣnιaᴛ choꞃι. Ᵹaιḃᴛhιꞃ ꝼleꝺuᴣuꝺ leu ꝺaꝺaιᴣ. Conᴣaιꞃ
ꝼꞃáeᴄ ᴣιlla ꝺι a munᴄιꞃ: "Aιꞃᴣ aꞃꞃ," ol ꞃe, "coꞃ ιn maᴣιn ιn
ʙeoᴄaꝺ-ꞃa ιꞃꞃ ιn uιꞃce. Eꞃcne ꞃoꞃaᴄʙaꞃa anꝺ—ꝺonuc ꝺo ꝼιnꝺ-
aʙaιꞃ, ⁊ ιꞃʙʙaꝺ ꝼeꞃꞃιn ꝼaιꞃ: ⁊ ꞃonaιᴄeꞃ ιnᴛ éᴄne lee commaιᴛh,
⁊ aᴛa ιnꝺ oꞃꝺ-naꞃc ιm meꝺón ιnꝺ éιcnι. Iꞃ ꝺoιᴣ lιm con ꝺeꞃꞃaꞃ
ᴄucann ιnnoᴄᴛ." Ᵹaꝺᴄhuꞃ meꞃca ⁊ aꞃuꞃꝺeιᴄᴄeᴛ cꝺola ⁊ aꞃꝼιcι.
Aꞃʙeꞃᴛ Aιlιll ιaꞃum: "Cucaιꝺ mo ꝼꝺoᴄu ꝺam-ꞃa húιlι," ol ꞃe.
Doʙꞃeᴛha ꝺó ιaꞃum com ʙaᴛaꞃ aꞃ a ʙelaιʙ. "Amꞃa, amꞃa," ol
cáᴄ. "Ᵹaιꞃιꝺ ꝺam-ꞃa ꝼιnꝺ-aʙaιꞃ," ol ꞃe. Doᴄaeᴛ ꝼιnꝺ-aʙaιꞃ
cucaι ⁊ coιca ιnᴣen ιmꞃe. "A ιnᴣen," ol Aιlιll, "ιnꝺ oꞃꝺ-naꞃc ʙo
ꞃaᴛu ꞃ-[ꞃ]a ʙuιᴄ-ꞃιu ιnuꞃaιꝺ—ιn maιꞃ laᴛᴛ? Cuc ʙam conʙacca-
ᴛaꞃ ιnꝺ óιc. Roᴛʙιa-ꞃu ιaꞃum." "Nι ꝼeᴛaꞃ," ol ꞃι, "cιꝺ ʙeꞃnaꝺ
ʙe." ꝼιnᴛa-ꞃu ém," ol Aιlιll: "ιꞃ eιcenꝺ a cunᴣιꝺ, no ᴄhanιm ʙo
ʙul aꞃ ʙo ᴄuꞃꞃ." "Nι cónꞃιu," ol ιnꝺ óιc; "aᴄá moꞃ ʙι maιᴄh
anꝺ chena." "Nι ꝼaιl nι ʙo'm ꝼéᴄaιʙ-ꞃe naʙ ᴄeι ʙaꞃ cenꝺ na
hιnᴣιne," ol ꝼꞃaeᴄ, "ʙaιᴣ ꞃuc ιn claιʙeʙ ʙam ʙo ᴣιull ʙo'm an-
maιn." "Nι ꝼuιl laᴛ ʙo ꝼéᴄaιʙ nι noʙoᴄᴄaιn manι aιꞃce úaιʙι
ιnꝺ oꞃꝺ-naιꞃc," ol Aιlιll. "Nι comᴄhá-ꞃa cumanᴣ ʙι a ᴛaʙaιꞃ,"
ol ιnꝺ ιnᴣen: "an ꞃoᴄaꞃa ʙaᴣne ʙιm-ꞃa." Cuṅᴣu ʙιa ᴄonᴣeꞃ mo
ᴄúaιᴄ, aᴛʙelaᴛ ʙo ʙeóιl, menι aιꞃce uaιᴄ," ol Aιlιll. "Iꞃ aιꞃe
conʙeᴣaꞃ ᴄucuᴛ uaιꞃ ιꞃ ʙecmaιᴣ, aꞃ ꞃoꞃeᴄaꞃ-ꞃa co ᴄιꞃaᴛ na
ʙóιnι aᴛʙaᴄhaᴛaꞃ o ᴄhoꞃꞃuch ʙomuιn, nι ᴄhιc aꞃꞃ ιn maᴣιn ιn
ꞃoláꝺ." "Nι conᴛιᴄꞃa ꞃι móιn na aʙlaιc ᴄhꞃa," ol ιnꝺ ιnᴣen:
"ιn ꞃeᴄ conneᴣaꞃ anꝺ—ᴄιaᴣ-ꞃa conʙaᴛuᴄ-ꞃa, uaιꞃ ιꞃ ᴄꞃιcc conʙeᴣaꞃ." "Nι ꞃeᴣa-ꞃu," ol Aιlιll: "ᴄaéᴛ neᴄ úaιᴛ ιmmoꞃo ʙι
a ᴛaʙaιꞃᴛ."

ꝼóιʙιꞃ ιnꝺ ιnᴣen a ιnaιlᴛ ʙι a ᴛaʙaιꞃᴛ, "Conᴣu-ꞃa ʙo ʙιa ᴄoṅ-
ᴣeꞃ mo ᴄúaᴄ, ʙιa ꞃaιᴣʙιᴄheꞃ nι conʙeꝺ-ꞃa ꝼo ᴄ' ᴄumaᴄᴄa-ꞃu ʙa
ꞃíꞃe, ʙιan ʙumꞃoιʙ ꝼoꞃ ꞃaꞃ-ol moᴣꞃeιꞃ. "Nι conᴣeʙ-ꞃa ón
ʙíᴄ-ꞃu ón cιʙ coꞃꞃ ιnn eᴄaιꞃe ᴄheιꞃι, ma ꝼoᴣaʙᴛaꞃ ιnꝺ oꞃꝺ-naꞃc,"
ol Aιlιll. Doʙeꞃᴛ ιaꞃum ιnꝺ ιnaιlᴛ ιn meιꞃ ιꞃꞃ a ꞃιᴣ-ᴄeᴄ ⁊ ιnᴛ

He then goes into the dun. All the hosts rise before him, and bid welcome to him, as if it were from another world he were coming. Ailill and Medb arise and do penance to him for the attack[21] they had made at him, and they make peace. Feasting commences with them at once. Froech calls a servant of his suite: "Go off," he says, "to the spot in which I went into the water. A salmon I left there—bring it to Find-abair, and let herself take charge over it; and let the salmon be well broiled by her, and the ring is in the centre of the salmon. I expect it will be set to us[22] to-night." Inebriety seizes them, and music and amusement delight them. Ailill then said: "Bring ye all my gems to me," he says. They were brought to him then, so that they were before him. "Wonderful, wonderful," says every one. "Call ye Find-abair to me," he says. Find-abair goes to him, and fifty daughters around her. "O daughter," says Ailill, "the ring I gave to thee last year—does it exist with thee? Bring it to me that the youths may see it. Thou shalt have it afterwards." "I do not know," she says, "what has been done about it." "Ascertain then," says Ailill: "it must be sought, or thy soul must depart thy body." "It is by no means worth," say the youths: "there is much of value there without it." "There is nought of my gems that will not go for the daughter," says Froech, "because she brought me the sword for pledge of my soul." "There is not with thee of gems anything that should aid thee unless she returns the ring from her," says Ailill. "I have by no means the power to give it," says the daughter; "what thou mayest like do it in regard to me." "I swear[23] the oath my territory swears, thy flesh shall perish unless thou returnest it from thee," says Ailill. "It is why it is asked of thee, because it is difficult, for I know until the persons who have died from the beginning of the world come, it comes not out of the spot in which it was flung." "Now it shall not come with gift or liking," says the daughter: "the gem which is asked in the case—I go that I may bring it to thee, since it is keenly it is asked." "Thou shalt not go," says Ailill; "but let one go from thee to bring it."

The daughter sends her maid to bring it. "I swear as an oath the oath of my territories, if it shall be found, I shall by no means be under thy power any longer, though I should be at great drinking continually." "I shall by no means bring it as a fault against thee, namely—that it were to the groom thou should'st go, if the ring is found," says éicne ṗonaiċe ṗuiṗṗe, iṡ ó ṗuilleċca ṗo mil boṡniċh laṡṡ inn inṡin co maiċh ⁊ bói inb oṗb-naṗc óiṗ ṗoṗṗ inb eicni anuaṡ. Doṗ-ṗeccai Ailill ⁊ Mebb. Da lei conbeṗcaṗ aṗ Ḟṗaeċ ⁊ boéccai a boṗ-ṗán. "Inbaṗ lemm iṡ la ceiṗc ṗoṗacbuṗ mo ċṗiṡṡ," ol Ḟṗáeċ. "Ḟoṗ ḟíṗ bo ḟlaċa," ol Ḟṗaeċ, "apaiṗ cib beṗnaiṗ b' inb oṗb-naiṗc." "Ni ċelcaṗ oṗuc ón," ol Ailill: "lemṗa inb oṗb-naṗc ṗobai iċ' boṗṗan, ⁊ ṗoṗecaṗ iṡ Ḟinb-abaiṗ boṗac buic. Iṡ iaṗum ṗolaṗa iṡṡ in Duib-linni. Ḟoṗ ḟíṗ ċhainiċ ⁊ ċ'anma, a Ḟṗoeiċ, aṗnbiċh cia cṗuch aṗṗalab a ċabaiṗc aṗṗ." "Ni celcaṗ ṗoṗc-ṗu," ol Ḟṗaéċ. "A cec la ṗoṗṗuaṗ-ṗa inb oṗb-naiṗc in boṗuṗ inb liṗṗ, ṗoṗecaṗ ṗoṗu ṗéc cáeim. Iṡ aiṗi boṗṗoiṗeċc-ṗa colleiṗ im' boṗṗán. Roċcualaṗ-[ṗ]a al laa boċoab bo'nb uiṗciu inb inṡen ṗoblaa immab oc a iaṗmoṗaċc. Aṗbeṗc-ṗa ṗṗie: "cia lóṡ ṗombia lacc aṗ a ṗaṡbail?" Aṗ-beṗc-ṗi ṗṗim-ṗa bombéṗab ṗeiṗċṁ bliabna bam-ṗa. Ecmainṡ niṗṗaṡbuṗ-[ṗ]a immṁm: ṗoṗ-ṗáċbuṗ i m' ċhaiṡ bi m' éiṗ. Ni comaiṗnecmaṗ-ni co comaiṗnec-maṗ oc cabaiṗc in ċlaibib iṡṡ inb abainb i m' láim-ṗe. Iaṗ ṗin aċċonbaṗc-ṗa in can ṗaoṗlaici-ṗiu inṁ boṗṗan ⁊ ṗollaiṗ inb oṗb-naiṗc iṡṡ in uiṗce, aċċonnaiṗc inn eicni boṗṗoeblainṡ aṗ a ċinb, coniboṡab inn a beolu. Ronṡabuṗ-[ṗ]a inn eicni iaṗum, caċnócaib iṡṡ inṁ bṗac, baṗoluṗ il láim na hinṡine. Iṡ hé inc eicne ṗin iaṗum ṗil ṗoṗṗ in méiṗ."

Ṡaibċhiṗ abmilliub ⁊ abampuṡub na ṗcel-ṗa iṡ ceṡlub. "Ni ṗ5iċuṗ-ṗa mo menmain ṗoṗ óclaċn aile in hEṗinn biaib-ṗiu," ol Ḟinb-abaiṗ. "Aṗocnaiṗc bó," ol Ailill ⁊ Mebb, "⁊ caiṗ ċucuṗṗni co ċ'búaib bo Cháin nam bó a Cuailinṡiu; ⁊ in can boṗeṡa-ṗu co ċ'búaib anaiṗ boṗibiṗi, ṗíbaib ṗinb [*recte* ṗunb?] inn aiḃi ṗin babaiṡ ⁊ Ḟinb-abaiṗ." Daṡén-ṗa aní ṗiu," ol Ḟṗáech. buic anb iaṗum co aṗn a baṗaċ. Ṡabaiṡ Ḟṗaeċ immi con a munciṗ. Cele-bṗaib iaṗum bo Ailill ⁊ Meibb. Documláic b'a cṗíchaib iaṗum.

Ecmonṡ ṗoṡacá a baé calleic. Canic a maċaiṗ ċuce. "Ni béoba bo ṗeccaṗ boċoaṗ: ṗoṗiṗṗe móṗn imnib buic," aṗ ṗi "Roṡacca ⁊ bo bai ⁊ bo cṗi meicc ⁊ bo ben conbaṗail oc Sléib Elpae. Acaac ceoṗa bae bíb in Albain cuaṗcaṗc la Cṗuchneḃu." "Ceṗc, ciḃ boṡen-ṗa?" ol ṗe ṗi a máchaiṗ. "Doṡena neṗhċheċc

Ailill. The maid then brought the dish into the palace, and the broiled salmon on it, and it dressed under honey which was well made by the daughter: and the ring of gold was on the salmon from above. Ailill and Medb view it. After that Froech looks at it, and looks at his purse. " It seems to me it was for proof I left my girdle," says Froech. "On the truth of the sovereignty," says Froech, "say what thou did'st about the ring." "This shall not be concealed on thee," says Ailill; "mine is the ring which was in thy purse, and I knew it is Find-abair gave it to thee. It is therefore I flung it into the Duib-linne. On the truth of thy hospitality and of thy soul, O Froech, declare thou what way the bringing of it out happened." "It shall not be concealed on thee," says Froech. "The first day I found the ring in the door of the *Less*, I knew it was a lovely gem. It is for this reason I put it up industriously in my purse. I heard, the day I went to the water, the daughter who put it out a-looking for it. I said to her—'What reward shall I have at thy hands for the finding of it?' She said to me that she would give a year's love to me. It happened I did not leave it about me; I had left it in my house behind me. We met not until we met at the giving of the sword into my hand in the river. After that I saw the time thou opened'st the purse and flungest the ring into the water—I saw the salmon, which leaped for it, so that it took it into its mouth. I then caught the salmon, took it up in the cloak, put it into the hand of the daughter. It is that salmon accordingly which is on the dish."

The criticizing and the wondering at these stories begin in the household. "I shall not throw my mind on another youth in Eriu after thee," says Find-abair. "Bind thyself for it," say Ailill and Medb, " and come thou to us with thy cows to the Spoil of the Cows from Cuailnge; and when thou shalt come with thy cows from the East back, ye shall wed here that night at once and Find-abair." "I shall do that thing," says Froech. They are in it then until the morrow. Froech sets about himself with his suite. He then bids farewell to Ailill and Medb. They depart to their territories then.

It happened his cows were all stolen. His mother came to him. "Not active of journey hast thou gone; it shall cause much of trouble to thee," she says. "Thy cows have been stolen, and thy three sons, and thy wife[24], so that they are at the mountain of Elpa. Three cows of them are in Alba of the North with the Cruthnechi."

ѽı a cungıb: nı chaıbrea t'a[n]maın ѝorru," ol rı. "Rocbıac
baı lem-ra chena," ol rı. "Nımcha ron," ol re; "ѽoѽoıѽ ѝor
m'eıneѽ ꞇ ѝor m'anmaın aırec co Aılıll ꞇ co Meıѽb co m' búaıb
ѽo chaın nam bѽu a Cúalngıu." " Nı roѽebcar," ol a máchaır,
"a conѽaıꞁı." Ceıcı úaѽ ıarum la roѽaın.

Ѽoѽumlaı rom arr ıarum crıb nonbaraıb ꞇ ѝıѽ-ѽuaѽ ꞇ cú
lomna leu, col luıѽ hı crıѽ Ulaѽ, co comarnaıc rı Conall
Cernaѽ oc bennaıb baırѽı. Raѽıѽ a ѽeırc ѝrı rıѽe. "Nı bu
rırran buıc," ol re rıѽe, "anı arѽoccá. Arѽoccá mórn
ımnıѽ," ol re, "cıѽ anѽ ѽobeѽ ѽo menma." "Ѽommaır-re,"
ol Ѝraeѽ rı Conall, "coꞃ ѽıchır .lemm naѽ ѝé conarneccmar."
"Raꞁaѽ-ra óm," ol Conall Cernach. Ѽocumlac arr a crıur car
muır, car Saxoın cuarcerc, car muırn hıѽc, co cuarcerc
Langѽarѽ, coꞃ rancacar rleıbce Elpae. Conaccacar ѝracc na
caın oc ınꞁarıu ѽaéreѽ ar a cınѽ. "Cıaꞁam anѽerr," ol Conall,
"a Ѝróıch, con acalѽam ın mnaı chall, eɔ anac arn oıc runѽ."
Locar ıarum ѽı acalѽaım. Arberc-rı: "Can ѽuıb?" Ѽı ѝeraıb
hErenn," ol Conall. "Nı bu rırran ѽo ѝeraıb hErenn óm,
cıchcaın ın cırı-re. Ѽo ѝeraıb hErenѽ óm mo machaır-re.
Ѽomꞃaır ar conѽaılbı." "Arnıѽ nı bún ѽı arn ımcheѽcaıb.
C'ınnar ın cıre ѽonancamar?" "Cırꞃ ѽuaıꞁn, uachmar coꞃ
ócaıb anꞃıb, reꞁaıc ѝor cech lech ѽo chabaırc bó ꞇ ban ꞇ brac,"
ol rı. "Cıѽ ar nuıѽem cucrac?" ol Ѝraéѽ. "baı Ѝraéѽ
meıcc Iѽaıch a ıarchur hErenѽ, ꞇ a ben ꞇ a crı meıcc. Unre
a ben lar ın rıꞁ; onѽac a baı ırr ın cır ar ѝarꞃ belaıb."
"Ѽonꞃaır-nı ѽo ѽóbaır," ol Conall. "Ir bec mo ѽumaꞁꞁ aѽc
eolar namma." "Ir re Ѝraéѽ ınro," ol Conall, "ꞇ ıc ó a baı
cucca." "In caırırı lıb-rı ın ben?" ol rı. "Cıѽ caırırrı lınѽ
ın can ѽolluıѽ, ber nı caırırrı ıar cıaѽcaın." "ben caıѽıꞁı nam
báu—aırꞁıѽ aѽoѽum: errıѽ ѝrıe ѝor coırc: ѽı ѝeraıb hErenѽ
a cenel: ѽı Ulcaıb ınѽ̇aınrıuѽ̇."

Cıaꞁaıc co ruıѽıu : arѽaꞁaıbec ꞇ norlaınѽec ѽı, ꞇ ѝeraır

"Query, what shall I do?" he says to his mother. "Thou shalt do a non-going for seeking of them; thou would'st not give thy soul for them," she says. "Thou shalt have cows at my hands besides them." "Not so this," he says: "I have pledged my hospitality and my soul to go to Ailill and to Medb with my cows to the Spoil of the Cows from Cuailnge." "What thou seekest shall not be attained," says his mother. At this she goes from him then.

He then sets off with three enneads [nines] and a wood-cuckoo (hawk), and a hound of tie with them, until he goes to the territory of the Ulaid, so that he meets with Conall Cernach[26] at Benna Bairchi. He tells his quest to him. "What awaits thee," says the latter, "shall not be lucky for thee. Much of trouble awaits thee," he says, "though in it thy mind should be." "It occurred to me," says Froech to Conall, "that thou would'st come with me any time we might meet." "I shall go truly," says Conall Cernach. They set off the three [that is, the three nines] over sea, over Saxony of the North, over the Sea of Icht, to the north of the Longbards, until they reached the mountains of Elpa. They saw the woman of the herd at tending of sheep before them. "Let us go south," says Conall, "O Froech, that we may address the woman yonder, and let our youths stay here." They went then to a conversation. She said, "Whence are ye?" "Of the men of Eriu," says Conall. "It shall not be lucky for the men of Eriu truly—the coming to this country. From the men of Eriu too is my mother. Aid thou me on account of relationship." "Tell us something about our movements. What is the quality of the land we have come to?" "A grim, hateful land with troublesome youths, who go on every side for carrying off cows and women and captives," she says. "What is the latest thing they have carried off?" says Froech. "The cows of Froech, son of Idath, from the west of Eriu, and his wife and his three sons. Here is his wife with the king; here are his cows in the country in front of you." "Let thy aid come to us," says Conall. "Little is my power, save guidance only." "This is Froech," says Conall, "and they are his cows that have been carried off." "Is the woman constant in your estimation?" she says. "Though constant in our estimation the time she went, perchance she is not constant after coming." "The woman who frequents the cows—go ye to her; tell ye her your errand; of the men of Eriu her race; of the Ulaid exactly."

They come to her; they receive her, and they name themselves to

ꝼαιlcı ꝼᚱıu. "Cıch ıbꝼoꝛuıꝛech?" ol ꝛı. "Ꝼoꝛꝛoꝛꝑeꝋ ımneꝋ,"
ol Conall: "lem na baı, ┐ ın ben ꝼıl ıꝛ ınꝋ lıꝛꝛ." "Nı bu ꝛıꝛꝛαn
ꝋúıb ém," ol ꝛı, "ꝋul ꝼo ꝋıꝛımm ınna mna: anꝋꝛu ꝋúıb ceꝋ ꝛéꝋ"
ol ꝛı, "ınꝋ naıchıꝛ ꝼαıl oc ımbeᵹαıl ınꝋ lıꝛꝛ." "Nı mchíꝛ-aınm,"
ol Ꝼꝛαeꝋ: "nı caıꝛıꝛꝛı lımm, aꝋ aꝛıꝛı-ꝛıu lımm: ꝛoꝼeꝋαmαꝛ n'ım-
meꝛα, uaıꝛe ıꝛ ꝋı Ulcaıb ꝋuıc." "Can ꝋı Ulcaıb ꝋúıb?" ol ꝛı.
"huınꝛe Conall Ceꝛnach ꝛunꝋ, laeꝋ aꝛ ꝋeꝋ la Ulcu," ol Ꝼꝛαeꝋ.
Ꝼocheıꝛꝋ ꝛı ꝋı láım ım bꝛαᵹıc Conaıll Ceꝛnaıch. "Reıꝛꝛ ınꝋ oꝛᵹaın
hı ꝼechc-ꝛα," ol ꝛı, "uaıꝛe ꝋonꝋαmıc ꝛıꝋe; uaıꝛ ıꝛ ꝋo ꝛuıꝋe
ꝋoꝛaıꝛꝛᵹeꝛeꝋ oꝛᵹaın ın ꝋuını-ꝛea. Cıaᵹ-ꝛα αꝛꝛ," ol ꝛıꝛꝛı: "nı
beo ꝼꝛıꝛ̇ bleᵹon nam bó. Ꝼαıceꝋ ın leꝛꝛn oıbela: ıꝛ me
nonꝼαꝋα. Aꝛbéꝛ ıꝛ ꝋe ól ꝛoꝋmeꝋaꝛ ınꝋ lóıᵹ. Cıꝛcaı-ꝛı ıꝛꝛ ın
ꝋun, αꝋꝋ comcalaꝋ: ıꝛꝛ anꝋꝛu ꝋúıb ınꝋ naıꝋıꝛ ꝼαıl oc on ꝋún:
ꝋolleıceꝋαꝛ ıl-cꝛαꝋa ꝋı." "Reᵹmaı, amın," ol Conall.
Ꝼuabbꝛαıc ın leꝛꝛ: ꝼocheıꝛꝋꝋ ınꝋ naıchıꝛ beꝋᵹ ı cꝛıꝛꝛ Cónaıll
Ceꝛnaıᵹ, eꝋ oꝛᵹαıc ın ꝋun ꝛoꝋeꝋóıꝛ. Ceꝛꝛαıᵹıc ıαꝛum ın mnáı
┐ na cꝛı maccu, ┐ ꝋobeꝛαꝋ an aꝛ ꝋeꝋ ꝛéꝋ ın ꝋúıne, ┐ leıcıꝋ Conall
ın nachıꝛ αꝛꝛ a chꝛıꝛꝛ, eꝋ nı beꝛᵹenı neꝋꝋαꝛꝋe olc ꝼꝛı a ꝋéıle.
Eꝋ ꝋochıαᵹαꝋ ı cꝛích Cꝛuıchen-cuache, co ꝼαca ceoꝛα bú ꝋı am
buaıb aꝛꝛαıꝋe. Concullaꝋαꝛ ꝋo Ꝋún Ollαıꝋ meıc bꝛıuın ꝼꝛıu,
com baꝋαꝛ ın αıꝛꝋ hUaꝛ̇ Echach. Iꝛ anꝋ αꝋbach ᵹılla Chonaıll
oc cımmaın nam bó .ı. bıcne mac Laeᵹαıꝛe. Iꝛ ꝋe aꝋα Inbeꝛꝛ̇
bıcne oc benchuꝛ. Coꝋucꝛαꝋ am bu caꝛꝛ ılleı. Iꝛ anꝋ
ꝛolaꝛαꝋ an aꝋaꝛca ꝋíb conıꝋ ꝋe aꝋα Cꝛαchꝛ̇ bencoꝛ. Luıꝋ
Ꝼꝛαeꝋ αꝛꝛ ıαꝛum ꝋı a cꝛíꝋ ıαꝛum, ┐ a ben ┐ a meıcc, ┐ a ꝋaı
laıꝛꝛ, conluıꝋ la Aılıll ┐ Meıꝋb ꝋo Chaın nam bó a Cualꝛ̇ᵹıu.

her, and she bids welcome to them. "What has led you forth?" she says. "Trouble has led us forth," says Conall: "ours are the cows and the woman that are in the *Less*." "It shall not be lucky for you truly," she says, "the going up to the multitude of the woman; more troublesome to you than every thing," she says, "is the serpent which is at guarding of the *Less*." "She is not my country-name," says Froech; "she is not constant in my estimation; thou art constant in my estimation; we know thou wilt not lead us astray, since thou art of the Ulaid." "Whence of the Ulaid are ye?" she says. "This is Conall Cernach here, the bravest hero with the Ulaid," says Froech. She flings two hands around the throat of Conall Cernach. "The destruction has come in this expedition," she says, "since he has come to us; for it is to him the destruction of this dun has been prophesied. I shall go out of it," she says; "I shall not be at the milking of the cows. I shall leave the *Less* opened; it is I who close it. I shall say it is for drink the calves were sucking. Come thou into the dun, when they are sleeping; more troublesome to you is the serpent[26] which is at the dun; several tribes are let loose from it." "We shall go truly," says Conall. They attack the *Less*; the serpent darts a leap into the girdle of Conall Cearnach, and they plunder the dun at once. They save off then the woman and the three sons, and they carry away whatever was best of the gems of the dun, and Conall lets the serpent out of his girdle, and neither of them did harm to the other. And they come to the territory of the Cruithen-tuath, until they saw three cows of their cows in it. They drove off to Dun Ollaich[27] Meic Briuin with them, until they were in Ard hUan Echach. It is there Conall's gilla died at driving of the cows, that is, Biene son of Loegaire; it is from it is Inber Bicne at Benchor. They brought their cows over it thither. It is there they flung their horns off them, so that it is from it is Trachm Benchoir. Froech goes away then to his territory after, and his wife, and his sons, and his cows with him, until he goes with Ailill and Medb for the Spoil of the Cows from Cualnge.

TAIN BO FRAICH.

NOTES.

[1] Ꝑꞃoeɔ. In the Tain Bo Cuailngi, Leb. na hUidre, Froech's father is called Idad (= our Idath), but in later writings he is called Fidach. Some have supposed that it is from our Froech "Carn Froich" beside Rath Cruachan has been named. This, however, is a mistake, for the Carn has been called after Froech, son of Conall of Cruachu, as we learn from the Dind-senchus, "Book of Lecan," fol. 243, b. From the same account, as well as from the "Tain," Leb. na hUidre, we learn that our hero was drowned in a ford at Sliab Fuait, a mountain in the county of Armagh, the highest of the "Fews" mountains, by his brother demigod Cu Chulaind; and, being a demigod, that immediately after he was carried off by the *Sidè* into an adjoining hill, which, from that circumstance, has been called "Sid Fraich.".

[2] ɑ Síoɪb: That is, from the "*Sidè* immortals," not from the "Sid hills," which would be ɑ Síoɑɪb. There are in Irish two words, which must not be confounded; namely, Síꝺ, an artificial structure, within which has been laid, that is to say, dwells a deified mortal; the other, Síꝺe, which means that deity himself. The former is the Lat. *situs*, a substantive, gunated *sétu*; the latter is *situs*, an adjective, gunated, and with -*ya* termination, *sétya*. The verbal root is *si* -, " to enclose," "to mound." For the former compare Hor. lib. 3, Od. 30:—
"Regalique situ pyramidum altius;" and for the latter, Cic. de Leg. lib. 2, cap. 22:—"Declarat Ennius de Africano: Hic est ille *situs*. Vere: Nam *siti* dicuntur ii qui mortui sunt." The two forms occur in the following passage at the close of the *Serg-ligi*:—conɪꝺ ꝑꝓɪꞃ nɑ ɔɑɪobɪ ꞃɪn ɑɔbeꞃɑɔ nɑ hɑɪneolɑɪᵹ Síꝺe ⁊ ꝺéꞃ Síꝺe: so that it is to those apparitions the unlearned give the name *Sidè* and the class of *Sid*. That the ancient Irish held this *rationale* of the word ꞃíꝺ, " a residence for the immortals" (knowing nothing of the mythic ꞃíꝺe, a blast of wind), is clear from the following, the most ancient Irish passage on the subject: — Síꝺ móꞃ hɪɔɑɑm, conɪꝺ ꝺeꞃuɪꝺɪb non-

naınmnıȝċeṇ ᵭeṇ Sḟᵭe: "it is a large *Sid* (structure) in which we are, so that it is from it that we are called the class of SID." This is the explanation of the *Sidè* goddess to Condla Ruad, when inviting him away to the "Lands of the Living" (Leb. na hUidre). I may observe that the *Sidè* government in ancient Erin was of the same federal form as that of the secular government; that is, a presidential king with provincial and sub-kings. This is evident from several passages.

³ Ꝺo ᵬoınᵬ. Boand, who gave her name to the Boyne, was the daughter of Delbaeth, a chieftain of the mythological Tuatha de Danann, and wife of Nechtan. See her story, "Battle of Magh Lena," p. 90, note p., ed. O Curry.

⁴ Ꝼınᵬ-aᵬaıṇ. That is, "Bright-beam," not "bright-brow," as hitherto interpreted. The gen. of aᵬaıṇ, "eye-lash," not "eye-brow," is aᵬṇac, while that of aᵬaıṇ in Ꝼınᵬ-aᵬaıṇ is aᵬṇach, as will be seen further on. This aᵬaıṇ is declined like nacḣıṇ, a serpent (gen. nacḣṇach); comp. the Lat. *apricum.* Find-abair appears conspicuous in our great Irish Wiliad, "The Spoil of the Cows of Cualnge," which gives a graphic account of her warlike mother's seven years' raiding in the lands of Ulster.

⁵ Maȝ ᵬṇeȝ. That is, "Campus Bregum," not "Planities amœna." ᵬṇeȝ is gen. pl., the nom. sing. of which would be in Gaulish *Brex*, like *rix* (Ir. ṇíȝ), a *g*-stem. This plain extends from the Liffey to the Boyne. See O'Donovan's supplement to O'Reilly.

⁶ Ꝼınᵬ-ṇuını. What this highly prized metal or metallic compound was, has not yet been determined. In the "Feast of Bricriu," Leb. na hUidre, Medb says: "The difference between bronze and findruine is between Loegaire and Conall Cernach, and the difference again between findruine and red gold is between Conall Cernach and Cu Chulaind." For works of art, then, it stands in value between bronze and red gold.

⁷ Ꝺṇúıch. This word is a masc. *a*-stem = *druta*, and means a "buffoon," a "satirist," while the word for druid is ᵬṇuí, gen. ᵬṇuaᵬ, a *d*-stem. See my "Faeth Fiada" (Journal of the Hist. and Archæol. Association of Ireland, April, 1869, p. 305, note *v*).

⁸ Ꝺo Chṇuchnaıᵬ. This dat. plur. may be from either Cṇuachu or Cṇuachan, both of which forms occur as nom. sing., the former an *n*-stem, and the latter an *a*-stem. We may, then, here write the English form Cruachan, or Cruachna.

⁹ bᵱeı. Accus. Plural; see further on.

¹⁰ ın cɑıʒe. In the "Feast of Bricriu," Leb. na hUidre, this palace is thus described:—Seċc cuɑᵱbɑ ɑnb ⁊ ᵱeċn ımbɑbɑ o ᴄoın co ᵱᵱɑıʒ. Aıᵱınıċ cᵱebumɑ ⁊ ɑuᵱᵱcɑᵱcɑb beᵱʒ-ıbɑıᵱ. Cᵱı ᵱceıll cᵱebumɑ ı cɑulɑıċ ın cɑıʒe. Ceb bɑᵱɑċ co cuıʒı ᵱlınneb. Dı ᵱenıᵱcıᵱ bec ɑnb co comlɑcɑıb ʒlɑınıbıb ᵱᵱıu. Imbuı Aılellɑ ⁊ Mebbɑ ım mebon ın cıʒe; ɑıᵱınıʒ ɑıᵱʒıbı ımpe ⁊ ᵱceıll cᵱebumɑ ⁊ ᵱleᵱc ɑıᵱʒıc oc onb ɑıᵱınuċ ɑᵱ belɑıb Aılellɑ, ɑbcomceb mıb-lıᵱᵱe ın cıʒe, ⁊ᵱ. . . . "Seven circles in it and seven apartments from fire to side-wall. Rails of bronze and a partitioning of red yew. Three plates of brass in the plinth of the house. A house of oak, with a roof of shingle. Twelve windows in it, with glass shuttings to them. Ailill and Medb's apartment in the middle of the house; silver rails around it, and a strip of bronze and a wand of silver at the rail in front of Ailill, which used to touch the girders of the house," &c.

In the "Tochmarc Emire," Leb. na hUidre, one of the palaces of Emain is thus described:—"Iᵱ ɑmlɑıb ıɑᵱum bɑı ɑ ceċ ᵱın .ı. ın Cᵱɑeb Ruɑb Con-ċobuıᵱ, ᵱo ınc [ᵱ]ɑmɑıl Cıʒe Mıb-ċuɑᵱbɑ .ı. noın ımbɑ ó cenıb co ᵱᵱɑıʒıb ɑnb; xxx. cᵱɑıʒeb ın ɑᵱbɑı ceċ ɑıᵱınıʒ cᵱebumɑ boı ıᵱ cıʒ. Eᵱᵱcɑᵱ be beᵱʒ-ıbɑᵱ ɑnb. Scıɑll ɑᵱċɑᵱúᵱ hé ıɑᵱn fóᴄoᵱ, ⁊ cuʒı ᵱlınbeb ıɑᵱn úɑċcoᵱ. Imbuı Con-ċobuıᵱ ın ɑıᵱenuċ ın cıʒı co ᵱcıɑllɑıb ɑıᵱʒıc, con úɑcnıb cᵱébu-mɑıb, co lıʒᵱɑb óıᵱ ᵱoᵱ ɑ cenbɑıb, con ʒemmɑıb cɑᵱᵱmocuıl ıncıb, combɑ comᵱoluᵱ lá ⁊ ɑbɑıʒ ıncı, con ɑ ᵱceıll ɑıᵱʒıc uɑᵱ ınb ᵱıʒ co ɑᵱb-lıᵱᵱ ınb ᵱıʒ-cıʒı. In um nobúɑleb Con-chobuᵱ co ᵱleıᵱc ᵱıʒbɑ ın ᵱceıll, concóıcıᵱ Ulɑıb ulı ᵱᵱıᵱ. Dɑ ımbɑı bec ın bɑ eᵱᵱeb beɑc ımmon ımbɑı ᵱın ımmɑcuɑıᵱb." "It is how accordingly that house was, that is, the Craeb Ruad of Con-chobur, under the likeness of Tech Mid-chuarta, that is, nine apartments from fire to side-wall in it; thirty feet in the height of each rail of bronze that was in the house. A partitioning of red yew in it. A jointed stripe is it according to base, and a cover of shingle on it according to top. The apartment of Con-chobar in the centre of the house with stripes of silver, with bronze pillars, with adornments of gold on their heads, with gems of carbuncle in them, so that co-bright were day and night in it, with its strip of silver above the king to the girder of the palace. The time Con-chobur used to strike the strip with a royal wand, the Ulaid all used to turn to him. The twelve apartments of the twelve champions about that apartment all round."

The Croeb Ruad is thus described in H. 2, 18 :—" Sciall apcopup bo bepɣɣ-ibup a ceɣ ꞁ na imbaba. Imba Con-chobuip pop láp in caiɣe. Cipiniɣ cpebuma impe com bappibaib apɣic, ꞁ eóin óip popp na haipenċaib, ꞁ ɣemma bo luic loɣmaip—ic ó púli nobicíp in a cennaib. Slacc apɣaic uap Chon-ċobup ꞁ ceopa ubla óip ḟuppi, ppi ċinċopc inc ḟlúaiɣ : ꞁ in can nocpoiċeb, no copchab pon a ɣoċa peppin, no ċóab in pluaɣ : ꞁ ce bopaibpab pnaċac pop láp in caiɣe, po cluinpibe lap in cui bicíp ap aipmicin pom."
"A jointed plate of red yew the house and the apartments. The apartment of Con-chobur on the centre of the house. Rails of bronze about it with tops of silver, and birds of gold on the rails; and gems of precious stone—they are the eyes that used to be in their heads. A rod of silver above Con-chobur and three apples of gold on it, for checking of the host; and the time he used to shake it, or used to raise the sound of his own voice, the host would become silent: and though a needle should fall on the floor of the house, it would be heard with the silence in which they used to be for reverence to him."

As the Tech Mid-chuarta of Temair, and its copy, [the Croeb Ruad, were oblongs, lying north and south, it is probable the palace of Cruachu was of the same form. For the compound pecc-apbb, "seven-rank," of our text, the "Feast of Bricriu" has pecc cuapba, "seven circuits;" and for our *sixteen* windows with *brass shuttings* it has got *twelve* with *glass*. These apparent discrepancies, however, might be reconciled. As both accounts give only seven apartments, I take the opbb of one and the cuaipb of the other to denote the space occupied by each apartment. These apartments were three on one side, three on the other, and one at the end; and this constituted a fourth part of the house from one door to another; that is, from the western to the eastern.

The royal *imdai* was always in the centre of the house, as we see from the preceding extracts. This location is sometimes expressed by in aipenuch, where the word aipenech is different from aipineċ, a rail. O'Clery, in his Glossary, explains it by "the principal place;" and so in the Prologue to the Felire of Oengus :—Ppim-puibe bo Nepainn in aipenach peíne : "a chief seat for Nero in the centre of pain." The auppcapcub, or eppcap, I take to mean the *wood-partitioning* within the house, or perhaps the *grand hall*. It cannot mean *area*, or any place external to the house, for it is said to be "in it." In H. 2, 18, the word is thus used as a verbal noun :—Ɗo uppcapcab na ſlóȝ oi Maiȝ Muɼɼemne : "for the separating (expelling) of the hosts from the Plain of Murthemne." In the phrase ın aulaıcħ ceóa ımbaı, the aulacħ bears the same relation to the ımbaı that ɼaulacħ, in the first extract, does to the whole house. Ɑulao = ſaulao (English, vault?) is the name given to a warrior's tomb or *bed* of stone. The ſoɼleſ, of which we sometimes find several on one house, was our *sky-light.* On a certain occasion Mider Bri Leith puts Etain under his right arm, and flies off with her by the ſoɼleſ of the palace of Tara, (Leb. na hUidre).

[11] Nı ba ouſaıſ, ⁊c. This phrase seems to be an old proverb; the translation is conjectural.

[13] Cáını. In this paragraph the three harpers are called the Chants and sons of Uaithne, the Dagda's harp, and their mother is said to be Boand from the *Sidè.* When this lady was in the pangs of triple child-birth, Uaithne played her a *Sorrow-strain,* at the commencement; a *Joy-strain,* towards the middle; and a *Sleep-strain* towards the close. When she awoke from her sleep, she addressed Uaithne, and accepted the three sons : and in anticipation of the future Spoil of the Cows of Cualnge, which formed a portion of her own Mag Breg, she predicted that as *sorrow, joy,* and *sleep* were to be the lot of the women and cows that were to fall by Ailill and Medb, so men should die by the hearing of the music of these three. This prediction was now being fulfilled.

Uaithne properly means *child-birth, puerperium.* "Puerperius," then, is the player on the harp, and this harp is Boand herself; and thus she is the mother of these Sidè strains, while "Puerperius" is the father. In the original it is hard to decide whether we have cſuıcɼ, a harp, or cſuıcɼıſe, a harper; the sense, however, is the same whether we take the *harp* or the *harper* of the Dagda. Meantime it must be stated that cſuıcɼ is written in full in the original with a sort of mark of contraction over it, and that Uaithne is the traditional harper of the Dagda. If then we take the "harper," we must give the translation somewhat thus; "she (Boand) had a cry of sorrow : *he* played : . . . which *he* played."

The reader will, no doubt, note the peculiar dress of these Chants of Uaithne. Born of a harp, they are, of course, of the form of harps, and consequently dressed as harps; and so the writer says:—"those forms used to run about the men all round." This is the old Iberno-Celtic method of representing spiritual beings under the embodiment of their functions. Thus in the "Vision of Adamnan," Leb. na hUidre :—Seċt mīle ainʒel ın ꝺelꝑaiꝺ ꝑꝑim-cainnel oc ꝑoilꝼiʒuꝺ ocuꝑ oc ınoꝑċuʒuꝺ na caṫꝑaċ mꝺcuaıꝑꝺ : "seven thousand angels in the *forms* of chief-candles at lighting and illuminating of the city (the celestial) all round."

The following is the dress of the ancient Irish harper, as given in the "Brudin da Derga," Leb. na hUidre :—Ꝺcconꝺaꝑc nonꝺuꝑn aıle ꝼꝑiu. Noı monʒae cꝛaeꝺaċa, caꝛꝛa ꝑoꝛaıꝺ: noım ꝺꝛoıc ʒlaꝛꝛa, luaꝛcaıʒ ımpu: noım ꝺelce óıꝑ ın am ꝺꝛacaıꝺ: noꝼ ꝑaılʒe ʒlano ım ꝺ lꝺma. Oꝛꝺ-naꝛc óıꝑ ım oꝛꝺaın cꝺċ ae: au-ċumꝑıuꝺn óıꝑ 'm ó ċaċ ꝑ-ıꝑ : muınce aıꝛcıc ım ꝺꝛꝺʒıc caċ ae. Noım ꝺuılc con ınċaıꝺ óꝛꝺaıꝺ hı ꝼꝛaıʒ: noı ꝑleꝛca ꝼınꝺ-aꝛcıc ınn a lamaıꝺ: "I saw another ennead [nine] by them. Nine branching, curling heads of hair on them : nine grey winding cloaks about them : nine brooches of gold in their cloaks: nine rings of pearl around their hands. A ring of gold around the thumb of each of them : an ear-tie of gold around the ear of each man : a torque of silver about the throat of each of them. Nine bags with golden faces in the side-wall : nine wands of white silver in their hands.

[12] Imꝺeꝛac ın ꝑıꝺchıll, ⁊c. That is, "Medb and Froech then play the chess." So further on : ꝑıꝺꝺaıꝺ ꝛunꝺ ınn aıꝺċı ꝛın ꝺaꝺaıʒ ⁊ Ꝼınꝺ-aꝺaıꝛ : "Ye shall unite here that night at once and Find-abair:" that is, thou and Find-abair. This is a form of expression occasionally met with in Irish; that is, an assertion, direct or dependent, is made in the plural of two subjects in the singular coupled by ocuꝑ (and), but with the first, or principal subject omitted. In the present case the principal subject, *Medb*, is omitted. The following are other examples: Ꝺolluıꝺ Pꝺcꝛıcc ó ṫemaıꝛ hı cꝛıch Laıʒen: conꝑancaraꝛ ⁊ Ꝺuꝺṫach macc U Luʒıꝛ: "Patric went from Temair into the territory of the Laigne : they met and Dubthach Mac U Lugir:" that is, Patric and Dubthach : . . . met (Book of Armagh). Ꝛoʒellꝛom ⁊ ın ꝼılı ucuc ım Ꝺıꝺıꝺ Ꝼoċaıꝺ Ꝺıꝛʒcıʒ. "We held a wager and yon poet about the destruction of Fothad Airgtech;" that is, myself and yon poet; (Stories of Mongan, Leb. na hUidre). It will be observed that the omitted subject here is a person of distinction as compared with the second and expressed subject, and this may be the true origin of the construction. In the following passage in the Tain Bo Cuailnge Fergus addresses Medb in the second person plural :—

Inꝺnaiꝺiꝺ ꝛunꝺ co ꞇíꝛa aꝛ inꝺ ꝼiꝺ, ocuꝛ níꝛ maꝺꝺaꝺ liꝶ ciꝺ cían co ꞇíꝛoꝛ : " Wait *ye* here until I come out of the wood, and let there be no wondering with *you*, though it be long until I come."

¹⁴ Cꝛi laa ꞁ ꞇeoꝛa aiꝺꝋi. This is the accus. of time, the only case of time in Irish. All our apparent genitives of time are simply ordinary dependents, though of course expressing *time ;* and accordingly the governing substantive always accompanies them. The example Oommaiꝛ Ꝼiaꝺo cach ꞇꝛaꞇha : " May God at every hour come to me," quoted by Dr. W. Stokes, Goidilica, p. 94, as a case of time, is in construction, " the God of every hour ;" and this is the construction of all his other examples. When there is no governing substantive we have the accus. ; as, maꞇain (not maiꞇne) ꞇancaꞇaꝛ a ꞇech : " in the morning they came home " (Brocan's Hymn) : Cocumlai aꝛꝛ maꞇꞇain muich : " he goes off at early morn :" (Tain Bo Cuailnge, Leb. na hUidre). ꝺa anꝺ conꞇuileꝺ caꞇn aiꝺꝋi : " it was in it she used to sleep every night :" (Tochmarc Etaine, Ib.). The use of the genitive is very extended in Irish ; the following are two examples ,—ocuꝛ máꝺ uꝛꝙuꝛ, maiꝛꝼiꝺ nónꝶoꝛ caꞇa uꝛꝙaꝛa : " and if it is a shot, it will kill an ennead of each shot ;" that is, each shot will kill nine, (Brudin da Derga, Leb. na hUidre) ; ocuꝛ ꝺoꝶeꝛaꞇ cloiꞇ caꞇ ꝼiꝛ leó ꝺo ꝱuꝛ ꝱaiꝛnꝺ : " and they bring a stone of each man with them to set up a cairn ;" that is, each man brings a stone with him to set up a cairn, (Ib.). In accordance with this peculiar construction, we have generally a dependent genitive where we should otherwise have an accusative of time.

¹⁵ Oo'nꝺ aꝶainꝺ. This river of Cruachu is the *Brei,* mentioned above, and that in which Froech bathes, a few lines further on. It must be the stream from the fountain *Clebach,* at which the two daughters of king Loegaire met St. Patric. These, like Find-abair and her maid, came at early morn to the fountain to wash. The Irish Tripartite (Royal Irish Academy), introduces this meeting as follows :—Ooluiꝺ Ꝑaꞇꝛic iaꝛ ꝛin Oo'n ꞇopuꝛ .i. Cliꝶech i ꝛleꝛaiꝶ Cꝛuachan ꝼꝛi ꞇuꝛcuꝶailn ꞃꝛeine. Oeꝛꞇiꞇaꝛ in chleꝛiꞃ ic on ꞇiꝛꝛaiꞇ. Ooloꞇaꝛ ꝺe inꞃin Loiꞃaiꝛi maic Neill com moch ꝺo'n ꞇiꝛꝛaiꞇ, ꝺo niꞃi al láim [*sic*] amail ha ꝶeꝛ ꝺoiꝶ .i. Eiꞇne Ꝼinꝺ ꞁ Ꝼeꝺelm Oeꝛꞇꞇ. Connaiꝛneꞇꞇaꞇaꝛ ꝛenaꝺ inna cleiꝛeꞇ ic on ꞇiꝛꝛaiꞇ con heꞇaiꞃiꝶ ꞃelaiꝶ ꞁ al liꝶaiꝛ aꝛ a [*sic*] ꝶelaiꝶ. Roinꞃanꞇaiꞃꝛeꞇ ꝺeilꝶ inna cleiꝛech: ꝺoꝛuimenaꞇaꝛ ꝶauꝛ ꝼiꝛ Siꞇhe, no ꝼanꞇaiꝛi: " Patric

after that went to the well .i. Clibech in the sides of Cruachu with the rising of the sun. The clerics sat down at the fountain. Two daughters of Loigare mac Neill came early to the fountain for the washing of their hands, as was their custom; that is, Eithne the White and Fedelm the Red. They found a synod of the clerics at the fountain with white garments, and their books before them. They wondered at the form of the clerics; they imagined them to be men of the *Side*, or a phantasy."

From this ancient authority we learn that the Lat. *lavare* of the Book of Armagh means "*washing* of hands," &c., not washing of *clothes;* and from it we learn also that in the celebrated passage "viros *Sidè* aut deorum terrenorum, aut phantassiam," "men of the *Sidè* or of terrene gods, or a phantasy," the words "deorum terrenorum" are merely explanatory of *Sidè.* See my "Daim Liacc," p. 8, where this passage has been for the first time so translated and explained. In our tract Froech goes to the river ɒo ınluc, and so do Find-abair and her maid, and this ınluc is the proper term for "washing of hands," &c. Thus in the *Serg-lige*: Ɒo ċaéc Goċaıɒ Iuıl ıaɲom ɒo ınluc a lám ɒo'n cıɲɲaıc: "Eochaid Iuil goes afterwards for the washing of his hands to the fountatn." The term for washing the head is ɲolcaɒ and for bathing the whole person, ɲoċɲacaɒ.

I may remark that the phrase ɲɲı cuɲcubaıln ʒɲéıne, which Colgan, Fifth Life of St. Patric, lib. 2, cap. 14, renders, contra ortum solis— "opposite the rising of the sun," means, in my opinion, *time,* not *locality.* The Book of Armagh, Betham's text, (I cannot get a sight of the Original) has a double phrase: "contra ortum solis, ante ortum solis," a confusion which goes to confirm my interpretation. The present phrase is lɑ eıɲʒhı na ʒɲeıne; the ancient ɲɲı, *ad,* is always lɑ in modern Irish. Compare la coɲcbáıl ɲoɲcela (Vis. of Adamnan), "cum ortu evangelii:" "with the rising of the Gospel."

It would seem, then, that it is not necessary to go to the east of Rathcroghan to look for the fountain *Clebach*, or the *Sen-domnach* (Old-church) which St. Patric founded beside it. At the same time it is as likely that both are to the east as to the west of the palace. It is impossible, however, that this fountain could have been three miles from the palace, as Dr. O'Donovan, in his Roscommon Ordnance Survey Letters, supposes: but it is not impossible, that the *palace* may have been two miles away from the spot now called Rathcroghan. He says nothing of the Brei, which must have been a considerable river, abounding in otters, and in that spot where Froech bathed so dark and deep as to merit the name Ꝺub-linꝺ, Black-pool. With the data developed in this note I think it would not be difficult to identify the fountain, river, and church of Cruachu.

[16] Oc on ᴄain : That is, at the "Tain Bo Cuailngi."

[17] Aᴄ maich in uᴘciu. Ailill induces Froech to get into the Brei, with the hope of his being drowned, for he was well aware of the prophecy that drowning was to be the ultimate fate of the son of Befind. His aunt Boand frequently cautioned his mother against allowing her heroic son to indulge in bathing, or by any chance to come in contact with Cu Chulaind. Thus in the Book of Fermoy, Boand says :—

> A bhebínn, bean an bo mac
> Ᵹan ṁnái ᴄᴘiallᴘuᴘ ꝺó ᴄóómaᴘc,
> Uaiᴘ an bliaꝺaiᴘ boꝺeᴘa
> Iᴘ anꝺ ᴄéilᵹᴘꝺ-ᴘa ꝺéᴘa.
>
> Na ᴄaóaiᴘ ᴘe Coin na cleᴘ,
> Uaiᴘ noóan anꝺ aᴄá bo leᴘ :
> Iᴘ e boᴘaᵹa ᴘe ᴘé—
> Macaṁ Ṁhuiᵹi Ṁúiᴘᴄeiṁne.
>
> Na ꝺena ᴘnaṁ boꝺúiᴘ ꝺúiꝺ
> Uaiᴘ iᴘ ann ᴘéᴘᴘaᴘ a ᴘuil :
> Na biꝺ a ᵹaiᴘciꝺ an ᵹll,
> Abaiᴘ ᴘe Ᵽᴘoeó, a ꝺébinn.

TRANSLATION.

O Befind, impress on thy son
Not to court a woman who shall come to him,
For the year he shall bring her—
It is in it thou shalt shed tears.

Contend not thou with Cu of the feats,
Since it is not in it thy advantage is :
It is he who shall come by time—
The youth of Mag Murthemne.

Let him not make the swimming of black water.
For it is in it he shall shed his blood :
Let not his armour be in pledge,
  Tell to Froech, O Befind.

[18] Capna pamaipci. A bath of this nature was made for Cethern Mac Fintain, who attacked Medb's camp single-handed, and as the result received innumerable wounds: Ip anbpin conaccacc Pinʒin Pachaɔ pmip-ammaip pop Coin Culainɔ ɔo ic ꝯ ɔo leiʒip Chechipn meic pincain. Canic Cu Chulainɔ peme in ɔunuɔ ꝯ il lonʒpopc pepn hepenɔ, ꝯ na puaip ɔ' almaiɓ ꝯ ɔ' eiciɓ ꝯ ɔ' inɓiliɓ anɔ—cuc leipp app iac: ꝯ ɔoʒni pmip-ammaip ɔiɓ, ecip peoil ꝯ cnamaiɓ ꝯ lechap. Ocup cucaɔ Cechepn mac Pincain ip in pmip-ammaip co cenɔ ceopa lá ꝯ ceopan aiɓche, ꝯ paʒaɓ ac ól na pmip-ampaɔ imme. Ocup paluiɓ in pmip-ammaip anɔ ecip a cneɓaiɓ ꝯ ecip a cpeccaiɓ, ɓap a alcaiɓ ꝯ ɓap a il-ʒonaiɓ. Anɔpin acpacc pom app in pmip-ammaip i cinɔ ceopa la ꝯ ceopan aiɓce, see 160. "It is then Fingin Fathach (the physician) asked Cu Chulaind for a *smir-ammair* for the saving and for the healing of Cethern mac Fintain. Cu Chulaind went forward to the fortress and to the encampment of the men of Eriu, and of what he found of flocks, and of herds, and of cattle there—he brought them with him out of it: and he makes a *smir-ammair* of them, between flesh and bones and hide. And Cethern mac Fintain was brought into the *smir-ammair* till the end of three days and three nights, and he set to at the drinking of the *smir-ammair* around him. And the *smir-ammair* went into him between his sores and between his scars, over his cuts and his many wounds. Then he arose out of the *smir-ammair* at the end of three days and three nights, and so forth." The word pmip-ammaip is a compound, of which the first member means "marrow;" what the second means I cannot say at present. In our tract, the phrase po chal ꝯ beuil is, I think, correctly rendered, beuil being = biail. The cál and bial are frequently associated; thus—"aep cáil ocup beli, adze—and axe-men" (O'Donovan's Supp. to O'Reilly). The *adze* to cut the flesh; the axe to chop up the bones.

[19] Siɔ Cpuachan. This *Sid*, the temple and burial vault of the royal family and clan, was, as we see, at some distance from the piʒ-ceɔ, palace, but probably within the *raths* or enclosures. Of these there were several, as we find the *chief-rath* spoken of, p. 138. The whole place was called *Cruachu*, or *Cruachan*, in the singular; or, *Cruachan* or *Cruachna*, in the plural. It was also called *Dun Cruachan*, and *Rath Cruachan*. In the History of the Cemeteries, Leb. na hUidre, it is called *Cathair Cruachan*. Every royal residence con-

sisted of three principal parts within the circumvallations; namely, the
pɩʒ-ceċ, palace; the *dun*, or fortified part, appropriated to visitors: and
the *less*, which comprised the whole space within the enclosure, save
what was occupied by the *palace* and *dun*. In this *less* were the stables,
cow-houses, and the houses of all the menial retainers of the king. On
coming up, Froech and his suite sat at the door of the *first-rath*.
Ailill orders them to be admitted into the *less*, p. 138. The fourth
part of the palace is then allowed them. Every *imdai* or apartment, with its occupants, was called the ceʒlaċ, or household of
the chief person in it. Thus ceʒlaċ Ƒnaich p. 142. Then there was
a cech ímacallmae, " house of conversation ;" and this was outside
the palace, though, perhaps, communicating with it; for Ailill and
Medb go out of the " house of conversation" into the palace, p. 144. I
have said above that the *dun* was the residence of visitors. This is
evident from the " Stories of Mongan," Leb. na hUidre, where we find
the poet Forgall and his company residing in it. This will explain
the use of the word *dun*, not *palace*, where it is stated, p. 142, that
Froech and his suite " stayed till the end of a fortnight in the *dun*."

[20] Ʒol-ʒaɩne ban Sɩve. This ancient air is still played by the
Irish harper and piper.

[21] Ꝺo'nꝺ eꞃ. The word eꞃ is of rare occurrence. We find it in
Fiacc's Hymn of St. Patrick: Ƒoꞃꞃuib a choɩꞃ ꝼoꞃꞃ ɩnꝺ leɩcc; ma-
ꞃaɩc a eꞃ, nɩ bꞃonna : " He pressed his foot upon the stone; its trace
remains, it wears not." In this passage eꞃ is glossed ꝼolliuċc, a mark.
In Zeuss., p. 473, *interlitus* is glossed ecaꝼꝼuɩllechca ; and in " Scela
na Eꞃeꞃʒe," p. 10, are read the words: Ƒuɩlliuċca na cneċ ꝼoꞃo-
ꝺamacáꞃ aꞃ Cꞃꞁꞃc: " the marks of the wounds which they suffered
for Christ."

[22] Cucann. This word is written cuca in MS., but with a hori-
zontal stroke over cuc, which I take to be intended for the final a. I
have, therefore, resolved as in text.

[23] conʒu. This conʒu = ꝺo-ꝼonʒu. Ƒonʒu is Lat. *pango*, another example of a primitive initial p becoming ꝼ in Irish. This
formula, occasionally slightly changed, is very common in the more
ancient manuscripts. It is always, so far as I know, put into the
mouth of the Gentile Irish ; never into that of a Christian. The more
usual form is—conʒu ꝺo ꝺɩa coɩnʒeꞃ mo ċuach: " I swear for an
oath the oath of my territories." In this form ꝺo ꝺɩa has hitherto

been rendered " to God." Now the words bo bia in the sense of " to God," besides being absurd in the mouth of a Pagan, are frequently omitted. I therefore render "for an oath," "as an oath." In O'Davoren's Glossary, bee is glossed minna, an oath, (Skrt. *divya* (?), id.), and this I take to be the word here. In the next paragraph Find-abair adopts the usual formula. Other forms are "conʒu bo bia," "I swear for an oath," (Lugaid in the Tain); conʒu a coinʒer mo cuac: "I swear the oath of my territories," the words bo bia not used (Fer. Rogain, Brudin da Derga). Cu Chulaind in the Tain has another form: conʒu a coinʒce Ulab: "I swear the swearings of the Ulaid." Even Cu Chulaind's charioteer swears in the same way. From this it will be seen that "my territories" does not mean *those in my possession*, but the territories in which I live; and it is in this sense that Find-abair swears in the same manner. It would appear that in ancient Eriu every tribe had a certain form of oath, and conse-quently a certain object to attest that oath, distinct from those of every other tribe.

²⁴ Do ben. This was Trebland, daughter of Froech, son of Aengus from the *Sid* of the *Brug*, as we learn from the "Courtship of Treb-land," Book of Fermoy. She was then, like himself, a semi-deity. The writer of the story says: ba balca bo Coirppe Mac Roʒa an Crebblann rin, uair bocleaccabair maici mac Mhib meic ⁊ inʒina bo alcrom bo rʒib na riʒ rolur-ʒlan, ba cóimhera bóib, ar báiʒ nac claecloʒbair ic na bhicc na blac in Erinb rri a linb: "This Trebland was a foster-child to Coirpre Mac Rosa, for the magnates of the sons of Miled were wont to foster the sons and daughters of the bright-pure *Sid's*, which were next to them, for the sake that neither corn, nor milk, nor bloom should decay in Eriu during their time."

²⁵ Conall Cernach. The second of the three great champions of the Ulaid; the first being Cu Chulaind, and the third Loegaire Bua-dach. See "Battle of Magh Rath," ed. O'Donovan, p. 83.

²⁶ Inb nachir. This serpent is found everywhere in our old Irish tales, as defending *duns*, native and foreign. The usual name is bíarc, or péirc, Lat. *bestia*, but frequently nacir, as here, and its usual abode the sea, lake, or other water, adjoining or within the dun. In the case of the serpent of Cruachu we find that Froech, though probably looked on with jealousy by the demon, swam un-harmed about the river until he touched the mystic rowan-tree. This

tree was guarded by the serpent, and accordingly in the Book of Fermoy it is said to have come from the root of the tree. Ailill knew this, but Froech was a demi-god, and consequently more than a match for the demon; and hence the result. Is not this the ancient serpent and the fruit-tree? The demon naturally took charge of that tree through which he brought death into the world, and cherished it with affection. But a Divine Being crushed the head of the serpent; and it is to be remarked that Froech did not completely cut off its head, but merely so as to have it hang on its side.

In the case of Conall Cernach the serpent entered into no contest with him, for he was a mere mortal; but not so on a certain occasion in the case of Cu Chulaind, a demigod, and a being whom I have already examined mythologically in my "Religious Beliefs of the Pagan Irish" (Journal of the Historical and Archæological Association of Ireland, April, 1869, p. 321). In the "Spirit-chariot of Cu Chulaind," Leb. na hUidre, it is related that St. Patric brought up Cu from the lower regions to speak to Loegaire, for the latter declared he would not otherwise believe. Cu addresses Loegaire in dark and mysterious language, but the king has a doubt if the stranger is really Cu. "If it is Cu that is in it," he says, "he should tell us about his great exploits." "That is true," says Cu. And then he recites for Loegaire some of his principal achievements. In the course of his narrative he says that he went once to Dun Scaith, a fort in the south of Skye, and there encountered and crushed a host of serpents and other venomous reptiles, who had their abode in a pit in the dun:—

ba cuiċe iꞃ in Ðún,
  Laꞃ in ꞃiꙅ, aðꞃeċ;—
Ðeiċ naċꞃaiꙅ boꞃoembaċaꞃ
  Ðaꞃ a óꞃ—ba beċ!

Iaꞃ ꞃin aċaꞃeċuꞃ-[ꞃ]a,
  Cia ꞃ' aðbol in ðꞃonꙅ,
Con beꞃnuꞃ an oꞃðneða
  Eċiꞃ mo bá boꞃnb.

Ċeð lán bo loꞃcannaib—
  Ðoꞃaꞃlaiċċe bún;
Míla ꙅéꞃa, ꙅulbenða,
  Rolelċaꞃ i m' ꞃꞃub, ꞃc.

There was a pit in the dun,
    Belonging to the king, it is related;—
Ten serpents burst
    Over its border—it was a deed!

After that I attacked them,
    Though vast the throng,
Until I made bits of them
    Between my two fists.

A house full of toads,
    They were let fly at us;
Sharp, beaked monsters,
    They stuck in my snout, &c.

This extract will illustrate the meaning of our phrase, "several tribes are let loose from her;" that is, tribes of serpents.

[27] Dún Ollaid. Now Dunolly, near Oban. See Dr. Reeves' edition of Adamnan's Life of St. Columba, p. 180.

V.—TOCHMARC BEC-FOLA.

TRANSLATED AND EDITED BY

B. O'LOONEY.

THE text of the following tale of Bec Fola and king Diarmait, son of Aedh Slane, is taken from a vellum MS. in the Library of Trinity College, Dublin, Class H. 2, 16, compiled about the year 1390 by Donogh Mac Firbis, of Lecan Mic Firbisighe in the county of Sligo. The tale commences on column 765, ninth line from bottom, and has been collated with another copy in a vellum MS. of the year 1509, Class H. 3, 18, in the same Library, p. 757.

According to the Annals of the Four Masters, king Diarmait, son of Aedh Slane, and his brother, Blathmac, assumed the sovereignty of Ireland A. D. 657, and ruled conjointly for eight years, till they were both cut off by the mortality called the Buidhe Connaill, A. D. 664.

This tale is of the class the knowledge of which constituted one of the literary and legal qualifications of an ollamh, or poet; and though not in the incomplete list of historical tales in the "Book of Leinster," printed by O'Curry, in his "Lectures on the Manuscript Materials of Irish History," p. 584, et seq., it contains internal evidence of antiquity. The language is old and well preserved, and the story is told in an ancient style of diction. It contains some minute descriptions of personal appearance, dress, and ornaments of gold and silver.

Of the lady Bec Fola I have found no mention elsewhere. The name means literally "small dowry." *Fola* is used here in the sense of *Coibche*, a price, reward, gift, or dowry; but in its technical legal sense it was the name for the first gift which a husband gave to his wife on marriage. The amount of the *Coibche* was defined by law in accordance with the grade of the parties, but, the coibche, whether great or small, secured the woman in her marriage rights, and saved her from personal dishonour. Professor O'Curry translated Bec Fola, "Woman of the small dowry," in his work on "The MS. Materials of Irish History," p. 283, where he has inadvertently printed Diarmait Mac Cerbeoil, for Diarmait Mac Aedh Slane. Diarmait Mac Cerbeoil was father of Aedh Slane, and grandfather of the hero of this tale, as mentioned in the following passages from the story of the birth of Aedh Slane, preserved in Leabhar na Huidri, in the Library of the Royal Irish Academy, pp. 52, 53 :—

 bde τρά món áınaó món peóτ anb h-í callcın la Oíaρmaιc mιc Ƿeηȝuρa Ceρbéoιl. "There was a great fair held one time at Taill-ten, by Diarmait son of Fergus Cerbeoil." * * * *

> " Compenτ Muȝaın mó caó olamb,
>   Oo mac cóıρ óubaıb óeρbaıll;
>   lanom oρ ρóen ρúamaó ρ6,
>   In n-Cléb ρáen ρlúaȝaó Slán6.

> Mugan bore, the greatest of all children,
>   To the right worthy son of Cerball;
>   After this over the heroic field he reigned awhile,
>   The noble Aedh Slane of hosts."

" Diarmait Mac Fergus Cerbeoil" died A. D. 592.

In illustration of some of the passages in the text, three Addenda are given :—

I. Dindsenchas of Dubthar, which identifies the places called Dubthar, Inis Fedach, and Inis Mic in Doill; and indicates the people called ua Feadach.

The contest of the ua Fedach referred to in the text may, perhaps, be identified with that of the sons of Dall Deas, of Inis Mic in Doill, given in the Dindsenchas as the origin of Fedach and Dubthar.

II. Dindsenchas of Loch n-Erne, illustrating the allusion to the "bearded heroes," and representing that Loch n-Erne afforded, in ancient times, a sanctuary for women.

III. A poem on the prohibitions of the beard, from the "Yellow Book of Lecan," in further illustration of the allusion to bearded heroes in the text, p. 180.

O'Curry considered this poem "to be a simple condensation of the law which regulated the wearing and responsibilities of the beard, and that it belonged to a period anterior to the year 900." He observed that "any person acquainted with the language of the earlier Irish MSS. will find no difficulty in ascribing the language and com-position of this poem to a period at least five hundred years earlier than the MS. in which it is preserved," which belongs to the year 1390.

τochmorc bec Fola.

Bαι Διαρμαιτ mac Αεδα Slane ιρριζι Cempach, Cριmchanδ mac Αεδα ι n-δαlcυρ δο, ocυρ ι n-ζιαllαιζεċτ ρρι lαιm o Lαιζνιδ. Lυιδρεom lαα n-ανδ ocυρ α δαlcα, .ι. Cριmchanδ, δα Αch Cρυιm h-ι Loeζαιρε, ocυρ oen ζιllα leo. Conacαταρ ιn mnαι δαρ ριν n-αch αnιαρ h-ι cαρραιc; δα mαel αρρα Finδρυιne ιmpe, δα ζem δο lιc loζmαιρ eιρτιδ, lene Fo δερζ ινδlαιτ oιρ ιmpe, δραc coρcρα, δealζ óιρ lánecαιρ co mδρeaċτραδ n-ζem n-ιlδαċhαch ιριν δρυτ [oρ α δρυιnne⁴], mυncι δι óιρ Foρloρce ιmα δραζαιc, mιnδ n-óιρ Foρ α cιnδ, δα each δυδ ζlαρα Fo nα cαρρατ, δα n-αll óιρ Fριυ, cυnζι co τυαζmιlαιδ αιρζδιδιδ Foραιδ.

"Can δο δeachαιδ αδean ?" oρ Διαρmαιτ. "Nι δο nach ceιn." oρ ρι; "Cιδ δο ċeιζ ?" oρ Διαρmαιτ, "Do cυιnδchιδ ριl cρυιch-neachτα, [oρ ρι]. Ατα δαζ ιchιρ lιm ocυρ nιmċα ριl α ċomαδαιρ." "Mαδ ριl ιn τιριρεα δαρ, αιl δυιτ," oρ Διαρmαιτ, "nι Fυιl δο δυl reachαmρα." "Nι oρυρ διn," αρ ρι "αchτ Fombια α loζ," "Roτ-δια αn δealζ m-δeaζ ρα," oρ Διαρmαιτ. "Ζεδċαρ διn," oρ ριρι.

Nomδeρ leρ δο chυm nα Cempach. "Can δon mnαι α Διαρ-mαιτ ?" oρ cach, "Nι Fo ρlοιnδι δαm διn," αρ Διαρmαιτ, "Cιδ δο ραταιρ ιnα cιnδρρα?" [oρ cach], "mo δealζ δec," oρ Διαρmαιτ. Ιρ δec ιnδ Fola oρ cach." "διδ eαδ α h-αιnm διn," oρ ιn δραι, "[.ι.] δec Fola."

---

¹ "*Ath Truim ui Laeghaire*," Trim, in the territory of *ui Laeghaire* in Meath.

² "*Findruine*," white bronze—a bronze generally considered to contain a large proportion of tin, or perhaps some alloy of silver, sometimes used for ornamenta-tion.

³ "*Lene* and *Lened*," a kilt, a kind of short petticoat worn outside.

⁴ Words inserted in [ ] are supplied from MS. H. 3, 18.

⁵ "*Muince*," a generic name for any kind of collar, ring, or necklace for men, women, horses, dogs, and for the hafts

COURTSHIP OF BEC FOLA.

IARMAIT, son of Aedh Slane, was in the sovereignty of Teamair,
Crimthand, son of Aedh, was in pupilage with him, and in hostage-
as pledge from the Lagenians. He and his pupil, i. e., Crimthand,
.t one day to Ath Truim, of ui Laeghaire,[1] and one servant with
n. They saw a woman coming eastward over the ford in a
:iot; she wore two pointless shoes of findruine,[2] two gems of pre-
.s stones in them, a lene[3] interwoven with red gold upon her, a
son robe, a brooch of gold fully chased and set with gems of
ous colours in the robe [over her bosom[4]], a muince[5] of burnished
l around her neck, a mind[6] of gold upon her head, two black-grey
ds to her chariot, two n-all of gold[7] to them, a yoke with trappings
ilver upon them.

"Whence have you come, O woman?" said Diarmait. "Not very
" said she. "Whither do you go?" said Diarmait. "To seek
l-wheat" [said she]. "I have good soil and I require suitable
l." "If it be the seed of this country you desire," said Diarmait,
)u shall not pass me." "I do not object indeed," said she, "if I
a log."[8] "I will give you this little brooch," said Diarmait. "I
l accept it," said she.

He brought her with him to Teamair. "Who is this woman,
)iarmait?" said they. "She has not given me her name indeed,"
. Diarmait. "What did you give as her tindscra?"[9] [said they].
.y little brooch," said Diarmait. "That is a Bec Fola," said they.
et that be her name then" said the druid, "i. e., Bec Fola."

---

ears where the head was inserted.
"Mind n-óir," a diadem or coronet
)ld.

"n-All of gold," All, a double-
ed chariot bridle, as distinguished
the sruth ean, srian or single
ed riding bridle.

[8] "A Log," a price, wages, or reward;
but here it means a log tanamnais, "bride
price," or coibche, a marriage gift.

[9] "Tindsora." See Additional Note,
A, p. 194, for an explanation of this word
in the sense in which it is here used.

Rola ρι bιn, [a] menmaιn ρορ a balταρom, .ι. ρορ Cριmchanb
mac n-Aeba, baι ocá ʒuιbι ocuρ ocá τochluʒab cen máιn.

Acchoτaρ bιn on ʒιlla, .ι. τubechτ aρ a cenbρι co Cluaιn
ba Chaιleach τρατ τειρτι bιa bomnaιc ba bρειch ρορ aιcheab.
Ro ιnbιρ ριbe bιa muιnτιρ. Ruρταιρmeρcaταρ ιαρum a munτιρ;
naca beρnab ben aρb-ριʒ h-Eριnb bo cabaιρτ aρ aιceab.

Αςραιʒ ρι bιn maιτιn moch bιa bomnaιʒ o Dιαρmaιτ, "Cιb ρο
a ben?" oρ ρε [Dιαρmaιτ]. "Nι cιb maιc," oρ ρι, "Inbιle ριl bam-
ρα[11] oc Cluaιn Da Chaιleach, ρορρacaιbρeτ na bachlaιch [ιaττ],
ocuρ bo chuabaρ ρορ τecheb." "Cιρρι ιnbιlι?" oρ Dιαρmaιτ.
"Sechτ lenτι cona n-ιmbenmaιb, ocuρ ρeττ n-belʒι óιρ, ocuρ τρι
mιnba óιρ. Iρ lιach a τeττ amuba." "Na τειʒ, oρ Dιαρmaιτ,
ιρ ιn bomnach, nι maιτ ιmaball ιn bomnaιch," "Neach lιmρa aρ,"
oρ ρι [ριu] "Nι ba h-uaιmρea on," oρ Dιαρmaιτ.

Luιb ρι on bιn ocuρ a h-ιnaιlc a τemρaιʒ ρobeρ coρραn-
ʒabaρ Dubchoρ laιʒen; boρ ρala ρορ meρuʒab ann co τρατ
b'aιbchι conτaρταταρ coιn alcaι co ρο maρbρab an ιnιlc, ocuρ
luιb ρι h-ι cρanb ρορ τecheb.

Am baι ιριn cρunb conρacaι ιn τenι ρορ laρ na caιllι. luιb
bochum ιn τeneb, conρacaι ιn oclach ιmon τenι oc uρʒnam na mucι.
Inaρ ριρecbaι ιme co n-ʒlan-coρcaιρ, ocuρ co cιρclaιb óιρ acaρ,
aρcaιτ, cennbaρρ bι óρ ocuρ aρʒuc ocuρ ʒlaιne ιm a cenn; mo-
coιl ocuρ ριchιρι óιρ ιm cach n-bual bιa ρulc conιcι claρ a bá
ιmbaι, bá uball óιρ ρορ bι ʒabal a muιnʒι, meb ρeaρ boρnn ceac
τaρnaι; a claιbeb óρ-buιρnn aρ a cριρ, ocuρ a bá ρleʒ coιcριnbι
ιcιρ leaτaρ a ρceιτ, co cobρuιb ριnbρuιne ρoρa;[18] bρuτ ιlbaτach
[leιρ]. A bá laιm lana bι ρaιlʒιb óιρ ocuρ aρcaιτ co a bι uιllιnn.

Τειτ ρι ocuρ ρuιbιb ocaι ocon τenι. Ruρbechαρταρ, ocuρ nι

---

[10] "*Cluain da Chaileach*," near Baltinglas, in the county of Wicklow.

[11] Ριl lιmρa ρεριn, which belong to
myself. MS. H. 3, 18.

[12] "*Sunday journey.*"　See Note B.,
p. 195.

[13] "*Dubthor Laighen,*" now Duffry,'a
district in the barony of Scarawalsh, Co.

of Wexford.　Duffry Hall, in ruins,
retains the name, in the parish of Temple-
shanbo : *vide* O'D. Suppl. ad O'R. Dict.
She probably went by *Bealach-Dubthair*
(road of *Dubthar*), now called *Bealach
Conglais* or Baltinglas.　See Four Masters, A. D. 594, p. 218, n. h.; and Addendum No. 1, p. 184.

She, however, fixed her mind on his pupil, i. e., on Crimthand, son
.edh, whom she continued to seduce and solicit for a long time.

She, at length, prevailed upon the youth to come to meet her at
ain Da Chaileach[10] at sunrise on Sunday in order to abduct her.
told this to his people; they then forbade him to abduct the wife
he high king of Eriu.

She rose early on Sunday morning from Diarmait. "What is the
ter, O woman?" said he [Diarmait.] "Not a good thing," said
; "some things of mine that are at Cluain da Chaileach, the
'ants have left them, and have fled away." "What are the
igs?" said Diarmait. "Seven lenes with their garniture, and seven
oches of gold, and three minds of gold, and it is a pity to let them
lost." "Do not go," said Diarmait, "on Sunday, the Sunday
rney is not good."[12] "A person will be with me from the place,"
l she. "Not from me indeed," said Diarmait.

She and her handmaid went then from Teamair southward till they
shed Dubthor Laigen;[13] she wandered about there for part of the
ht till wild hounds came[14] and killed the handmaid, and she fled into
:ee to avoid them.

When she was in the tree she saw a fire in the middle of the wood.
: went to the fire, and saw a young warrior at the fire cooking a
. He wore an inar[15] of silk of bright purple, and with circlets of
d and silver, a ceann barr[16] of gold and silver and crystal upon his
id, bunches and weavings of gold around every lock of his hair reach-
: down to the tips of his two shoulders, two balls of gold upon the
o prongs of his hair, each of them as large as a man's fist; his gold-
ted sword upon his girdle, and his two fleshmangling spears in the
ther of his shield, with bosses of findruine[17] upon it;[18] he wore a
ny-coloured cloak. His two arms were covered with failgib[19] of gold
l silver up to his two elbows.

She went and sat with him at the fire. He looked at her, but

---

[4] "*Wild hounds*," *Coin allta*, wolves,
es, any kind of beasts of prey, &c.

[5] "*Inar*," a tunic, a frock.

[3] "*Ceann barr*," a diadem, an orna-
at or cover for the head.

[17] "*Findruine*." See *ante*, note 2, p.
174.

[18] ꝑⱥⱦⱀ, upon it. MS. H. 3, 18.

[19] "*Failgib*" (Nom. Sing. *Fail*) of
gold. See Note C., p. 196.

concapò a moò cocaipnic[20] òo puine na muice. Òo ʒni iapum
bpoòmuc òia muic, inòmaiò a lama, luiò on ceni; luiò pi òin ina
òiaiò co piʒi in loch.

Lonʒ cpeòumae i meòon in lacha. Ronò cpeòumu i meòon ip
in luinʒ icip, ocup ponò aile ipin n-inòpi bai f meòon inò lacha. Òo
ppenʒa in loech in luinʒ, ceic pi ip in luinʒ pemipeom, pacabaip
inò lonʒ illonʒ-ciʒ cpeòa ap bopap na h-inòpi, ceic pi pemi ipa
ceʒ; ampa in ceʒ h-i pin icip ippcapcaò ocup òepʒuòa. Òepiò-
peom, òepiò pf òin inna pappaòpom; piʒiò a laim peachu [ina
puiòi] co cuc meip co m-biuò òoib. Lonʒaicpom biblinaiò ocup
ebaic; co nap ba meapcai[23] neaċ òib. Ni boi òuine ipin ciʒ,
ni manaplapcap òoib. Luiòpeom ina liʒi, òopleic pi po bpac-
pom, ecuppu ocup ppaiʒh; nochop impo òin ppiapi co maicin,
cocualacap maicin moch an n-ʒaipm pop popc na h-inòpi, .i.
"caipp imach a Plainò òo pil na pipu." Acpaiʒ puap lapòbain
ocup ʒebiò a ċpelam paip, ocup luiò imach; luiò pi òia òepcin
co òopup in ciʒi, conacai in cpiap popp in pupc. Comchpoca,
comaepa, comòelba ppipium a cpiup. Conacai òin cechpop ap
puc na h-inòpi ocup a pceich a paenʒabail ina lamaib; acpaiʒ-
peom òin a cechpop [a n-òoċum in ceaċpap ele]; ima cuapcac
òoib[24] com bo òepc cach òib òia pailiu. Co n-òeachaiò cach òib
ppi copʒa a lechi; luiò [Plann a òenap] ina inòpi apiòipi.

"òuaiò ċheniʒ òuic," op pi, "ip loechòa in ʒleo pin." "òa
maiċ checup maò ppi naimòiu," op pe. "Can òona hocaib?"
op pipi. "Mac bpachap òampa[25]," op pe; "cpi bpachaip òam
òin na h-i aili." "Ciò po ċopnaiò?" op in ben. "Inò inip[26]," op pe.
"Cia h-ainm na h-inòpi?" op pi. "Inip Peòaiʒ Mic in Òaill," op
pe. "Ocup cia h-ainmpiu?" op pipi. "Plann ua Peaòaich," op
pe; "h-ui peòaiò òin pil icconò imchopnum."

IS maiċ iapam in n-inòpi, .i. ppainò ceic icip biaò oocup linn

---

[20] Concaipnic. H. 8, 18.

[21] "Brodmuc," a spitted pig, a cooked
pig roasted or browned on the brod or
spit; a side or slice of roast bacon is also
called brodmuc. See MS. T. C. D. H. 3,
18, p. 368.

[22] "Creduma." The usual meaning
of this word is bronze, but it is also used
for the ore of copper, gold, or silver.

[23] Conbaò mepcai, till they were
drunk. H. 3, 18.

[24] A ceaċpap a n-òoċum in cea-

wed no further attention on her until he had finished the cooking
ɔ pig. He then made a brodmuc[21] of his pig, washed his hands, and
away from the fire; she followed him till they reached the lake.
. ship of creduma[22] was in the middle of the lake. A cable of cre-
ι from the middle of the ship to the land, and another cable from
:o the island which was in the middle of the lake. The warrior
ɔd in the ship, she went into the ship before him, they left the
in a ship-house of bronze at the port of the island, she went before
into the house; the house was admirable both in carvings and
. He sat down, she sat near him; he reached his hand across [her
er seat], and drew forth a dish with food for them. They both
ιnd drank, but so that neither of them got drunk.[23] There was no
r person in the house, nor were they interrupted. He went into
)ed, she lay under his garment, between him and the wall; he did
turn towards her till morning, when they heard the call at early
ning on the port of the island, i. e., "come out, Fland, the men are
).." He rose up instantly, put on his armour, and went out; she
.t to look after him to the door of the house, and saw the three
ι on the port. In features, age, and form, the three were like him.
then saw four men moving along the island holding their shields
ʼn in their hands; the four men then advanced [against the other
: men];[24] they struck each other till each party was red from the
ɔr. Then each party of them went off to his own side; he [Flann
ιe] went into the island again.

"The triumph of your valour to you," said she, "that was a heroic
ιt." "It would be good, truly, if it were against enemies," said he.
Vho are the warriors?" said she. "One of them is my brother's
,"[25] said he; "the other three are my three brothers." "What do
contend for?" said the woman. "This island," said he. "What
he name of the island?" said she. "Inis Fedach Mic in Daill,"[27]
1 he. "And what is your name?" said she. "Flann ua Fedach,"
1 he; "it is the ui Fedach who are contending for it."

The island is good, indeed, i. e., the dinner of one hundred men[28]

ɪn (ele), ʒabaɪꝺ aʒ comꞇuaɲʒaɪn
ele, &c., the four men advanced to-
rds the other four, and each com-
nced to strike another, &c. H. 3, 18.
ɪ5 Ɱac bɲaꞇaɲ aꞇaɲ ꝺaɱꝼa, the
ι of my father's brother. H. 3, 18.

[26] Inꝺ ɪnꝼɪꝼɪ, this island. H. 3, 18.
[27] "Inis Fedach Mic in Daill." See
Addendum I., p. 184.
[28] "Dinner for one hundred men." See
Note D, p. 197.

ıꞃe a h-ımᴄaıꞃec cecha nona, cen pꞃıᴄh̄znam[30] o bunıu oca; [aꞃeıꞃ] nı ꞃaıb achᴄ bıaꞃ ınᴄı, nıꞃ ᴄaıꞃıc achᴄ a ꞃoıꞃᴄu.

"Ceꞃc," oꞃ ꞃı, "Cıb na h-anımꞃea ʟaᴄꞃu?" "Iꞃ bꞃoch banaıꞃ buıᴄꞃıu ceᴄuꞃ," oꞃ ꞃeꞃem. "anab ʟımꞃa ocuꞃ ꞃı h-Θꞃenb bo ꝼaobaıʟ, ocuꞃ beıᴄ buıᴄ ꞃoꞃamꞃa, ocuꞃ a ᴄeꞃoꞃ ım bıaıbꞃı."

"Cıb na compaıcım?" oꞃ ꞃı, "Na ᴄo bon chuꞃꞃa," aꞃ ꞃeꞃem, mab ʟımꞃa ımoꞃꞃo ınb ınıꞃ, ocuꞃ bıa maıꞃem ꞃeꞌzaᴄꞃa aꞃ bo chennꞃo, ocuꞃ ıꞃ ᴄuꞃu bıᴄh ben bıaꞃ ım ꝼaꞃꞃab, ocuꞃ aıꞃcꞃeo bon chuꞃꞃa."

"Saeᴄ bam mo ınaıʟᴄ bo ꝼacbaıʟ," oꞃ ꞃı. "Aᴄa ı m-beaᴄ-aıb ı m-bun ın chꞃoınn cheᴄnaı," oꞃ ꞃeꞃem; "ʟaız na h-ınbꞃı ꞃo-ꞌzabꞃeb ımmꞃı ocuꞃ ꞃeꞌzᴄaıꞃ bıaꞃ n-ıbʟocon." ba ꝼıꞃ ꞃon.

Rıc ꞃı a ᴄez, co ꞃaꞃnıc ınnı Dıaꞃmaıc oc eıꞃzıu ıꞃın bomnac ceᴄnu. "Amꞃa ꞃın aben," oꞃ Dıaꞃmaıc, "na beaꞃnaıꞃ ımabaʟʟ ın bomnaıc baꞃ aꞃ n-uꞃzaıꞃı," "Nı ꞃoʟamaꞃ ꞃon[32]," oꞃ ꞃı, "ımchım bo bꞃeıᴄhꞃıꞃıu," amaıʟ na ᴄeıꞃeb ꞃı eᴄeꞃ : ba h-e a h-aen [ꝼ]ocaʟ ón uaıꞃ ꞃın na bec ꝼoʟab.

> "Daꞃa abaız ıꞃın choıʟʟ
> ⠀⠀Iᴄız ınbꞃı mıc ın baıʟʟ[33]
> ⠀⠀Cıaꞃ bo ʟa ꝼeꞃ nıꞃ bo choʟ,
> ⠀⠀In ᴄan ꞃcaꞃꞃom nıꞃ ba ꞃom[34]
>
> Inıꞃ Feabaıb Mıc ın Doıʟʟ[35]
> ⠀⠀Iᴄꞃ́ʀ ʟaızın ı n-Dubᴄaıꞃ
> ⠀⠀Cıaꞃo ꞃocuꞃ bo ꞃooᴄ
> ⠀⠀Nı ꞃazbaıb oız uʟchaız."[36]

ba h-ınznab ʟa cach n-oen ın n-aᴄeꞃc ꞃın. Aʟʟa ꞃın bın, cınb bʟıabna boı, Dıaꞃmaıc ꞃoꞃ a beꞃzab, ocuꞃ a ben, .ı. beo Foʟa, conacabaꞃ ın ꝼeꞃ ꞃeach boꞃuꞃ ın ᴄızı, ocuꞃ ꞃe achzoıᴄı, .ı. Fʟanb, ıꞃ anb aꞃbeꞃᴄ bec Foʟa.[37]

> "Foꞃzaʟo ꝼeꞃ bıꞃu amıꞃıꞃ
> ⠀⠀Don bebaıb ı n-Dam Inıꞃ
> ⠀⠀Inab ın ceᴄhꞃuıꞃ ꞃo bꞃıꞃ
> ⠀⠀Foꞃ ceachꞃuꞃ ı n-Dam Inıꞃ."

[29] "*Linn.*" See Note D., p. 197.

[30] "*Frithgnam.*" See Note D., p. 197.

[31] "*Calves of this island.*" See Note E., p. 197.

[32] Nı ꞃoʟamaꞃꞃıum. I should not have dared. H. 3, 18.

[33] "*Inis Mic in Daill,*" i. e. Damh Inis. See Addendum, No. 1, p. 184.

[34] In ᴄan ꞃcaꞃꞃomne ba ꞃomh

of food and linn[29] is its supply every evening, without any frith-
n[30] from the people; there were only two persons in it [last night],
e came but their supply.

" I ask," said she, "why should I not remain with you?" " It
ld be a bad espousal for you, indeed," said he, "to remain with
and to abandon the King of Eriu, and you [i. e. your blame] to
upon me, and its vengeance to follow me."

" Why should we not dwell together?" said she. " Let us not this
?," said he, "but if the island be mine, and that I live, I will go
you, and you shall be my constant wife residing with me, but depart
r for the present."

" I am grieved to leave my handmaid," said she. " She is alive at
foot of the same tree," said he; " the calves[31] of the island sur-
nded her and detained her to screen us." This was true.

She reached her house, and found Diarmait there rising on the same
nday. " It is well, O woman," said Diarmait, " that you have not
rneyed on the Sunday against our prohibition." " I should not have
·ed to do that,"[32] said she, "to disobey your order," just as if she
l not gone at all: her only word from that time forth was, the Bec
lad.

> " I was a night in the wood
>   In the house of Inis Mic in Daill:[33]
>   Though it was with a man, there was no sin,
>   When we parted it was not early.[34]
>
> Inis Feadaid Mic in Daill,[35]
>   In the land of Laigen in Dubthar,
>   Though it is near unto the road,
>   Bearded heroes do not find it." [36]

Every person wondered at these words. At the end of a year from
at day, however, Diarmait was upon his bed, with his wife, i. e. Bec
la, they saw a wounded man passing the door of the house, i. e.
.and, it was then Bec Fola said:[37]—

> " Superior in valour of fierce men, I ween,
>   In the battle of Damh Inis,
>   The four men who conquered
>   The [other] four men in Damh Inis."

hen we parted it was early. H. 3, 18.
[35] "Inis Feadaid Mic in Daill," now
amh Inis. See Addendum, No. I.,
184.

[36] "Bearded heroes." See Addendum,
No. III., p. 190.

[37] ᚐᚏᚁᚓᚂᚈᚏᚔᚁᚓ .ι. ᚁᚓᚑ ᚠᚑᚂᚐ, said
she, i. e., Bec Fola.

Inυe υιχιτ Ꞟlanυ:

"ᾳ bean na bean ιꞟ n-aτhbeꞟ[38]
Ꞟoꞟ na h-oυu υια n-aτ̇lιᵹ;
Nι υατ ᵹαlα ꞟeꞟ ꞟo clol,
ᾴότ ꞟιꞟ con uꞟbαιᵹ ꞟoꞟ ᵹαι."[39]

" Nι ꞟo ꝼaᵹbαιm," oꞟ ꞟιꞟι " aꞟ ᵹαιl υunι υ-ꝼulaτταιn, τꞟaτ̇ ιꞟ
ꞟoꞟ Ꞟlanυ υo υeꞟcaυ,[40] a comlunn ιn τ̇omoτταιꞟ laꞟoυαιn noꞟ,"
leιcι uαιυιυ aꞟ ιn τιᵹ ιna υιαιυ cona h-αꞟꞟuꞟ. "Noꞟ leιcιυ, uαιb,"
oꞟ Ꙅιαꞟmαιτ, " a n-uꞟτ̇oυ, aꞟ nι ꝼeaꞟ cια τheιτ, no cια τhuυchαιυ."

ᾳm bαταꞟ ꞟoꞟ a n-ιmꞟαιτιυ conacaταꞟ ceτhꞟuꞟ mac cleιꞟech
ιꞟan τech. "Cιυ ane?" oꞟ Ꙅιαꞟmαιτ, "ιn meιc cleιꞟιᵹ oc ιm-
τeaτ̇τ ιꞟιn υomnuch !"[41] Lα τobαιꞟτ a bꞟuιτ υαꞟ a cenυ conach aꞟ
ꞟαcα ιτιꞟ.

"Iꞟ comαꞟlecuυ ꞟꞟuιτ́ υonꞟuc," oꞟ na meιc cleꞟιch, "nιm-
τholτα, .ι. Molαꞟι Ꙅam-Inυꞟι[42] υonꞟαιυ υo τ'acallαιm, .ι. columun
υo muιnτιꞟ Ꙅam-Inυꞟι ꞟo buι oc aιꞟeꞟᵹι abo ιꞟιn maτιn, ꞟe, ιnυιu,
conꞟαca ιn ceτhꞟaꞟ ꞟo naꞟmαιυ cona ꞟcιατhαιυ ꞟoιnᵹαbαlα
ιαꞟ ꞟuτ na h-ιnυꞟe; conꞟαca υιn ιn ceaτhꞟoꞟ αιle aꞟa cιnυ: Im-
moꞟτuαιꞟceτ co cloꞟ ꞟon ιnυꞟe n-uιle ᵹαιꞟ na ꞟcιaτ̇ ocon n-
ιmτuaꞟᵹαιn, comma τoꞟchαιꞟ υoιb aτ̇τ aen ꝼeꞟ aτhᵹoιτι aꞟꞟulαι
aꞟ namma."

" Ro aυnachτα lα Molαιꞟι ιn moꞟꞟeꞟιuꞟ ele; ꞟoꞟ ꞟacαιυ ꞟeaυ,
ιmoꞟꞟo, υι óꞟ ocuꞟ aꞟᵹuτ aιꞟι υeꞟι uannι, .ι. υo neoch ꞟo buι ꞟo
m-bꞟoταιυ, ocuꞟ ιm a m-bꞟαιᵹυιb, acaꞟ ιm a ꞟcιατhαιυ, acaꞟ a
n-ᵹóo, acaꞟ a clαιυβιu, acaꞟ ιm a lamα, acaꞟ ιm a n-ιnαꞟα. Co
ꞟeꞟαꞟαꞟu υo chuιτ υιnυ n-óꞟ acaꞟ υιnυ n-aꞟᵹaυ ꞟιn."

"Na τ́o," oꞟ Ꙅιαꞟmαιτ, " an υo ꞟaυ Ꙅια υoꞟom noτ̇o τ̇uιτιτ̇ꞟα
ꝼꞟιꞟ. Ꙅenαιτheꞟ a ꞟeτhlα[44] laιꞟeom υe." υα ꝼιꞟ ꞟoιn.

Iꞟ υιnυ n-aꞟᵹuυ ꞟιn, ιmoꞟꞟo, acaꞟ υon óꞟ ꞟocumυαιᵹeυ
mιnna Molαιꞟι,[46] .ι. a ꞟcꞟιn,[47] acaꞟ a mιnιꞟτιꞟ[48] acaꞟ a bατ̇all. Ꙅo
choιυ, ιmoꞟꞟo, bec Ꞟolα lα Ꞟlann uα Ꞟebαιch, acaꞟ nι chαιnιc
beoꞟ. τochmoꞟc bec ꝼolα ꞟιn. Ꞟιnιτ.

[38] ᾳ bean na beιꞟ aꞟ n-αιchꞟeꞟ
ꞟoꞟꞟ na h-ócu υιαꞟ n-aτ̇lιᵹ. H.
3, 18.

[39] " *Men with charms on their spears.*"
See Additional Note, F., p. 198.

[40] Inaτ Ꞟlann, ꞟoꞟ ꞟo υeꞟᵹaυ aꞟ

υαυ, in revenge of Fland I shall wound
them. H. 3, 18.

[41] " *Clerics travelling on Sunday.*" See
Note B., p. 195.

[42] " *Molasa of Dam Inis*, who sent us,"
&c. See Note G., p. 199.

Then Fland said :

> "O woman, cast not thy reproach[38]
> Upon the heroes to disparage them ;
> It was not manly valour that vanquished them,
> But men with charms on their spears."[39]

"I cannot help," said she, " from going to oppose the valour of the l, because it was Fland that was wounded[40] in the conflict of the it," and so she went from them out of the house after him to his a abode. "Let her depart from ye," said Diarmait, "the evil, we know not whither she goes or whence she comes."

While thus conversing, they saw four ecclesiastical students coming the house. "What is this?" said Diarmait, "the clerics travel- on Sunday!"[41] Thus saying, he drew his cloak over his head so t he might not see them at all.

"It is by order of our superior we travel," said the ecclesiastical dents, "not for our pleasure, i. e. Molasa of Damh Inis[42] who sent us parley with you, i. e., a farmer of the people of Dam Inis[43] while rding his cows this morning—to-day, saw four armed men with ir shields slung down traversing the island; he then saw four n more coming against them: they struck each other so that the ngour of the shields was heard all over the island during the nflict, till they all fell but one wounded man who alone escaped."

"Molaisa buried the other seven; they left, moreover, the load of ro of us of gold and silver, i. e. of that which was upon their garments, d upon their necks, and upon their shields, and upon their spears, d upon their swords, and upon their hands, and upon their tunics. o ascertain thy share of that gold," [we have come, said they.]

"Not so," said Diarmait; "what God has sent to him, I will not rticipate in. Let him make his fethla[44] of it." This was true.

It was with this silver now, and with this gold, Molaisa's minda[45] ere ornamented, namely, his shrine[46] and his ministir[47] and his crozier. ec Fola, however, went off with Flann ua Fedach, and she has not ince returned. That is the courtship of Bec Fola. FINIS.

---

[43] "*Dam-Inis*," now Devinish Island Loch Erne. See Addendum, No. I. 184.

[44] *Fethal*, pl. *Fethla*, an ornamental acing or covering, as of shrines, cases, nd sacred reliquaries.

[45] "*Minda*," here sacred reliquaries, &c.

[46] "*Shrine of Saint Molasa*." See Additional Note, G., p. 199.

[47] "*Ministir*," a portable box or case, a safe in which the sacred vessels and Gospels or Lectionary for the service of the altar were preserved and carried.

Oinosenchas Ouibchir.

Ouibchir canar ro h-ainmniʒeò? nin. òa mac porpacaiò
ʒuairi Mic in òoill, .i. ʒuairi ʒann acar Oairi Ouibchear-
cach. Co ro marò ʒuairi in Oairi oc Oaim Inir coniò òe roleach
Fiò acar mochar[48] òar Crich n-ʒuairi òon Finʒail rin òo roinòe
ʒuairi ror in Oairi n-Oubchearòach[49] ror a brachair,—ror a
chineaò olroòain, unòe òicicur Ouibchir Oairi òia n-eòraò.

Ouibchir ʒuari ʒnim òa[50] Fuil,
  Ir rcel Fin, co Fearaòairi,
  òai rel nar òo òuchor òor
  In crich cruchach comrolair.

Oa mac porpacaiò Oall Oear
  ʒuaine Oall Oairi Oilear
  Imon crich can òuilʒe
  Oeniòòar cuiòòe comroinòe.

Fillir ʒuairi ʒnim n-earbach
  For an Oairi n-Ouibòearcaò,
  Co corchair leir Oaine in òaiʒ
  Can ʒne n-ailiò n-imcoroich

On lo ro ʒaeò ʒuairi òron
  A n-Inir Oaim can òichor,
  Ir Fich, co m-buaine mochair,
  Crich ʒuairi òon chomochain.[51]

[48] "*Mothar*," an enclosure, a place
studded with bushes or brushwood.
[49] For an Oaire n-òian n-òuibòear-
caò. Upon the vehement Daire Duib-
cheastach. Book of Ballymote, referred
to hereafter by the letter B.

[ADDENDUM, No. I.]

DINDSENCHAS OF DUBTHAR.

Book of Lecan (fol. 251 *a.b.*)

)uibthir, why so called? Answer. Two sons that were left by ıre Mac in Doill, i. e. Guaire Gann and Daire Duibhcheastach. ıre killed Daire in Dam Inis. A wood and a mothar[48] overspread land of Guaire on account of that fratricide which Guaire commit- upon Daire Dubcheasdach[49] i. e. upon his brother,—upon his race , unde dicitur Duibthir Dairi, of which was said :—

Duibthir Guari, the deed whence it is,
It is a true story, be it known to you,
There was a time when it was not a bushy Duthor,
The broad delightful region.

Two sons were left by Dall Deas,
Guaire Dall and Daire Dileas,
Of that region, without contention,
They made an appropriate equal division.

Guaire wrought a wicked deed
Upon Dairi Dubcheastach,
And he killed Daire the good,
Without shade of blemish or disgrace.

Since the day that powerful Guaire slew
In Inis Daim, without provocation,
It is a heath, a perpetual mothar,
The land of Guaire of the foul treachery.

50 Gnim dia puil. H. 2, 18, and B. 51 Compochain. B.

Mairg da gni fingal co h-om
Gnim do na timgar torad
Crich Guairi can chosnum de
Fil na dos-mag Duibthire. D.

Nomsaera ar fill is ar olc
A crist rochind[52] mo chaem chorp
Ari subach na sine[53]
Nir bum dubach duibthire. D.

[ADDENDUM, No. II.]

DINDSENCHAS LOCHA N-EIRNE.

Loċ n-Eirne canar ro h-ainmniged? Nin. Fiacha Labraindi do rad caṫ[55] and do Ernaib conad and ro mebaid in loch ros thír, unde Loch n-Erne dicitur no for Ernaib.

Ailetes Erni, ingen buirc buireadaich mac Maċoin mic Machon[56] ban-tairech ingenraid na Cruachnai, acas ban-choimedaich do chiraib acas do cloirib[57] Meidbi Cruachan.

Fecht and do luid Olcai[58] a h-uaim Chruachan do comrod[59] fri h-Aimirgin Margiudach[60] dia ro fai le Findchaim ingin Magach, conad and rochroich Olcai a ulcha acas ro bean a deda,[61] co n-deachaid Erne cona h-ingenaib for fualang ar a imomon co riacht loch n-Erne co ro baidead and diblinaib, unde loch n-Erne dicitur.

Eirne chaid can chuaird chnedaig
Ingen buirc bain buireadaig
Ba saragad saer trin son ban
Mac Maichin mic Machon.[62]

52 "Rochind." Who rules. B.

53 Ari na subaid, n a sine, O king of the joys [of the] elements. B.

54 "*Fiacha Labrainde.*" See Note H., p. 202.

55 Do breta caṫ, gave battle. B.

56 Mac mainċin, son of Mainchin. B.

57 Cleraib. B.

58 Olccai. B.

59 Comrug, to contend. B.

60 h-aimirgin mairgiunnaċ. B. See Additional Note, I., p. 202.

Woe to him who commits a cold fratricide,
  A deed of which no profit comes;
  The land of Guaire is through it unprotected,
  A bushy plain of Duibtihr. D.

Save me from treachery and from evil,
  O Christ, who seest[52] my comely body,
  O benign king of the elements[53]
  That I be not a sorrowful Dubthor. D.

[ADDENDUM, No. II.]

DINDSENCHAS OF LOCH ERNE.

Book of Lecan R. I. A. (fol. 250 b. b.)

Loch n-Eirne, why so called? Answer. Fiacha Labrainde[54] that
ɜ battle there to the Ernans and it was then the lake burst
h over the land, unde Loch n-Erne dicitur, or it was over the Ernans
came].

Or Erni, daughter of Burc Buireadach, son of Machin,[56] son of Ma-
n, mistress of the maidens of Cruachan, and mistress in charge of
 combs and caskets of Medb of Cruachan.

At one time Ulchai came out of the cave of Cruachan to contend with
nirgin Mairgiudach who had espoused Findchaom, daughter of
ɩgach, and it was then Ulchai shook his beard and he gnashed his
th, so that Erne and her maidens fled precipitately through fear
him till they reached Loch n-Erne and they were all drowned in it,
de Loch n-Eirne dicitur.*

      Eirne chaste without shade of stain,
        Daughter of Burc Buireadach the fair,
        It was an insult to the honour of her noble father;
        He was the son of Maichin, son of Mochon.[62]

[61] Deca, teeth. B.

[* Eleven stanzas follow here on the
ɜt derivation, which do not, however,
ɩar on our subject.]

[62] ba ꞃaꞃaᵹaꝺ ꞃaeꞃ cꞃɩaꞃ ɩꞃ ꞃoꞃ baꞃ
  Maᴄ maɩꞃchɩꞃ maᴄ mochoꞃ. B.,

The following is the text of H 2. 18,
which is followed in the translation with
the correction indicated in brackets:

    ba ꞃaꞃaᵹaꝺ ꞃaeꞃ [a] chɩꞃ ɩꞃ ꞃoꞃ
    ba Maᴄ Maɩchɩꞃ mɩo mochoꞃ.

          H. 2, 18, fol. 154, a. a.

Eipne noipech cen eamain[63]
   Fa coipech fop ingenaib
   Ipaich Cpuachan na peb peib,[64]
   Nip uachab ben ca bich-péip.

Aici po bibip pe meap[65]
   Min peoib meabba na mop cpeap,
   Acip pa chioip can chlob
   Iap na cinol bo bepg óp.[66]

Co canaic a cpuaich cheapa
   Olcai co n-uach n-imchana,[67]
   Cop chpoich a ulcha ap in plog,
   In gapb fep, baigep baich mop.[68]

Ro pcanpab pa Chpuaich Cheapa
   Na h-anpi na h-ingena
   Caibpin a chpocha, pochóip.
   Glan pin[69] agocha glopaich.

Ro cheich Epne ilap m-ban
   Co Loch n-Epne nach inglan
   Cop bail caipppi in cuile chuaib,
   Co pup baib uili a n-aen uaip.

Giamab uabib ip bpeach cheapc,[70]
   Fiab na pluagaib ni paeb peacc,
   Ip caipm cap cpocha po chaipg
   Ainm Locha Epni imaipb. L.

A aipb pi peibil, pip bám
   Failci bemin bom bibnab;
   Fop nim co m-buabaib pombae,
   A pip cuapcaib Loch Epne. L.

---

[63] cen n-eamain. H. 2, 18, fo. 154, a. a.
[64] Reb peib, Lecan, is peb peb. In B.
Book of Leinster has—
   I paic cpuachan na cpeab bo cein
   Nip b'uachab ban ca Compeip.
   In Rath Cruachan of wounds of old.
   Not few the women in her charge.
H. 2, 18, fol. 154, a. a.

[65] bibip pia meap, had them in charge
to care. B.
[66] A cip, a cpioll can chlob.
   Cona n-biol bo beapg óp.
   Her combs and caskets without stain.
   With their adornments of red gold.
H. 2, 18, fol. 154, a. a. and B.

Eirne noble without guile
  Was mistress of the maidens
  In Rath Cruachan of heroic feats,
  Not few the women in her constant charge.

Hers was the task to care
  The polished jewels of Medb of great battles,
  Her combs and caskets without stain
  When embellished with red gold.

Till from Cruach Ceara came
  Olcai of flight-causing visage,[67]
  And shook his beard at the host,
  The fierce man, terrific, hideous-coloured.[68]

Over Cruach Ceara in fright they fled,
  The timid youths and the maidens,
  On beholding his form, though comely.
  Clear was the sound[69] of their resounding voices.

Erne with her many maidens fled ·
  To Loch n-Erne which is not impure
  Till the rude wave rolled over them,
  And drowned them all at the one time.

Though it be from these, it is a right judgment,[70]
  Before the hosts 'tis not a trifling cause,
  The overwhelming sudden deaths proclaimed
  The name of Loch Erne aloud. L.

O high King of Mercy, give to me
  A true welcome to protect me ;
  In heaven in joys may I be,
  O man, who caused the eruption of Loch Erne. L.

---

[67] Co canaic i Cruachan caip.
  Olccai con li blac amnaip.
  Till to Cruachan of valour came.
  Olocai of beautiful bold countenance.
[68] In ganb fen baic baigep mop.

[69] Ꝃlan pin, Lecan, is ganb pin,
rough sound. H. 2, 18, 154 a. a.
[70] Ciambab uaoib ni paeb peoc
though it were from them it is no trifling
cause. B.

ᵹeısı ulcaı.

———•———

Coneıᵹıuᵱ ᵭuıᵭ ᵹeıᵱı ulċaı
   ın caċ ınᵭaıᵭ.
Ɍeᵭıl ᵱaᵭlaıᵭ, olc ᵭo anmaın ;
   Cᵱom ᵭo mıᵭlaıᵹ.
Αϲa ceıϲıᵱn ᵭıan ϲoıᵭ ulċaı
   Nı ᵭaᵱ ᵭaelı—
Αᵱᵭᵱuım ϲuaċ ocuᵱ muıᵱe
   Ocuᵱ laϲ ᵹaelı.
Saeᵱ ċlanna ᵱıᵹ ᵱeᵭᵹa alluᵭ
   Α huıċϲ ᵭuıᵭean ;
Αn cınᵹıᵭ loeċ ᵱᵱıᵱ na ᵹeᵭċeᵱ
   comᵭonn ᵹuıneaċ,
Maᵭ aᵱ chena ceᵭoᵱ leceaᵭ,
   Nıᵱ o ᵭeᵱıl [ᵭıᵱıl .ı. ᵭeıᵱeoıle]
Moo a meᵭal ᵭı, cıᵭ a ᵱoıᵱeaᵱ
   Maᵭ ᵱo ᵹeᵱıᵭ.
Ɣeᵱ ᵭı nomaıᵭe na ᵭeaᵱᵹᵱaıᵭeaᵱ lé ᵱınᵭı,
   Ceaᵭ maᵭ uıllı ;
Ɣeıᵱ ᵭı ᵹᵱıan ᵭo ϲuᵱcᵭaıl ᵱuıᵱᵱı
   ına lıᵹı.
Ɣeıᵱ ᵭı eıᵹem oan a ċoᵭaıᵱ
   Maᵭ ᵭo ᵹneϲeᵱ,
Ɣeᵱ ᵭı ᵹen ᵹaıᵱı ᵭıa cᵱoċaᵭ ;
   Ɣeıᵱ ᵭı ϲecheᵭ ;
Comᵱuc ᵱᵱı loech, ıᵱ ᵱeıᵭm ınᵹneaċ,
   Ɣeıᵱ ᵭı oᵱaᵭ,

PROHIBITIONS OF BEARD.

———◆———

H. 2. 16. *T. C. D. col.* 919.

I shall relate to you the prohibitions of a beard
    At all times.
Curled and hedgy, 'tis bad for the timid ;
    'Tis too heavy for the coward.
There are warriors who are entitled to a beard
    Who are not cowardly—
Noble chiefs by land and sea
    And battle champions.
Noble sons of kings who inflict wounds
    In the front of battalions ;
The kingly champion over whom is not gained
    The woundful battle,
If then he should suffer reproach
    It shall not be from pusillanimity.
Its disgrace will be the greater, should it come
    Under the prohibitions.
A prohibition of it, a nomaid[71] unreddened with spears,
    If oftener it is allowable ;
A prohibition of it, the sun to rise on it
    In its bed.
A prohibition of it, to hear a moan without relieving it
    If made to him ;
A prohibition of it, to laugh when shaken ;
    A prohibition of it, to retreat ;
To battle with a champion, to fight with the nails
    A prohibition of it, to refuse.

[71] " *Nomaid,*" a space of time: sometimes it means one day, but in the Irish Laws it is generally put for nine days or the ninth day.

Cıb beaɔ, ɲo beɔ, ıcıɲ ıcıɲ,
   ʒeɲ ɓı obaɲ;
ʒeɲ ɓı ʒualach oɔuɲ mıanach;
   Iɲ oɲɓ ɲnımaċ;
ʒeɲ ɓı alcɲom ʒeɲ ɓı caɲcaɓ,
   ʒeɲ ɓı cıɲaɓ.
ʒeɲ ɓı ɲloıɓı mna no ʒılla,
   Iɲ oɲɓ melı.
Aċc a ɲoıach aɲ ɲoaċ a ɲıʒı,
   ʒeɲ ɓı eɲı;
ʒeɲ ɓı ʒlun ɲalaċ a h-ımbaıɓ—
   Nı ɓaıl ɓulbċaı;
Na nı on leanuɓ ɔo ɲaıłóı
   Inɲa n-ulċaı.
Ceċ maɔ aċaıch, aċ ɲoɲ ɲaıċech,
   Seɲnaɓ ɲupu,
Poemaı ɔoɲmaılıɲ ıɲ ɓacu
   Fɲıɲ na buɔɔu.
Ro ɲela ɓam, ɔonɓa ćolaċ
   ɲaıɲɲı aɲ chulɲaı.
Feaɲ ecna moıɲ amaıl ıɲ ɔoıɲ
   Fɲı ɔeċ n-ulċaı.
Ceɲɓa, ʒobaınɓ, ɲaıɲ luınɓ,
   Leʒa le ıɔeaɓ labaıɲ,
Oıa beıċ ɓıa ɲcıɲ beɲɲaɓ ɔeċ mıɲ
   Aɲ a naıʒıb.

However small, ever so small, at all, at all,
    A prohibition of it to labour ;
A prohibition of it to mine for coals or mineral,
    And to wield the sledge;
A prohibition of it to nurse ; a prohibition of it to shovel ;
    A prohibition of it to kiln-dry.
A prohibition of it to abuse women or boys,
    And the habit of a sluggard.
Save his shield sheltering his arm,
    A prohibition of it to carry a burthen ;
A prohibition of it, to bring an unclean knee into a bed,—
    Not an unreasonable condition ;
Nor anything filthy from the child
    In the beard.
Every son of an Athach, if rich,
    Grows the wisps [beard],
They desire to be like in appearance and colour
    To the bucks [he-goats].
It has been revealed to me, therefore I know
    The privileges of the collars [whiskers].
I am a man of great knowledge of what is lawful
    For every kind of beard.
Artificers, smiths, house-builders,
    Physicians who cure the infirm,'
Because of their fatigue they shave every month
    [The beard] on their faces.

ADDITIONAL NOTES.

(A.) " *Tindsora.*" *Tinscra*, a gift, price, reward or dowry: here it is used in a general sense to represent the "Bride Price," the "marriage gift," and the "morning gift." *Bec Fola* having consented to receive King Diarmait's brooch as her *Folad*, which is also called Tinscra in this passage, (p. 174), and this being the only pledge or price given her, it represents the three; and, with the adjective *Bec*, little or small, affixed to it, it forms the name *Bec Fola*, or little dowry, as O'Curry has rendered it in his work on "The MS. Materials of Irish History," p. 283. The following passages show that the word meant "Bride Price" and "morning gift."

Ʈabραιὸ ὸαmρα, ϝορ Oenʒuρ, ὸο mnαι Ɛιʌnι, .ι. ϝuρ n-ὸαlʌα, acaρ ὸο bϝρρα ϝeρανὸ ὸuιb na ʌιnρcρα .ι. ϝeρανὸ ϝιl ὸαmρα lα oρραιʒe ϝρινὸ α n-ὸeρ, acaρ ιρ cec ὸuιbριu αραρρινʒuὸ ϝοραιb.

" Give me, said Oengus, Eithne as wife, namely, your foster child, and I will give you land as her *Tinscra*, namely, land which I have near to Ossory by us on the south, and it shall be permitted to you to make it more extensive for yourselves."—*Leabhar na h-Uidhri*, p. 54, col. 2, top.

Ὸο ʒnι̇ʌeρ ιmacallαιm oc Ulʌαιb ιmon cαιnʒιn ριn: ιρρeὸ ιαροm comαιρle αριċʌ léo, Ɛmeρ ὸο ϝeιρ lα Concobαρ αn αιὸċι ριn, acaρ Ϝeρʒuρ acaρ Caʈbαὸ α n-oen lepαιὸ ϝριu ὸο coιmeὸ enιʒ Conculαινὸ; acaρ bennacʌ Ulaὸ ὸon lαnαmαιn αρ α ϝαemαὸ. Ϝαemαιὸ αn nι ριn, acaρ ὸο ʒnιec ραmlαιὸ. Icuὸ Concobaρ ʌιnρcρα Ɛmιρe ιαρ na mαρuċ, acaρ ὸο bρeʌαι eneclανὸ ὸο Conculαινὸ, acaρ ϝαιὸeρ ιαρ ριn lια bιn ċelα, acaρ nι ρο ρcαρραʌ ιαρρubιu co ϝuαραʌαρ bαρ bιblιnαιb.

" The Ultonians held a consultation on this difficult question: the counsel on which they determined was to have Emer to sleep with Conchobar that night, and Fergus and Cathbadh in the same bed with them to protect the honour of Cuchulaind; and the thanks of the Ultonians were offered to the pair for agreeing to this. They consented to this, and it was so done. Conchobar paid Emer's *Tinscra* on the morrow, and he gave *eneoland* (honour price) to Cuchulaind; and he embraced his wife after that, and they did not separate afterwards till they both died."—" *Leabhar na h-Uidhri*," p. 127, col. 1.

(B.) "Clerics travelling on Sunday." This is an allusion to the *Cain Domnaig*, a rule for the observance of Sunday as a day free from every kind of labour; the copy of the tract preserved in the " Yellow Book of Lecan," T. C. D., Class H. 2, 16, col. 217 opens thus :—" Iɼeƀ mɼo poɼuɼ chana m ƀomnaiʒ ƀoɼɼuc Conall mac Ceolmaine ƀi chuaƀ ƀia ailicɼi ƀo Ꞃoím acaɼ ɼo ɼcɼiƀ a láim ꝼéin aɼ m eiɼiɼcil ɼo ɼcɼiƀ láim ƀé ꝼoɼ nim a ꝼiaƀnaiɼi ꝼeɼ nime acaɼ ɼolaƀ ꝼoɼ alcoiɼ ɼecaiɼ aɼɼcail iɼm Ꞃóim. " This is the knowledge of the *Cain Domnaig*, which was brought by Conall, son of Ceolman, who went on his pilgrimage to Rome, and was written by his own hand out of the epistle which was written by the hand of God in heaven, in presence of the men of heaven, and which he placed upon the altar of Peter the Apostle in Rome." This account is repeated in the version of the rule incorporated with the ancient laws preserved in Cod. Clarend. Brit. Mus., vol. 15, fol. 7, p. 1 a. b., and in the following stanzas from the metrical version of the Cain Domnaig which follows it in the same MS. :—

> Ꞁeaƀaɼ ƀo ɼaƀ lám ƀé móiɼ
> Ꝼoɼ alcoiɼ ɼecaiɼ iɼ póil;
> Iɼ ꝼɼic iɼa leƀuɼ ceaɼc
> Ꝟan ƀomnaƀƀo caiɼmceaƀc.

> Comaɼba ɼeƀaiɼ iɼ póil,
> Ꝼuaiɼ an leaƀaɼ ꝼa oécóiɼ,
> Ocuɼ ɼo leiʒ an leƀaɼ
> Ꞃaɼ ƀuƀ leiɼ ƀu lan meƀaiɼ.

> A book placed by the hand of the great God
> Upon the altar of Peter and Paul;
> It has been found in the appropriate book
> That the Sunday should not be transgressed.

> It was the Comarb of Peter and Paul,
> Who found the book first,
> And he promulgated the book
> As he had it well in memory.

> Cod. Clarend. Brit. Mus., vol. 15, fol. 7, p. 1, col. a. b.

Saint Conall, son of Ceolman, who is said to have brought the Cain Domnaig from Rome, was founder of a church on Inis Cail, now the Island of Iniskeele, near the mouth of the Gweebara bay, in the barony of Boylagh, and county of Donegal. His name is commemorated in the Festology of Aengus Céle Dé in the Leabhar Breac, fol. 34, a., at 11th May.

The Cain Domnaig enjoins under severe penalties that every class shall abstain from all kinds of work on Sunday, and that none shall travel on that day ; but wherever one happens to be on Saturday evening, there he should remain till Monday morning. To this there were some exceptions, such as bringing a physician to a sick person, relieving a woman in labour, saving a house from fire, &c. A priest was forbidden to travel on Sunday or Sunday night, or from vesper time on Saturday night till Monday morning, unless to attend a sick person supposed to be likely to die before the following morning, in which case the Cain says :—

> Feaρ ꝿρáib bia bomnaiꝿ ꝑoρ ρéb
> bo coρρuma neich bíρ ρe n-éꝿ,
> bo cabaiρc bo ouiρρ Cρiρc cáin,
> ma boiꝿ a éꝿ ρe mabain.

> A priest may journey on a Sunday
> To attend a person about to die,
> To give him the body of Christ the chaste,
> If he be expected to expire before morning.

Thus to see a priest travelling on Sunday was considered an omen of disaster, or of immediate death to some member of the *Fine* or tribe into whose house or territory he came; and hence King Diarmait's astonishment at perceiving the young priests approaching him on Sunday morning.

(C.) " *Failgib óir*," rings, or bracelets of gold; the *Failge* was a kind of open ring or bracelet for the wrist, arm, ankle, or finger, worn by men and women : by men in token of deeds of valour, as in the case of Lugadh Lagadh, who is said to have killed seven kings in successive battles, and who wore seven *Failgib* upon his hand in token of these deeds, of whom Cormac Mac Airt, monarch of Eriu (whose father was one of the seven) is recorded to have said, " ní čeil a boib ꝑoρ laꝿa ρo bič ρiꝿa boρiꝿai, .ı. a ρeačc ꝑailꝿi óiρ ima laim ;" i. e. " His hand does not conceal of Laga the number of kings he has slain, i. e. he has seven *Failgib* of gold upon his hand." Book of Lecan, R. I. A., folio 137 b. a. top; and the same occurs again in the same MS. fol. 124 a., margin col. mid. where the *Fail* is called a *Buindi* (i. e. a twisted ring) "ıp ce apbepc copmac ꝼꝛıꝛ, nı oeıl a boıb ꝼop laᵹa pobı pıᵹa .ı. a pécc m-buınbı óıp ıma boıb no ma meoıp." "His hand does not conceal of Laga that he has slain kings, i. e. he has seven *Buinnes* (twisted rings) of gold upon his hand or on his fingers." The *Fail* was used by women for the double purpose of personal ornament and munificence, as in the present instance, and in the case of King Nuada's wife, who is said to have had her arms covered with *failgib* of gold for the purpose of bestowing them on the poets and other professors of arts who visited her court.

(D.) "*Dinner for one hundred men each night of food and Lin*" (p. 179). This allusion shows that Bec Fola's sojourn was in the house of a king, and that *Inis Fedach Mic in Doill* (now Devinish Island), was the residence of a *Righ Buiden* (king of companies). According to an ancient law tract on the constitution and legal rights and duties of the different ranks of kings, preserved in vellum MS. T. C. D., Class H. 3. 18. p. 1 *et seq.*, four score men was the lawful retinue of a king, in addition to which he had his *Foleith* or leet of twelve men, his five tribemen, his wife, and his judge, making in all one hundred men, which constituted the legal *Dam* (company) of a *Righ Buiden* (king of companies), and he was entitled as *Frithgnam* (supplies) to their free maintenance from his people. This tract will appear with a translation and notes, by W. K. Sullivan, in the Appendix to O'Curry's Lectures on the Manners and Customs of the People of ancient Eriu, Vol. II., p. 532.

"*Lin*," often used for ale or other malt drinks; but in the laws it means the full amount of any thing, and here it appears to mean the full amount of food accompaniments that constituted the lawful dinner of the *Dam*, or company of the king.

(E.) "*Calves of this island.*" *Laegh*, a calf. But here, as in many other instances, it is applied to the young of the deer, e. g. "ap ann pın bo concabap na cleıpe eılıc allca uaca ap an pliab acap laeᵹ pe na h-aıp. And then the clerics saw a wild deer from them on the mountain, and a calf (fawn) near her." Life of St. Findbar, O'C. MS. C. U. I., p. 4; and Ordnance Survey of Cork, R. I. A., vol. ii., p. 622.

(F.) "*Men with charms on their spears.*"—There are many references to charmed swords and spears to be met with in our ancient writings. In the tale of the battle of the second or northern Magh Tuireadh, we find the following:—

Iʀ an cat ʀin bin ꝼuaiʀ Oʒmai cʀen-ꝼeʀ Oʀnai, claibem Cechʀa, ʀí Ꝼomoiʀe. Coꝼoʀlaic Oʒma in claibem ocuʀ ʒlanaiʀ ó Iʀ anb inbiʀ in claibem nach a n-beʀnab be, aʀ ba béʀ bo cloibmib. in can ʀin bo coʀʀilciciʀ bo abbabiʀ na ʒnima bo ʒnícea bib. Conib be ʀin bleʒaib cloibme cíʀ a n-ʒlancai iaʀ na coʀlucab. Iʀ be bno ꝼoʀcomecaʀ bʀeicca h-i claibme ó ʀin amac. Iʀ aiʀe ʀin no labʀaibiʀ bemna b'aʀmaib iʀ in aimʀiʀ ʀin, aʀ no abʀaibiʀ aiʀm o bainib iʀ in ʀe ʀin ; acaʀ ba bo comaiʀcib na h-aimʀiʀe na h-aiʀm.

"It was in this battle that Ogma the champion obtained Ornai, the sword of Tethra, king of the Fomorians. Ogma opened the sword, and cleaned it. Then the sword related all the deeds that had been performed by it; for it was the custom of swords at this time to recount the deeds that had been performed with them. And it is therefore that swords are entitled to the tribute of cleaning them whenever they are opened. It is on this account, too, that charms are preserved in swords, from that time down. Now the reason why demons were accustomed to speak from weapons at that time was, because arms were worshipped by people in those times, and arms were among the protections (or sanctuaries) of those times."—*MS. Brit. Museum, Egerton,* 5280, *and see O'Curry,* vol. ii. p. 254, *et seq.*

On those charms and their venomous effect, the same tale has the following :—

Imma comaiʀnic be Luc acaʀ bo boluʀ biʀuʀbeʒ eʀ in cat. Suil millbaʒac leʀeom. Ni h-oꝼʀcailcie in ʀoul acc iʀʀoi Cacae namma. Cecʀaʀ cuʀcbanb amalaiʒ bie ꝼol Conu bʀolum omlichi, cʀie na malab. Sluoao bo n-eceub beʀ ʀan ʀól nin ʒeʀciʀ ꝼʀi h-occo cie ʀibiʀ liʀ ilmili. Eʀ be boi innem ʀin ꝼuiʀʀiʀ : .i. bʀuic a acaʀ bocaʀ oc ꝼuluic bʀaiʒeccae, canacʀeum acaʀ ʀo beaʀc ,caʀ ʀan ꝼunbeoic, con becaib be en ꝼoulachcae ꝼuici ʒonib ꝼoʀ ʀan ʀuil bo becoib nem an ꝼoulacca ieʀ ʀin.

"Lug and Balor Birurderg met in the battle. He (Balor) had a destructive eye. This eye was never opened but in the field of battle. Four men were required to raise the lid off the eye with a hook which was passed through its lid. A whole army that he looked upon out of this eye could not prevail against [a few] warriors, even though they were many thousands in number. The cause why this poison was on it was this, namely : his father's druids had been boiling a druidical spell, and he came and looked in through the window, so that the fume of the boiling passed under it, and it was upon the eye that the poison of the brewing passed afterwards."—See *" Battle of the Second or Northern Magh Tuireadh,"* MS. Brit. Mus. Egerton, 5280 O'Curry, MSS., Catholic University.

(G.) *" Molasa of Damh Inis, who sent us,"* &c. (p. 183). This was Saint *Molaisa* or *Laisren*, patron of the island of *Damh-Inis*, i. e. Ox Island, now Devenish, an island in Lough Erne near the town of Fermanagh. He was Molaisa or Laisren, son of Nadfraech, whose day is 12th September, to be distinguished from *Molaisa* or *Laisren*, son of Declan, Saint of Inis Murry (12th August), and from *Molaisa* or *Laisren*, son of Cairell of Leighlin (18th April).

See Annals of the Four Masters, A. D. 563, n. t. See also *Felire Aenguis*, and O'Clery's Calendar, &c.

The Shrine of Saint *Molaisa* of *Damh Inis*, alluded to in the text (p. 183), and referred to in note 46, is now preserved in the Museum of the Royal Irish Academy, and popularly known as *Soisceal Molaisa*, or Molaisa's Gospel. For some account of it see Proceedings of R. I. A. Vol. VII., p. 331, and Academy Registry. The allusion in the text to the battle spoils of the fallen warriors may be illustrated by the following extracts from the Laws of Waifs and Strays, preserved in Brehon Law MS. Rawlinson, 487, Brit. Mus. fol. 62, p. 2, col. a. *et seq.*

In this law, the Waifs and Strays of a *Fine* (tribe) are divided into seven classes, and special laws are laid down for the recovery and appropriation of every class of waif found within the *Fine* as follows :—

Ʈáiʈ ρeʈʈ ρρíʈhé la ρéine, .i. a ʈáiʈ ρeʈʈ ρρíʈhe ʙo ʒaʙuρ ʙa n-aiρneiʙenn in ρéineʈuρ : Ρρiʈhe ʈρeiʙe, .i. ʙo ʒaʙuρ iρ in ʈρeiʙ. Ρρiʈhe caʈhρach, .i. ʙo ʒaʙuρ iρin caʈhρaiʒ ʈall. Ρρiʈhe ρaiʈhe, .i. ʙo ʒaʙuρ iρin ρaiʈʈhe, .i. iρ na ceiʈρi ʒoρʈaiʙ iρ neρum ʙon ʙaile. Ρρiʈhe ρaiʈe, .i. iʈiρ ρaiʈʈe acaρ ʙiρρainn. Ρρiʈhe ρoρiʙa, .i. ʙo ʒaʙuρ iρin ρoρíʙ. Ρρiʈhe ρléiʙe, .i. ʙo ʒaʙuρ iρin ʈ-ρliaʙ. Ρρiʈhe ʈρaʈʈa, .i. ʙo ʒaʙuρ iρin ʈρaʈʈ. Ρρiʈhe ρaiρʒe, .i. ʙo ʒaʙuρ aρ in ρaiρρʒe amuiʒ.

" There are seven waifs in the *Fine* (tribe), i. e. there are seven waifs which are found, of which the *Fenechus* takes cognizance :—*Frithe Treibe*, i. e. the waif which is found in the *Treb* (family home). *Frithe Cathrach*, i. e. the waif which is found in the distant *Cathair* (city). *Frithe Faithche*, i.e. the waif which is found in the *Faithche*, i.e. in the four fields which are nearest to the *Baile*. *Frithe Raite*, i. e. the waif which is found on the road between the *Faithche* and the *Dirrainn* (mountain). *Frithe Rofida*, i. e. the waif which is found in woody places. *Frithe Sleibhe*, i. e. the waif which is found on the mountain. *Frithe Trachta*, i. e. the waif which is found on the strand. *Frithe Fairrge*, i.e., the waif which is found abroad on the sea."—Rawlinson, 487, folio 62-63.

Ɍ̄ɼiche ɸaiche, .ı. ꝼɼiche ꝺo ꝣabuꝛ iꝛin ɸaiꞇꞇe, a ꞇꝛian aꝛa h-eccoimꝺıꝣ, acaꝛ aleꞇ aꝛ a coimꝺıꝣ. Iꝼꝛeꝺ coimꝺıꝣ ɸaiꞇꞇe anꝺ a ꞇulꝺain acaꝛ a ınaꝺa aiꝛeꞇꞇaiꝛ, no iꝼꝛéꝺ iꝛ coimꝺıꝣ ɸaiche anꝺ, aꝛliꝣꞇi acaꝛ a ınaꝺa ꝛéıꝺe aꝛꝺa, acaꝛ na h-ınaꝺa a m-bí aꞇıꝣi caɼch. Iꝼꝛeꝺ iꝛ écoimꝺıꝣ ınꞇı a ımꞀı acaꝛ a cúꞇa, no iꝼꝛeꝺ iꝛ eccoimꝺıꝣ ɸaiꞇꞇe anꝺ a cabana, acaꝛ a h-ınaꝺa ꝺıamꝛa, acaꝛ ın baile nach aıꞇıꝣınꝺ caꞇ aıꝛe. Iꝼꝛeꝺ iꝛ ɸaiche anꝺ na ceıchꝛı ꝣuiꝛꞇ iꝛ neaꝛa ꝺon baili, .ı. ꝣoꝛꞇ caꝥa aıꝛꝺı, ıme, acaꝛ cıꝺ hé ın ꝼꞀiab buꝺ neꝛa ꝺon baili, ꝛo ba aṁaıꞀ ɸaiche. Iꝼꝛeꝺ iꝛ ꝛeꞇꞇaꝛ ɸaiche ann ın aıꝛeꞇ acaꝛ ꝛo ꝛoıch cuaıꝛꝺ ınꝣelꞇa on ɸaiche amach, na iꝼꝛeꝺ iꝛ ɸaiche anꝺ an ꝛo ꝛaıꝣ ꝣuꞇh an cluıꝣ.

" *Frithe Faithche*, i. e. the waif which is found in the *Faithche*, one-third of it [goes to the finder] out of the *Ecoimdig*, and one-half out of the *Coimdig*. The *Coimdig* of a *Faithche* are its hills and its places of assembly, or the *Coimdig Faithche*, in it are its roads and its clear high places, and the places resorted to by the people. The *Ecoimdig*, in it are its border lands and its obscure places, or, the *Ecoimdig*, of a *Faithche* are its secluded places, and its obscure places, and the places not frequented by every *Aire*. A *Faithche*, in it are the four *guirt* (fields, Nom. Sing. *Gort*,) which are nearest to the *Baile*, i.e. a field on each side, around it, and even though the mountain happens to be nearest to the *Baile*, it is considered equal to a *Faithche*. A *Sechter Faithche*, in it is the distance which the grazing land extends out from the *Faithche*, or the *Faithche* is the distance at which the sound of the bell is heard from it."— Rawlinson, 487, fol. 62, p. 2, col. b. fol. 63, p. 1.

After having thus particularized the places and the circumstances of the different kinds of waifs, this law goes on to say :—

In ᵇuine ꝼuaiꞃ no ꝓoᵹebuiᵭ ꝼꞃíⱄⱦ, iꞃ na h-inaⱦa ꞃin iꞃeᵭ ᵭleᵹaꞃ ᵭe. Mɑꞃa ꝓꞃíⱄⱦe ⱄꞃe, ɑ eꞃⱄaiꞃe aꞃeᵭⱦ n-inaⱦa a ᵇeiꞃ ᵭliᵹe, ⱱo ꝓí, ⱱo h-aiꞃⱱinᵭeⱨ, ⱱo ꝓꞃimᵹaᵇainᵭ ⱦuaiⱨe, ⱱo ᵇꞃiuᵹaᵭ, ⱱo ᵇꞃeiⱨemain, ⱱo muilinᵭ ⱦuaiⱦe, ꝼia luᵭⱦ aen liꞃ, aⱄaꞃ oen ᵭaile.

Mɑꞃa ꝼꞃíⱦe ꝼaiꞃᵹi, ᵭleᵹaꞃ a eꞃⱄaiꞃe ⱱo ᵇuine maiⱦ in ⱄaⱨ ⱄꞃiⱨ ⱱo na ⱦꞃí ⱄꞃíⱨaiᵭ iꞃ neꞃa ᵭo, no ⱄoma ꞃeᵭⱦ n-inaⱦa in ⱄaⱨ ⱄꞃíᵭ ᵭiᵭ, aⱄaꞃ muiꞃ in ⱄeⱦꞃama ⱄꞃíⱨ; aⱄaꞃ ᵭa m-ᵭeⱦaiꞃ ᵭaíne aꞃ in muiꞃ, iꞃ a n-eꞃⱄaiꞃe ᵭóiᵭ.

Ma ꞃo eꞃⱄaiꞃe ꝼia ᵭáine, aⱄaꞃ ⱱo ꞃinᵭe ᵭliᵹe ꝼꞃíⱨe aⱄaꞃ ꞃo maiꞃ ⱄo iaꞃ n-ᵭeⱨma, iꞃ lan ⱄuiⱦ a ꝼꞃiⱨe ᵭo.

Muna ᵭeꞃna a ᵭliᵹeᵭ ꝼꞃíⱨe, aⱄaꞃ ꞃoⱱaiⱦ ꝼia n-ᵭeⱨmaiᵭ, iꞃ lɑn ꝓiaⱨ ᵹaiⱄi uaᵭ. Mana ᵭeꞃna a ᵭliᵹeᵭ ꝼꞃíⱦe, aⱄaꞃ ꞃomaiꞃ aiⱄe ⱄo iaꞃ n-ᵭeⱨmaiᵭ, no mɑ ⱱo ꞃoine a ᵭliᵭe ꝼꞃíⱨe, aⱄaꞃ ꞃo ⱨaiⱦ ꝼia n-ᵭeⱨmaiᵭ, ⱄin ⱄaiⱦe ꝼꞃíⱨe ⱱo aⱄaꞃ ⱄin ꝓiaⱨ ᵹaiⱄi uaᵭ aᵭⱦ aiⱨᵹin in ꝼꞃiⱨe.

" The person who has found, or who shall find a waif in those places, this is what he is bound to do. If it be a land waif, to proclaim it in the seven places specified by law [i. e.] to the king, to the *Airchindech*, to the chief smith of the *Tuath* (territory), to the *Brughadh*, to the judge, at the mill [miller] of the *Tuath* (territory), to the people of the same *Lios*, and the same *Baile*.

" If it be a sea waif, he is bound to proclaim it to a good man in every *crich* of the three *cricha* which are nearest to him, or he might proclaim it in seven places in every *crich* of them, and the sea makes the fourth *crich ;* and if there be people upon the sea, it is right that it be proclaimed to them.

" If he have proclaimed it before people, and have fulfilled the waif law and it [the waif] remained [unclaimed] till after the tenth day, he is entitled to the full amount of his proportion of his waif.

" If he have fulfilled the waif law, and have consumed (appropriated) it before the tenth day, he is liable for the full amount of a theft liability. If he have not fulfilled the waif law, and that the waif remain with him till after the expiration of the tenth day, or if he have fulfilled the waif law, and if he have consumed (appropriated) it before the expiration of the tenth day, he is entitled to the consideration of a waif wasting, and he is bound to forfeit the debts of a charge of theft all but the restitution of the waif."—Rawlinson, 487, fol. 63, p. 1, col. b.

(H.) "*Fiacha Labrainde*" was monarch of Ireland from A. M. 3728 to A. M. 3751, when he was slain by Eochaidh Mumho of Munster, in the battle of Bealgadan, now Bulgadan, a townland in the parish of Kilbreedy Major, near Kilmallock, in the county of Limerick. The Four Masters record this battle, fought by him against the Ernans, and the eruption of Loch n-Erne, under the year A. M. 3751. There is a curious poem of sixteen verses on the reign of Fiacha Labrainde preserved in the Book of Leacan, in the R. I. A., folio 30, a. a.

(I.) Ꝺimiɼᵹin Ꝏaiɼᵹiuꝺach ꝺia ɼo ꝼai le Ꝼinꝺchaim inᵹin Ꝏaᵹach. "Aimergin Mairgiudach,-who had espoused Findchaem, daughter of Magach." These names frequently occur in our oldest tales and best MSS.; but Amergin is more generally styled Ꝺmaɼᵹin iaɼnᵹiunaiᵹ than maiɼᵹiuꝺach, as in the text, and Findchaem is more generally made daughter of Cobthad than of Magach. Their names occur in the story of Bricriu's feast in Leabhar na h-Uidhri, p. 103, col. 2, where she is mentioned as one of the eleven princesses who accompanied Queen Mugan, wife of Conchobar Mac Nessa, King of Ulster, at the feast: "Ꝼinꝺcaem inᵹen Caꞇbaꝺ ben Ꝺmaɼᵹin iaɼnᵹiunaiᵹ—Findchaem, daughter of Cathbad, wife of Amargin Iarngiunach." They are also mentioned in the bean ɼeancaɼ eɼenꝺ or history of the noteworthy women of Eriu in the Book of Leacan, as father and mother of the hero Conall Cearnach of Emania. The passage is as follows :—"Ꝼinꝺchaem inᵹen Chaꞇhbaiꝺ bean Ꝺimiɼᵹin iaɼnᵹiunaiᵹ maꞇhaiɼ Ċonaill Cheaɼnaiᵹ. Findchaem, daughter of Cathbad, wife of Aimirgin Iarngiunach, mother of Conall Cearnach." See Leabhar na h-Uidhri, R. I. A., p. 103, col. 2, line 22, and Book of Leacan, folio 204, a. a. &c.

Celtic Languages.

NATIONAL MEMORIAL
OF THE LATE
REV. DR. TODD, S.F.T.C.D., ETC.

ROYAL IRISH ACADEMY HOUSE,
Dawson-street, Dublin;
1st of March, 1870.

THE eminent services rendered by the late Rev. JAMES HENTHORN TODD, D.D., S.F.T.C.D., to the elucidation of our long-neglected ancient Irish literature, are admitted by all Celtic Scholars at home and abroad. For more than a quarter of a century he devoted a large portion of his time to this object, and spared neither means nor exertion to promote the scientific study of the Irish and other Celtic languages, as well as of the archæology and history of this country. To enumerate all his labours in this direction would be unnecessary.

These services claim a distinguished recognition from the people of Ireland, and from all those who appreciate the high and enduring agencies for social advancement which spring from the cultivation of a sound National Literature.

At a public meeting held at the Molesworth Hall, Dublin, (the Very Rev. W. Atkins, D.D., Dean of Ferns, in the chair,) it was decided, on the motion of J. T. Gilbert, Esq., F.S.A., M.R.I.A., seconded by the Rev. Professor Jellett, F.T.C.D., [since elected President of the Royal Irish Academy,] that the most suitable Memorial would be to endow a Professorship of the CELTIC LANGUAGES, the study of which is becoming every day of increasing importance at home and abroad.

It is proposed to call this Foundation—which is to be connected with the Royal Irish Academy, of which body Dr. Todd was formerly President—" The Todd Professorship ; " and while it will perpetuate his name, it will greatly promote the knowledge of the IRISH LANGUAGE, and further the publication and translation of the vast mass of the Irish, Welsh, Scottish, and other Celtic MS. materials which are to be found in many of the great libraries of this country and of the continent.

This form of memorial has the fullest approval of the immediate relatives of the late Dr. Todd.

Those who desire to join in this effort, will kindly send their subscriptions to the Honorary Treasurers of the Todd National Memorial Fund :—

W. H. HARDINGE, Esq., Tr. R.I.A.; and J. T. GILBERT, Esq., F.S.A.
Royal Irish Academy House,
Dawson-street, Dublin ;

or to one of the Local Hon. Secretaries *(see next page)* ; or lodge them to the credit of "The Todd National Memorial Fund," at the Bank of Ireland, or the London and Westminster Bank or at any of their branches.

By order of the Committee,

WILLIAM REEVES, D.D., LL.D., M.R.I.A.
HENRY BROOKE DOBBIN, LL.B. } *Hon. Secs.*
JOHN RIBTON GARSTIN, M.A., M.R.I.A., F.S.A.

[TURN OVER.

LIST OF THE COMMITTEE.

(April 26th, 1870.)

The Lord Primate.
The Archbishop of Dublin.
The Lord Chancellor of Ireland.
The Duke of Devonshire.
The Marquess of Kildare, M.R.I.A.
The Earl of Derby.
The Earl of Meath.
The Earl of Desart.
The Earl of Dunraven, K.P., F.S.A., V.P.R.I.A.
The Viscount Gough, M.R.I.A.
The Viscount Monck, M.R.I.A.
Lord George Hill.
The Bishop of Winchester.
The Bishop of Peterborough.
The Bishop of St. David's.
The Bishop of Meath, M.R.I.A.
The Bishop of Limerick, Ex-Pres. R.I.A.
The Bishop of Brechin, D.C.L.
The Lord Talbot de Malahide, Ex-Pr. R.I.A.
The Lord Clermont, M.R.I.A.
The Lord Houghton, D.C.L.
The Rev. The Lord O'Neill.
Right Hon. The Chief Secretary.
Right Hon. The Lord Mayor of Dublin.
Right Hon. Sir Frederick Shaw, Bart.
Right Hon. Sir Joseph Napier, Bart., M.R.I.A.
Right Hon. Abraham Brewster.
Col. Right Hon. W. Monsell, M.P., M.R.I.A.
Maj. Gen. Right Hon. Sir T. A. Larcom, Bart.
Right Hon. The Master of the Rolls.
Right Hon. The Lord Chief Baron.
Right Hon. Dr. J. T. Ball, M.P., Q.C., V.G.
Right Hon. G. A. Hamilton, M.R.I.A.
Sir John Esmonde, Bart., M.P.
Sir John Conroy, Bart.
Sir James Y. Simpson, Bart., M.D., D.C.L.
Sir Arthur Guinness, Bart., M.A.
The O'Conor Don, M.P.
Hon. David Plunket, M.P.
Sir J. B. Burke, LL.D., C.B., M.R.I.A., *Ulster*.
Sir W. R. Wilde, M.D., V.P.R.I.A.
The Solicitor-General, M.P.
William Brooke, Esq., Master in Chancery.
Gerald Fitzgibbon, Esq., Master in Chancery.
The Dean of Cork.
The Dean of Ferns.
The Dean of Down.
The President of the Royal Irish Academy.
The President of the College of Physicians.
The President of S. Patrick's College, Maynooth.
The Archdeacon of Cashel, M.R.I.A.
The Archdeacon of Cork, V.G.

The Archdeacon of Tuam.
Rev. J. A. Malet, D.D., S.F. and Librarian T.C.D
Rev. Dr. Salmon, F.R.S., Reg. Prof. Div.
The President of Carlow College.
The Warden of St. Columba's.
Rev. Alexander Irwin, Precentor of Armagh.
Rev. J. Graves, Treasurer of S. Canice's, M.R.I.A
Anthony Lefroy, Esq., M.P.
Jonathan Pim, Esq., M.P.
Edward de la Poer, Esq., M.P.
Matthew O'Reilly Dease, Esq., M.P.
Augustus W. Franks, Esq., V.P.S.A.
Henry Bradshaw, Esq., University Librarian Cambridge, *Local Hon. Sec., Cambridge.*
Rev. Benj. Dickson, D.D., F.T.C.D., M.R.I.A.
Rev. Professor Mahaffy, F.T.C.D.
Rev. Professor Gibbings, D.D.
Rev. Maxwell Close, M.R.I.A.
Rev. F. W. Farrar, F.R.S.
Rev. F. Turnour Bayly, F.S.A.
Professor Acland, M.D., Oxford.
William Stokes, Esq., M.D., D.C.L., F.R.S., V.P.R.I.A., Reg. Professor of Physic, Dub.
J. Kells Ingram, Esq., LL.D., F.T.C.
W. K. Sullivan, Esq., Ph. D., M.R.I.A.
Professor Max Müller, *Local Hon. Sec., Oxford.*
Professor Apjohn, M.D.
M. Adolphe Pictet.
John Hastings Otway, Esq., Q.C.
Samuel Ferguson, Esq., LL.D., Q.C., V.P.R.I.A.
W. C. Kyle, Esq., LL.D., M.R.I.A.
W. J. O'Donnavan, Esq., LL.D., M.R.I.A.
W. Stokes, Esq. LL.D. *Local Hon Sec., Calcutta*
Jasper R. Joly, Esq. J.P., LL.D., V.G.
Major L. E. Knox, D.L.
Fleetwood Churchill, Esq., M.D., M.R.I.A.
R. D. Lyons, Esq., M.D., M.R.I.A.
Thomas Beatty, Esq., M.D., M.R.I.A.
F. R. Cruise, Esq., M.D., M.R.I.A.
Colonel Meadows Taylor, C.S.I., M.R.I.A.
Denis Kelly, Esq., D.L., M.R.I.A.
Francis Robinson, Esq., Mus. Doc.
Aubrey de Vere, Esq.
J. Sheridan Le Fanu, Esq.
John Henry Parker, Esq., F.S.A.
Dr. Caulfield, F.S.A., *Hon. Sec. for Cork.*
Thomas Maxwell Hutton, Esq., J.P.
Thomas L. Kelly, Esq., J.P.
Arthur O'Conor, Esq., J.P., D.L.
Charles O'Donel, Esq., J.P.
Matthew Arnold, Esq.

Sir Wm. Tite, M.P., F.R.S., V.P.S.A.,
42, Lowndes Square, London, S.W., and
William Chappell, Esq., F.S.A.,
Heather Down, Ascot, Berks ;

} "On behalf of the 'Society of Antiquaries of London,'" (under resolution of their Council.)

Local Hon. Treasurers and Secretaries for London.

WITH THE

HON. TREASURERS :
W. H. Hardinge, Esq., Tr., R.I.A.
J. T. Gilbert, Esq., F.S.A., M.R.I.A.

HON. SECRETARIES :
William Reeves, D.D., LL.D., M.R.I.A.
Henry Brooke Dobbin, LL.B.
John Ribton Garstin, M.A., F.S.A., M.R.I.A.

COMMITTEE ROOMS : *Royal Irish Academy House,*

N.B.—The Names are arranged alphabetically.

Name	£	s.	d.
J. G. Adair, Esq.	2	0	0
Professor Apjohn, M.D., F.R.S.	3	0	0
Andrew Armstrong, Esq., M.R.I.A.	5	0	0
Matthew Arnold, Esq.	1	0	0
Very Rev. Wm. Atkins, D.D., Dean of Ferns	2	0	0
George Atkinson, Esq., M.B.	1	0	0
Very Rev. D. Bagot, V.G., Dean of Dromore	1	1	0
J. T. Banks, Esq. M.D., President of the Coll. of Physicians	5	0	0
James B. Ball, Esq.	10	0	0
Rev. F. T. Bayly, F.S.A.	2	2	0
W. C. Begley, Esq., M.A., M.D.	3	0	0
E. H. Bennet, Esq., M.D.	1	0	0
Charles Benson, Esq., M.D.	1	1	0
Edward Bewley, Esq., Moate	1	0	0
Henry Bewley, Esq.	1	0	0
W. M. Bourke, Esq., Calcutta	2	0	0
J. Boxwell, Esq., Bengal C.S.	5	0	0
Henry Bradshaw, Esq., University Librarian, Cambridge	25	0	0
R. R. Brash, Esq., M.R.I.A. (£2 per annum for 3 years)	6	0	0
Right Hon. A. Brewster	5	0	0
William Brooke, Esq., M.C.	5	0	0
Sir Bernard Burke, C.B., LL.D., M.R.I.A., *Ulster*	3	0	0
William M. Burke, Esq., M.D.	1	0	0
The Most Rev. Samuel Butcher, D.D., Bishop of Meath, M.R.I.A.	10	0	0
Nathaniel Callwell, Esq.	5	0	0
Ven. John Cather, Archdeacon of Tuam	3	3	0
Richard Caulfield, Esq. F.S.A., LL.D.	1	0	0
William Chappell, Esq., F.S.A.	1	1	0
The Lord Clermont, M.R.I.A.	20	0	0
Rev. Maxwell Close, M.R.I.A.	5	0	0
Samuel H. Close, Esq.	2	0	0
Sir John Conroy, Bart.	5	0	0
Eugene A. Conwell, Esq., M.R.I.A.	5	0	0
Lieut. Col. Cooper, D.L., Markree	5	0	0
J. R. Corballis, Esq., LL.D., M.R.I.A.	5	0	0
C. P. Cotton, Esq., C.E.	1	0	0
Ven. Henry Cotton, D.C.L., M.R.I.A., Archdeacon of Cashel	5	0	0
H. A. Cowper, Esq.	1	0	0
Dr. Croker	1	0	0
Rev. J. A. Crozier, Chaplain to the Forces	1	0	0
F. R. Cruise, Esq., M.D.	2	2	0
The Right Rev. Robert Daly, D.D., Bishop of Cashel	10	0	0
M. O'Reilly Dease, Esq., M.P.	5	0	0
Edmond de la Poer, Esq., M.P.	3	0	0
Earl of Derby	5	0	0
Aubrey de Vere, Esq.	1	0	0
Duke of Devonshire	20	0	0
Rev. Benjamin Dickson, D.D., F.T.C.D., M.R.I.A.	5	0	0
Leonard Dobbin, Esq.	5	0	0
R. Dowse, Esq., M.P., Solicitor-General	5	0	0
Thomas Drew, Esq., F.R.I.A.L.	1	1	0
The Earl of Dunraven, K.P., F.S.A., V.P.R.I.A.	20	0	0
Very Rev. W. Edwards, Dean of Cork	2	2	0
George Ellis, Esq., M.B.	1	0	0
Sir John Esmonde, Bart.	3	0	0
Rev. F. W. Farrar	1	0	0
Rev. Thomas Farrelly, D.D., Bursar, Maynooth	2	2	0
Samuel Ferguson, Esq., Q.C., LL.D., M.R.I.A.	5	0	0
Rev. John Finlayson, M.A.	1	0	0
The Right Rev. William Fitzgerald, D.D., Bishop of Killaloe, M.R.I.A.	5	5	0
A. Fitzgibbon, Esq.	5	0	0
Gerald Fitzgibbon, Esq., M.C., M.R.I.A.	5	0	0
Christopher Fleming, Esq., M.D.	2	2	0
Charles H. Foot, Esq., M.R.I.A.	1	0	0
Right Rev. A. P. Forbes, D.C.L., Bishop of Brechin	5	0	0
Messrs. Forster and Co.	2	2	0
Right Hon. Chichester Fortescue, M.P., Chief Secretary	20	0	0
Augustus W. Franks, Esq., V.P.S.A.	10	0	0
Rev. Abraham S. Fuller, A.M.	1	0	0
M. H. Gaidoz, Paris	1	0	0
Rev. Professor Gargan, D.D., Maynooth	1	1	0
John Ribton Garstin, Esq., F.S.A., M.R.I.A.	5	0	0
Rev. Professor Gibbings, D.D.	3	0	0
J. T. Gilbert, Esq., F.S.A., M.R.I.A.	5	0	0
M. H. Gill, Esq.	5	0	0
Rev. Andrew J. Gillmor	1	0	0
The Viscount Gough, M.R.I.A.	10	0	0
Archdeacon Goold	2	2	0
Babu Gopal Chendra Chattopadhaya	0	10	0
Right Rev. Charles Graves, D.D., Bishop of Limerick, Ex-Pres. R.I.A.	10	0	0
Rev. James Graves, Treasurer of S. Canice's	1	0	0
Rev. R. P. Graves, M.A.	2	0	0
Sir Arthur E. Guinness, Bart.	20	0	0
Edward Cecil Guinness, Esq.	10	0	0
Right Hon. G. A. Hamilton, LL.D.	10	0	8
Anthony Hanagan, Esq.	2	0	0
W. Neilson Hancock, Esq., LL.D.	2	2	0
W. H. Hardinge, Esq., Treasurer R.I.A.	5	0	0
Pandit Hari Har Das	0	10	0
John Hatchell, Esq., J.P., M.R.I.A.	1	0	0
Lord George Hill	5	0	0
Alfred Hudson, Esq., M.D., M.R.I.A.	1	0	0
Rev. James Hughes, Junior Dean, Maynooth	2	2	0
Mrs. Hutton	2	2	0
T. Maxwell Hutton, Esq., J.P.	2	0	0
Mrs. T. M. Hutton,	1	0	0
J. K. Ingram, LL.D., F.T.C.	5	0	0
T. Dunbar Ingram, Esq., Calcutta	5	0	0
Rev. Alexander Irwin, M.A., Precentor of Armagh	10	0	0
Rev. Professor Jellett, F.T.C.D., President, R.I.A.	5	0	0
Thomas Jones, Esq., Manchester	1	0	0
P. W. Joyce, Esq., M.R.I.A.	1	0	0
William F. de Visme Kane, M.R.I.A.	3	0	0
Very Rev. Dr. Kavanagh, Carlow College	2	2	0
Denis Kelly, Esq., D.L., M.R.I.A.	10	0	0
Thomas Laffan Kelly, Esq., J.P.	5	0	0
Evory Kennedy, Esq., M.D.	2	2	0
J. C. F. Kenney, Esq., M.R.I.A.	5	0	0
The Marquess of Kildare, M.R.I.A.	5	0	0
Edward Hudson Kinahan, Esq., J.P.	5	0	0
G. Henry Kinahan, Esq.	1	0	0
J. J. Kirby, Esq.	1	0	0
Rev. J. Torrens Kyle, B.D.	1	0	0
Ven. S. M. Kyle, V.G., Archdeacon of Cork	2	0	0
William Cotter Kyle, Esq., LL.D., M.R.I.A.	5	0	0

[TURN OVER.]

	£	s.	d.
John J. Lalor, Esq., M.R.I.A.	5	0	0
Right Hon. Sir Thomas A. Larcom, Bart.	5	0	0
Rev. Alexander Leeper, D.D.	1	0	0
Anthony Lefroy, Esq., M.P.	10	0	0
The Duke of Leinster	10	0	0
John Lindsay, Esq., Co. Cork	1	0	0
Daniel Litton, Esq.	2	0	0
Rickard Lloyd, Esq., M.A.	1	0	0
Daniel McCabe, Esq.	1	0	0
Rev. Professor McCaul, King's Cull. London	1	0	0
T. M. McCormick, Esq , M.D., T.C.D.	2	0	0
Robert McDonnell, Esq., M.D., F.R.S.	2	2	0
Miss L. MacDougall	1	0	0
William MacDougall, Esq.	2	2	0
Macmillan and Co.	2	2	0
Hon. A. G. Macpherson, Judge of the High Court, Fort William	2	0	0
Rev. Michael Malone, C.C., Limerick	1	0	0
Brinsley Marlay, Esq., D.L.	3	3	0
M. Henri Martin, Membre de l'Institut	1	0	0
Theodore Martin, Esq.	2	2	0
Earl of Meath	5	0	0
John Mollan, Esq., M.D., M.R.I.A.	3	0	0
Viscount Monck	10	0	0
D. Moore, Esq., Ph. D., Glasnevin	1	0	0
Right Hon. William Monsell, M.P.	5	0	0
Professor Max Muller	1	0	0
Mrs. W. Murphy	5	0	0
J. A. Nicholson, Esq., M.R.I.A.	5	0	0
Miss O'Brien	5	0	0
Sir Patrick O'Brien, Bart. M P.	1	0	0
J. C. O'Callaghan, Esq.	1	0	0
The O'Conor Don, M.P.	5	0	0
Arthur O'Conor, Esq., D.L., Elphin	5	0	0
Peter O'Connor, Esq., Sligo	5	0	0
Mr. John O'Daly	1	0	0
Charles O'Donel, Esq., J.P.	2	0	0
W. J. O'Donnavan. Esq., LL.D., M.R.I.A.	5	0	0
Standish H. O'Grady, Esq.	5	0	0
Right Hon. T. O'Hagan, Lord Chancellor	10	0	0
Rev. Thaddeus O'Mahony, M.A., Professor of Irish, T.C.D.	1	0	0
The Rev. Lord O'Neill	10	0	0
J. P. O'Reilly, Esq., C.E.	1	0	0
Miss O'Rorke	5	0	0
Alexander Parker, Esq., J.P.	2	2	0
Mrs. Paulet	1	0	0
Mrs. Pereira, Edinburgh	1	0	0
Anthony Perrier, Esq., J.P., Cork	1	0	0
Rev. Louis Perrin	2	0	0
F. Lloyd Phillips, Esq.	1	1	0
Rt. Hon. D. R. Pigot, Lord Chief Baron	10	0	0
D. R. Pigot, Esq.	2	2	0
Jonathan Pim, Esq., M.P.	5	0	0
Alderman Plunket	1	0	0

	£	s.	d.
Hon. and Rev. William Conyngham Plunket, Precentor of S. Patrick's	2	2	0
G. H. Porter, Esq., M.D.	2	2	0
Rev. Thomas H. Porter, D.D.	5	0	0
Right Hon. B. Purdon, Lord Mayor of Dublin	2	2	0
Dr. Radford	1	0	0
Archdeacon Redmond	1	0	0
Rev. William Reeves, D.D., M.R.I.A.	10	0	0
Rev. Robert Rice, M.A., Warden of Saint Columba's College	2	2	0
John Ringland, Esq., M.D.	2	0	0
Francis Robinson, Esq., Mus. Doc.	5	0	0
Dr. Rogers, Exeter	1	0	0
Bartholomew W. Rooke, Esq., M.A.	1	0	0
Very Rev. Charles W. Russell, D.D., M.R.I.A., President of S. Patrick's, Maynooth	5	0	0
Rev. Professor Salmon, D.D., D.C.L., F.R.S., V.P.R.I.A.	5	0	0
M. W. Savage, Esq.	2	2	0
Vincent Scully, Esq.	1	0	0
Right Hon. Sir Frederick Shaw, Bart.	5	0	0
Rev. R. Corbet-Singleton, M.A., York	5	0	0
George Smith, Esq., Ballybrack	2	2	0
Rev. R. Travers Smith, M.A.	3	0	0
R. W. Smith, Esq., M.D.	2	0	0
Rev. Robert Staveley, B.D.	1	0	0
H. H. Stewart, Esq., M.D., M.R.I.A.	25	0	0
William Stokes, Esq., M.D., F.R.S., M.R.I.A.	5	0	0
Whitley Stokes, Esq., LL.D., Calcutta	5	0	0
Right Hon. Edward Sullivan, Master of the Rolls	10	0	0
The Lord Talbot de Malahide, Ex-Pres. R.I.A.	10	0	0
Colonel Meadows Taylor, C.S.I.	2	2	0
Right Rev. Connop Thirlwall, D.D., Bishop of St. David's	5	0	0
Alexander Thom, Esq., M.R.I.A.	5	0	0
Sir William Tite, M.P., F.R.S., V.P.S.A.	21	0	0
Arthur Todd, Esq.	1	0	0
Hon. Judge Townsend	1	1	0
Thomas Cooke Trench, Esq.	2	2	0
Most Rev. R. C. Trench, D.D., Archbishop of Dublin	5	0	0
T. J. Tufnell, Esq.	1	0	0
Charles Vignoles, F.R.S., Pres. Ins. C.E.	1	1	0
Laurence Waldron, Esq., D.L.	3	0	0
Rev. James Walsh, M.A., Limerick	1	0	0
G. S. Walters, Esq.	10	0	0
James Whitehead, M.A., Manchester	1	0	0
Rev. John Wilson, D.D.	1	1	0
Sir William Wilde, M.D., V.P., R.I.A.	1	0	0
S. G. Wilmot, Esq., M.D.	1	0	0
Edward Perceval Wright, M.D., Professor of Botany, T.C.D.	3	0	0

PUBLICATIONS OF THE ROYAL IRISH ACADEMY.

TRANSACTIONS:—Vols. I. to XXIII.

    ,,   Vol. XXIV.:—SCIENCE, Parts I. to XV.

    ,,   ,,   POLITE LITERATURE, Parts I. to IV.

    ,,   ,,   ANTIQUITIES, Parts I. to VIII.

PROCEEDINGS:—Vols. I. to X.

CATALOGUE OF THE ANTIQUITIES IN THE MUSEUM. By Sir W. R. Wilde, M.D. Vol. I. Price 14s.

           Vol. II. Part I.—ANTIQUITIES OF GOLD. Price 3s. 6d.

*** The following Parts of the TRANSACTIONS are lately Published:—

Part X.—" On Ziphius Sowerbyi (Mesoplodon Sowerbiensis, *Van Beneden*). By WILLIAM ANDREWS, M.R.I.A., &c.

Part XI.—" On the Histology of the Test of the Class Palliobranchiata." By Professor W. KING.

Part XII.—" On Bicircular Quartics." By JOHN CASEY, A.B.

Part XIII.—" Contributions towards a knowledge of the Flora of the Seychelles." By E. PERCEVAL WRIGHT, M.D., F.L.S., Professor of Botany and Zoology, Trinity College, Dublin.

Part XIV.—" Contributions to the History of the Terebenes.—On Colophonine and Colophonic Hydrate (new substances procured from the products of the destructive distillation of Resin)." By CHARLES R. C. TICHBORNE, F.C.S., &c.

Part XV.—" On a New Step in the Proximate Analysis of Saccharine Matters." By JAMES APJOHN, M.D., Professor of Chemistry and Mineralogy in the University of Dublin.

In the Press.

SCIENCE, Part XVI.—" On the Small Oscillations of a Rigid Body about a Fixed Point under the Action of any Forces, and, more particularly, when Gravity is the only Force acting." By ROBERT STAWELL BALL, A.M., Professor of Applied Mathematics and Mechanism, Royal College of Science for Ireland.

ANTIQUITIES, Part IX.—" On an Ancient Chalice and Brooches lately found at Ardagh, in the County of Limerick." By the Right Honourable the EARL OF DUNRAVEN AND MOUNT-EARL, F. R. S., Vice-President of the Academy.

DUBLIN:

ACADEMY HOUSE, 19, DAWSON-STREET;

HODGES, SMITH, & FOSTER, GRAFTON-ST.

LONDON:

WILLIAMS & NORGATE, HENRIETTA-STREET, COVENT GARDEN.

CONTENTS.